Study Guide

Understanding Management
Fourth Edition

Richard L. Daft

Vanderbilt University

Dorothy Marcic

Vanderbilt University

Prepared by

Stephen R. Hiatt

Catawba College

THOMSON

SOUTH-WESTERN

Australia · Canada · Mexico · Singapore · Spain · United Kingdom · United States

THOMSON

SOUTH-WESTERN

Study Guide to accompany Understanding Management, 4th Edition

Richard L. Daft and Dorothy Marcic

Prepared by Stephen R. Hiatt

VP/Editorial Director:
Jack W. Calhoun

VP/Editor-in-Chief:
Michael P. Roche

Acquisitions Editor:
Joe Sabatino

Developmental Editor:
Emma F. Guttler

Senior Marketing Manager:
Rob Bloom

Production Editor:
Emily S. Gross

Manufacturing Coordinator:
Rhonda Utley

Media Developmental Editor:
Kristen Meere

Media Production Editor:
Karen L. Schaffer

Senior Design Project Manager:
Michelle Kunkler

Cover Designer:
Lou Ann Thesing
Cincinnati, OH

Cover Images:
© Digital Vision and
© PhotoDisc, Inc.

Photography Manager:
Deanna Ettinger

Printer:
Globus Printing, Inc.
Minster, Ohio

Preface

This *Study Guide* has many features to help you learn, remember, and apply the information in your text, *Understanding Management*, 4e, by Richard L. Daft and Dorothy Marcic.

Each chapter of the *Study Guide* includes the following:

- *Chapter Outline* that will provide a framework for the material you will be learning.
- *Key Terms* that you can review to make sure you understand the vocabulary related to each area of management you will study.
- *Learning Objectives* to supply direction to your study time.
- *Chapter Review* to help you test your comprehension of what you have learned. Here you will answer 30 multiple choice, 10 true/false, and 4 short answer questions that will help you focus on important material presented in the chapter.
- *Manager's Workbook* to help you apply what you have learned; these activities are designed for individual work. This section includes the *Manager's Workbook* activities found in your textbook, plus new activities. The textbook activities are reprinted in the *Study Guide* for those who prefer carrying to class and writing in the *Study Guide* rather than their textbooks.
- *Manager's Workshop* to provide further opportunities to apply what you have learned. These exercises are designed for group effort and take the form of questionnaires, scenarios, and activities that provide opportunities for students to work in teams. As in the *Manager's Workbook* section, you will find textbook exercises as well as new exercises for each chapter.
- *Study Guide Solutions* to check your answers to the *Chapter Review* questions and to find suggested answers to the *Manager's Workbook* and *Manager's Workshop* activities and exercises.

Using various learning approaches during your study time and using the tools contained in this *Study Guide* will help to increase your interest in management and move you from being a passive learner to an active learner. Becoming an efficient and effective manager requires you to become actively involved in the learning process in order to gain the knowledge and practice the skills associated with successful management. And remember that management knowledge and skills are necessary not only for those who have a management job title, but they are also of value to anyone who has personal and career resources they wish to manage well.

Good luck in your pursuit of gaining knowledge and skills in an area that has the potential to enhance your personal and career success.

Stephen R. Hiatt

Contents

Part VI   Controlling

Chapter 1

Managing the New Workplace

Chapter Outline

I. The Definition of Management

II. Organizational Performance

III. Management Skills

IV. Management Types

V. What Is It Like to Be a Manager?

    A.   Manager Activities

    B.   Manager Roles

VI. Managing in Small Businesses and Not-for-Profit Organizations

VII. Management and the New Workplace

    A.   Forces on Organizations

    B.   New Management Competencies

    C.   Application: Managing Crises and Unexpected Events

    D.   The Learning Organization

    E.   Managing the Technology-Driven Workplace

VIII. Management and Organization

IX. Classical Perspective

    A.   Scientific Management

    B.   Bureaucratic Organizations

    C.   Administrative Principles

X. Humanistic Perspective

    A.   The Human Relations Movement

    B.   The Human Resources Perspective

    C.   The Behavioral Sciences Approach

XI. Management Science Perspective

    A.   Total Quality Management

Key Terms

Management: the attainment of organizational goals in an effective and efficient manner through planning, organizing, leading, and controlling organizational resources.

Organization: a social entity that is goal directed and deliberately structured.

Effectiveness: the degree tow which the organization achieves a stated goal.

Efficiency: the use of minimal resources—raw materials, money, and people—to produce a desired volume of output.

Performance: the organization's ability to attain its goals by using resources in a efficient and effective manner.

Role: a set of expectations for one's behavior.

Learning Organization: an organization in which everyone is engaged in identifying and solving problems, enabling the organization to continuously experiment, improve, and increase its capability.

e-business: work an organization does by using electronic linkages.

Intranet: an internal communications system that uses the technology and standards of the Internet but is accessible only within the company.

Extranet: a company communications system that gives access to suppliers, partners, and others outside the company.

e-commerce: business exchanges or transactions that occur electronically.

Enterprise resource planning (ERP): systems that unite a company's major business functions—order processing, product design, purchasing inventory, etc.

Knowledge management: the efforts to systematically find, organize, and make available a company's intellectual capital and to foster a culture of continuous learning and knowledge sharing.

Social forces: the aspects of a culture that guide and influence relationships among people—their values, needs, and standards of behavior.

Political forces: the influence of political and legal institutions on people and organizations.

Economic forces: forces that affect the availability, production, and distribution of a society's resources among competing users.

Classical perspective: a management perspective that emerged during the nineteenth and early twentieth centuries that emphasized a rational, scientific approach to the study of management and sought to make organizations efficient working machines.

Scientific Management: a subfield of the classical management perspective that emphasized scientifically determined changes in management practices as the solution to improving labor productivity.

Bureaucratic organization: a subfield of the classical management perspective that emphasized management on an impersonal, rational basis through such elements as clearly defined authority and responsibility, formal recordkeeping, and separation of management and ownership.

Administrative principles: a subfield of the classical management perspective that focused on the total organization rather than the individual worker, delineating the management functions of planning, organizing, commanding, coordinating, and controlling.

Humanistic perspective: a management perspective that emerged around the late nineteenth century that emphasized understanding human behavior, needs, and attitudes in the workplace.

Hawthorne studies: a series of experiments on worker productivity begun in 1924 at the Hawthorne plant of Western Electric Company in Illinois; attributed employees' increased output to managers' better treatment of them during the study.

Human relations movement: a movement in management thinking and practice that emphasized satisfaction of employees' basic needs as the key to increased worker productivity.

Human resources perspective: a management perspective that suggests jobs should be designed to meet higher-level needs by allowing workers to use their full potential.

Behavioral sciences approach: a subfield of the humanistic management perspective that applies social science in an organizational context, drawing from economics, psychology, sociology, and other disciplines.

Management science perspective: a management perspective that emerged after World War II and applied mathematics, statistics, and other quantitative techniques to managerial problems.

Total quality management (TQM): a concept that focuses on managing the total organization to deliver quality to customers. Four significant elements of TQM are employee involvement, focus on the customer, benchmarking, and continuous improvement.

Learning Objectives

1. Explain the difference between efficiency and effectiveness and their importance for organizational performance.

2. Define ten roles that managers perform in organizations.

3. Discuss the transition to a new workplace and the management competencies needed to deal with issues such as diversity, globalization, and rapid change.

4. Describe the learning organization and the changes in structure, empowerment, information sharing that managers make to support it.

5. Understand how historical forces influence the practice of management.

6. Identify and explain major developments in the history of management thought.

7. Describe the major components of the classical and humanistic management perspectives.

8. Discuss the management science perspective and its current use in organizations.

9. Explain the major concepts of total quality management.

10. Explain the leadership skills needed for effective crisis management.

Chapter Review

Multiple Choice: Please indicate the correct response to the following questions by writing the letter of the correct answer in the space provided.

_____ 1. The management function concerned with setting organizational goals is called
    a. organizing.
    b. leading.
    c. planning.
    d. controlling.
    e. coordinating.

_____ 2. The figurehead role is being filled by a manager when he or she
    a. seeks current information from periodicals.
    b. handles symbolic activities for the department.
    c. transmits important information to subordinates.
    d. allocates equipment to departments.
    e. negotiates with a supplier about a late shipment.

_____ 3. Managers may perform up to ten different roles as part of their everyday jobs. The roles are divided into three categories:
    a. personal, private, and public.
    b. interpersonal, informational, and decisional.
    c. semi-private, informational, and public.
    d. interpersonal, informative, and interesting.
    e. decisional, argumentative, and disruptive.

_____ 4. Conceptual skills are needed by _____ managers, but especially by _____ managers.
    a. few, first-line
    b. all, middle
    c. intellectual, personnel
    d. all, top
    e. few, middle

_____ 5. The learning organization is one in which
    a. everyone is expected to have a college degree.
    b. the CEO teaches everyone else how to act.
    c. everyone in the organization participates in identifying and solving problems.
    d. formal courses are offered to all employees.
    e. employees can easily learn how to progress up the career ladder

_____ 6. Technical skills are most needed by _____ managers.
    a. top level
    b. middle level
    c. first-line
    d. staff
    e. project

_____ 7. A manager who is not a good communicator is failing to perform the _____ role well.
   a. negotiator
   b. figurehead
   c. leader
   d. monitor
   e. spokesperson

_____ 8. A manager who is known for innovation is successfully filling the _____ role.
   a. figurehead
   b. disseminator
   c. monitor
   d. entrepreneur
   e. negotiator

_____ 9. Planning, organizing, leading, and controlling are referred to as the _____ of management
   a. principles
   b. objects
   c. functions
   d. antitheses
   e. nemeses

_____ 10. In telling an employee how to correctly do a task which he formerly did incorrectly, you are engaged in the _____ function of management.
   a. planning
   b. organizing
   c. leading
   d. controlling
   e. coordinating

_____ 11. Efficiency and effectiveness in the same organization
   a. is a practical impossibility.
   b. is not a desirable outcome.
   c. can both be high.
   d. must be achieved by different persons.
   e. none of the above are true.

_____ 12. The allocation of resources is done as part of the management function of
   a. planning.
   b. organizing.
   c. staffing.
   d. directing.
   e. controlling.

_____ 13. Not-for-profit organizations
  a. are a major source for management talent and innovation.
  b. represent a model for poor management.
  c. do not use human skills very much.
  d. illustrate that organizations can succeed without management.
  e. ignore the community in which they exist.

_____ 14. The classical management perspective
  a. recognized environmental influences.
  b. viewed workers as the same as managers.
  c. ignored rationality in favor of human relations.
  d. emphasized a rational, scientific approach.
  e. failed to recognize the importance of individual productivity.

_____ 15. The _____ approach to management initiated the careful study of tasks and jobs.
  a. scientific management
  b. classical management
  c. administrative principles
  d. systems theory
  e. contingency

_____ 16. The general approach of scientific management includes
  a. flexibility of standards for performing each job.
  b. selecting workers with appropriate abilities for each job.
  c. training workers in methods according to individual abilities.
  d. providing autonomy to workers in planning their own work.
  e. eliminating wage incentives since they are counterproductive.

_____ 17. Fayol's principle of unity of command means that
  a. top management must all be of one mind before issuing orders.
  b. each subordinate should receive orders from one—and only one—superior.
  c. after a command is received, subordinates have the duty of rallying behind the command even if they disagree with it.
  d. only one person should make a decision because group decision making is less efficient.
  e. similar activities in an organization should be grouped together under one manager.

_____ 18. According to Chester Barnard's acceptance theory of authority,
  a. workers need to learn to accept the authority of managers.
  b. managers need to learn to accept the authority vested in them.
  c. people have free will and can choose whether to follow management orders.
  d. people have the tendency to accept authority regardless of their perceptions.
  e. all of the above

_____ 19. Weber designed a bureaucracy mainly because
- a. he was a German and therefore liked paperwork.
- b. he worked for the government and saw how rational such an organization really was.
- c. he objected to European organizations which were managed by favoritism and subjective methods.
- d. he had studied the writings of Frederick W. Taylor and felt Taylor's ideas could be applied to government structures also.
- e. he objected to the way organizations were so impersonally managed in his day.

_____ 20. According to the text, the bureaucratic model works just fine at
- a. Boeing Corporation.
- b. United Parcel Service (UPS).
- c. research laboratories.
- d. Apple Computer Company.
- e. times when technology is changing rapidly.

_____ 21. In a bureaucracy _____ is separate from ownership.
- a. rationality
- b. funding
- c. management
- d. authority
- e. status

_____ 22. Which of the following is not a significant element of Total Quality Management (TQM)?
- a. strict control of quality by top management
- b. employee involvement
- c. focus on the customer
- d. benchmarking
- e. continuous improvement

_____ 23. Although team leadership is critical in learning organizations, the traditional boss
- a. is still in charge of everything.
- b. must still make the tough decisions.
- c. is practically eliminated.
- d. must be maintained.
- e. is still very important.

_____ 24. The assumption that the average human being learns, under proper conditions, not only to accept but to seek responsibility is an assumption of
- a. Theory Y.
- b. Abraham Maslow.
- c. contingency theory.
- d. Theory X.
- e. Frederick W. Taylor.

_____ 25. The behavioral sciences approach draws from
     a. anthropology.
     b. economics.
     c. psychology.
     d. sociology.
     e. all of the above.

_____ 26. _____ is/are the management science application which is used in the physical production of goods and services.
     a. Operations research
     b. Operations management
     c. Management information systems
     d. Queuing theory
     e. Scientific management

_____ 27. When work is done by using electronic linkages it is called
     a. E-business.
     b. E-commerce.
     c. enterprise resource planning.
     d. knowledge management.
     e. cyber management.

_____ 28. According to Theory X, the average human being has an inherent _____ work.
     a. understanding of
     b. liking for
     c. feeling, either positive or negative, towards
     d. dislike for
     e. trust in

_____ 29. When a company sets up an internal communications system that uses the technology and standards of the Internet, but it is accessible only to people within the company, it is called a(n)
     a. extranet.
     b. internal Internet.
     c. intranet.
     d. cyber communications system.
     e. E-commerce system.

_____ 30. ERP stands for
     a. Electronic Research Process.
     b. Enterprise Resource Planning.
     c. Elective Research Planning.
     d. Electronic Risk Probability.
     e. Enterprise Risk Planning.

True/False: Please indicate whether the following statements are true or false by writing a T or an F in the blank in front of each question.

_____ 1. It is impossible for an organization to be both efficient and effective at the same time since efficiency may use the resources in such a way as to preclude effectiveness.

_____ 2. A manager who is presenting an award is filling an informational role.

_____ 3. A first-line manager is most concerned with accomplishing day-to-day objectives.

_____ 4. When a manager is resolving a conflict between two subordinates, he or she is filling the disturbance handler role.

_____ 5. Most managers usually find time for quiet reflection, which is why many subordinates feel that managers do not work very hard.

_____ 6. Frank and Lillian Gilbreth, who had 12 children, were used by Frederick W. Taylor as an example of the disadvantages of not using scientific management.

_____ 7. According to Chester Barnard, people have free will and can choose whether to follow management orders.

_____ 8. While popular in the academic world, the behavioral sciences approach has never really been tried by any businesses.

_____ 9. Operations research consists of mathematical model building and other applications of quantitative approaches to managerial problems.

_____ 10. The learning organization refers to a company in which everyone is encouraged to complete a college degree.

Short Answer: Please indicate your answer in the space provided.

1. How would you define management to a friend who is unfamiliar with the term?

2.   What are the four functions of management?

3.   Discuss the advantages and disadvantages of Taylor's Scientific Management.

4.   What are the primary characteristics of a learning organization?

Manager's Workbook

Management Aptitude Questionnaire *(Also available on page 43 of text.)*

Rate each of the following questions according to this scale:

5 I always am like this.
4 I often am like this.
3 I sometimes am like this.
2 I rarely am like this.
1 I never am like this.

_____ 1   When I have a number of tasks or homework to do, I set priorities and organize the work around the deadlines. C

_____ 2   Most people would describe me as a good listener. H

_____ 3   When I am deciding on a particular course of action for myself (such as hobbies to pursue, languages to study, which job to take, special projects to be involved in), I typically consider the long-term (three years or more) implications of what I would choose to do. C

_____ 4   I prefer technical or quantitative courses rather than those involving literature, psychology, or sociology. T

_____ 5   When I have a serious disagreement with someone, I hang in there and talk it out until it is completely resolved. H

_____ 6   When I have a project or assignment, I really get into the details rather than the "big picture" issues.* C

_____ 7   I would rather sit in front of my computer than spend a lot of time with people. T

_____ 8   I try to include others in activities or when there are discussions. H

_____ 9   When I take a course, I relate what I am learning to other courses I have taken or concepts I have learned elsewhere. C

_____ 10   When somebody makes a mistake, I want to correct the person and let her or him know the proper answer or approach.* H

_____ 11   I think it is better to be efficient with my time when talking with someone, rather than worry about the other person's needs, so that I can get on with my real work.

_____12   I know my long-term vision for career, family, and other activities and have thought it over carefully. C

_____13   When solving problems, I would much rather analyze some data or statistics than meet with a group of people. T

_____14   When I am working on a group project and someone doesn't pull a full share of the load, I am more likely to complain to my friends rather than confront the slacker.* H

_____15   Talking about ideas or concepts can get me really enthused and excited. C

_____16   The type of management course for which this book is used is really a waste of time. T

_____17   I think it is better to be polite and not to hurt people's feelings.* H

_____18   Data or things interest me more than people. T

Scoring:

Add the total points for the following sections. Note that starred * items are reverse scored, as such:

    1 I always am like this.
    2 I often am like this.
    3 I sometimes am like this.
    4 I rarely am like this.
    5 I never am like this.

1, 3, 6, 9, 12, 15   Conceptual skills total score —————
2, 5, 8, 10, 14, 17   **H**uman skills total score —————
4, 7, 11, 13, 16, 18   Technical skills total score —————

The above skills are three abilities needed to be a good manager. Ideally, a manager should be strong (though not necessarily equal) in all three. Anyone noticeably weaker in any of the skills should take courses and read to build up that skill. For further background on the three skills, please refer to the model on page 8.

*reverse scoring item
NOTE: This exercise was contributed by Dorothy Marcic.

Who is a Manager?

After studying the roles of a manager in class Don became involved in a conversation about whether various persons he knew were "managers" or not. Help Don decide this by placing a yes or not in the appropriate spaces below.

ROLE	MANAGEMENT PROFESSOR	BASKETBALL COACH	FATHER OF A FAMILY
Figurehead			
Leader			
Liaison			
Monitor			
Disseminator			
Spokesperson			
Entrepreneur			
Disturbance Handler			
Resource Allocator			
Negotiator			

Manager's Workshop

The Worst Manager (Also available on page 44 of text.)

1. By yourself, think of two managers you have had—the best and the worst. Write down a few sentences to describe each.

The best manager I ever had was...

The worst manager I ever had was...

2. Divide into groups of 5-7 members. Share your experiences. Each group should choose a couple of examples to share with the whole group. Complete the table below as a group.

	Management principle followed or broken	Skills evident or missing	Lessons to be learned	Advice you would give managers
The best managers				
The worst managers				

3. What are the common problems managers have?

4. Prepare a list of "words of wisdom" you would give as a presentation to a group of managers. What are some basic principles they should use to be effective?

Sam Slick

You are the manager of a used car lot. The policy of the company is that your sales force never sells a car for below the established base price. Each sale results in a 5% commission for the salesperson. You have recently had some complaints from some of your employees regarding the actions of one of your best salespersons, Sam Slick. It seems that Sam has been selling cars for below the established base price. When you confront him about this practice, he points out that while the established base price gives the company a nice profit, no profit is realized if a car just sits on the lot forever. Consequently, he has been selling some of these slower-selling cars. A little profit is better than no profit at all he reasons.

Divide into groups of four persons. Each group will be designated as a *Taylor* group, a *Mayo* group, a *Deming* group, or a *Referee* group. Depending on your group type, answer the question below. After five minutes each group present its solution. The Referee group will then pick the best solution and explain its choice.

Taylor Group

You are a believer in scientific management. How would you handle this situation? Elect a spokesperson group to explain how and why you will handle it this way. This spokesperson will explain your rationale to the rest of the class.

Mayo Group

You follow the human relations approach to management. How might you handle this situation? Elect a spokesperson for the group to explain how and why you will handle it this way. This spokesperson will explain your rationale to the rest of the class.

Deming Group

You follow the management science approach to management. How might you handle this situation? Elect a spokesperson for the group to explain how and why you will handle it this way. This spokesperson will explain your rationale to the rest of the class.

Referee Group

You will listen to the groups present their approaches to solving this problem. Decide on the criteria for judging their solutions while they are working out their solutions.

Criteria

Which approach do you think would be best in this situation? Take a simple vote from all the referees to determine the best solution. Elect a spokesperson for the group to explain your choice to the rest of the class.

Study Guide Solutions

Chapter Review

Multiple-Choice Questions

1	2	3	4	5	6	7	8	9	10
C	B	B	D	C	C	C	D	C	D

11	12	13	14	15	16	17	18	19	20
C	B	A	D	A	B	B	C	C	B

21	22	23	24	25	26	27	28	29	30
C	A	C	A	E	B	A	D	C	B

True/False Questions

1	2	3	4	5	6	7	8	9	10
F	F	T	T	F	F	T	F	T	F

Short Answer Questions

1. Management is defined as the attainment of organizational goals in an effective and efficient manner through the employment of the four management functions of planning, organizing, leading, and controlling organizational resources.
2. The four functions of management are planning, organizing, leading, and controlling.
   a. PLANNING simply means deciding what it is you want to do and how you will go about it.
   b. ORGANIZING means deciding who does what.
   c. LEADING involves motivating and communicating with subordinates.
   d. CONTROLLING means setting standards, comparing results with those standards, and then making adjustments as needed.

3. The **advantages** of scientific management included the standardization of work, the systematic study of work, the linking of performance and pay, and improved productivity. The **disadvantages** included its failure to consider the social context within which work took place and its failure to appreciate workers' needs, other than their need for money.

4. The primary characteristics of a learning organization are—
   a. leadership
   b. team-based structure
   c. empowerment
   d. communications/information sharing
   e. emergent strategy
   f. strong culture

Manager's Workbook

Management Aptitude Questionnaire: Scoring and interpretation provided with exercise.

Who is a Manager?

Answers to this application will vary according to perceptions of each student. A discussion of the answers in class would be interesting.

ROLE	MANAGEMENT PROFESSOR	BASKETBALL COACH	FATHER OF A FAMILY
Figurehead	YES	YES	YES
Leader	YES	YES	YES
Liaison	YES	YES	YES
Monitor	YES	YES	YES
Disseminator	YES	YES	YES
Spokesperson	YES	YES	YES
Entrepreneur	MAYBE	YES	MAYBE
Disturbance Handler	YES	YES	YES
Resource Allocator	NO	YES	YES
Negotiator	NO	YES	YES

Manager's Workshop

The Worst Manager. Answers to this application will vary according to perceptions and unique experiences of each student.

Sam Slick

Taylor Group

As a believer in scientific management, you would try to convince Sam that there is one best way to sell used cars. You would try to train Sam in the company's prescribed way, including sticking to the established base price. You would also try to explain to Sam that by selling at a lower price he is reducing the amount of his commission. Since you believe that money is a prime motivator, this should convince him. You would also explain to him that it is management's job, not the employees', to establish procedures.

Mayo Group

You would explain to Sam that his actions were causing the other employees to complain and would not make him very popular with them. You would also emphasize the importance of teamwork. You would ask him if he had any ideas to solve this problem himself.

Deming Group

Since you subscribe to the management science approach, you would probably explain to Sam the quantitative rationale behind the present procedure. You would use logic to convince him that it is in his best interest to follow the procedure.

Referee Group

Some of the criteria you might consider using include practicality of the proposed solution, how well Sam will accept the solution, and the effect of the solution on the rest of the company.

Chapter 2

The Environment and Corporate Culture

Chapter Outline

I.   The External Environment

    A. General Environment

    B. Task Environment

II. The Organization-Environment Relationship

    A. Environmental Uncertainty

    B. Adapting to the Environment

III. The Internal Environment: Corporate Culture

    A. Symbols

    B. Stories

    C. Heroes

    D. Slogans

    E. Ceremonies

IV. Environment and Culture

    A. Adaptive Cultures

    B. Types of Cultures

V.   Shaping Corporate Cultures for the New Workplace

    A. New Demands for Managing Corporate Cultures

    B. Cultureal Leadership

Key Terms

Organizational environment: all elements existing outside the organization's boundaries that have the potential to affect the organization.

General environment: the layer of the external environment that affects the organization indirectly.

Task environment: the layer of the external environment that directly influences the organization's operations and performance.

Internal environment: the environment within the organization's boundaries

International dimension: portion of the external environment that represents events originating in foreign countries as well as opportunities for American companies in other countries.

Technological dimension: the dimension of the general environment that includes scientific and technological advancements in the industry and society at large.

Sociocultural dimension: the dimension of the general environment representing the demographic characteristics, norms, customs, and values of the population within which the organization operates.

Economic dimension: the dimension of the general environment representing the overall economic health of the country or region in which the organization functions.

Legal-political dimension: the dimension of the general environment that includes federal, state, and local government regulations and political activities designed to influence company behavior.

Pressure group: an interest group that works within the legal-political framework to influence companies to behave in socially responsible ways.

Customers: people and organizations in the environment who acquire goals or services from the organization.

Competitors: other organizations in the same industry or type of business that provide goods or services to the same set of customers.

Suppliers: people and organizations who provide the raw materials the organization uses to produce its output.

Labor market: the people available for hire by the organization.

Culture: the set of key values, beliefs, understandings, and norms that members of an organization share.

Symbol: an object, act, or event that conveys meaning to others.

Story: a narrative based on true events that is repeated frequently and shared by organizational employees.

Hero: a figure who exemplifies the deeds, character, and attributes of a strong corporate culture.

Slogan: a phrase or sentence that succinctly expresses a key corporate value.

Ceremony: a planned activity that makes up a special event and is conducted for the benefit of an audience.

Learning Objectives

1. Describe the general and task environments and the dimensions of each.

2. Explain how organizations adapt to an uncertain environment and identify techniques managers use to influence and control the external environment.

3. Define corporate culture and give organizational examples.

4. Explain organizational symbols, stories, heroes, slogans, and ceremonies and their relationship to corporate culture.

5. Describe how corporate culture relates to the environment.

6. Define a symbolic leader and explain the tools a symbolic leader uses to change corporate culture.

Chapter Review

Multiple Choice: Please indicate the correct response to the following questions by writing the letter of the correct answer in the space provided.

_____ 1. The task environment usually includes all of the following except
          a.   production technology.
          b.   competitors.
          c.   suppliers.
          d.   customers.
          e.   labor market.

_____ 2. The _____ environment refers to the external environment that affects the organization indirectly.
          a.   task
          b.   general
          c.   internal
          d.   corporate
          e.   outlying

_____ 3. _____ can cause the organization trouble by engaging in foreign production, making the price of entering the market high, or starting a price war.
          a.   Customers
          b.   Suppliers
          c.   Governments
          d.   Competitors
          e.   Joint ventures

_____ 4. A current trend affecting the labor supply is
   a. fewer expectations for democracy in the workplace by realistic, high-achieving workers.
   b. the increasing shortage of workers in some areas and a surplus in others.
   c. an increasing percentage of unionized workers.
   d. a pledge by large unions, especially the AFL-CIO, to unionize more companies.
   e. a decreasing number of college graduates as more workers are anxious to enter the job market.

_____ 5. The sociocultural dimension includes
   a. norms and values.
   b. demographics.
   c. geographic population distribution.
   d. educational levels in the community.
   e. all of the above.

_____ 6. The _____ environment widely dispersed and all its elements affect the organization about equally.
   a. task
   b. general
   c. internal
   d. corporate
   e. outlying

_____ 7. Which of the following is a characteristic of the organic organizational structure?
   a. rigidly defined tasks
   b. many rules and regulations
   c. centralized decision making
   d. low flexibility to the external environment
   e. employee teamwork

_____ 8. The U.S. population trends include
   a. the elderly population continues to increase.
   b. by 2050, non-Hispanic whites will make up only about half of the population
   c. by 2050 Hispanics are expected to make up nearly a quarter of the U.S. population
   d. the U.S. will continue to receive a large number of immigrants from Asia and Mexico.
   e. all of the above.

_____ 9. Visible organizational activities that illustrate corporate culture include everything except a
a. symbol.
b. slogan.
c. hero.
d. story.
e. supplier.

_____ 10. A special occasion that reinforces valued accomplishments is called a
a. symbolic meeting.
b. ceremony.
c. story event.
d. slogan maker.
e. hero-izer.

_____ 11. _____ is forcing a massive restructuring of power companies in several states.
a. Deregulation of electric utilities industry
b. The price of foreign oil
c. The "War on Terrorism"
d. Micorsoft
e. Foreign competition

_____ 12. To remain competitive in the global economy most companies have had to
a. move to Asia
b. move to Mexico
c. cut prices
d. get government financial support
e. resort to e-commerce

_____ 13. The _____ defines and uses signals and symbols to influence corporate culture.
a. cultural leader
b. pseudo-leader
c. ineffective leader
d. e-katzu
e. yheory Z

_____ 14. The internal environment includes
a. current employees.
b. production technology.
c. organization structure.
d. physical facilities.
e. all of the above.

_____ 15. Which of the following would be a customer of a hospital?
   a.   doctors
   b.   nurses
   c.   suppliers
   d.   patients
   e.   florists

_____ 16. A sociocultural trend in recent years has been
   a.   the trend toward greater interest in spirituality
   b.   the movement toward the work ethic.
   c.   greater savings by families.
   d.   increased homogeneity among consumers.
   e.   a return to the family farm.

_____ 17. Strategies for adapting to change include
   a.   centralized decision making.
   b.   boundary-spanning roles.
   c.   decreased planning and forecasting.
   d.   a structured hierarchy.
   e.   all of the above.

_____ 18. When the *Miami Herald* launches a Spanish-language newspaper, *El Nuevo Herald*, with articles emphasizing Hispanic, Cuban, and Latin American news and sports, it is responding to changes in _____ environment.
   a.   sociocultural
   b.   technological
   c.   economic
   d.   competitors
   e.   suppliers

_____ 19. The _____ has given increased power to customers and enabled them to directly impact the organization.
   a.   government
   b.   development of foreign competition
   c.   Internet
   d.   consumer movement
   e.   court system

_____ 20. If a manager does not have sufficient information about environmental factors to understand and predict environmental needs and changes, he is in a condition of
   a.   precarious guessing.
   b.   forecast ambiguity.
   c.   competitive advantage.
   d.   environmental stability.
   e.   uncertainty.

_____ 21. The _____ culture is characterized by a stable environment and an external strategic focus.
   a. adaptability
   b. achievement
   c. clan
   d. bureaucratic
   e. technology

_____ 22. Culture must fit the needs of the external environment and
   a. company strategy.
   b. government legislators.
   c. lobbyists.
   d. stockholders.
   e. competitors.

_____ 23. One of the elements of the corporate culture at the surface or visible level is
   a. a story.
   b. language.
   c. a ceremony.
   d. a value.
   e. a norm.

_____ 24. OSHA's 1992 mandatory regulations for workers exposed to blood-borne disease is an example of the
   a. technological dimension.
   b. sociocultural dimension.
   c. task environment.
   d. legal-political dimension.
   e. economic dimension.

_____ 25. A narrative based on true events that are repeated frequently and shared among organizational employees is called a
   a. story.
   b. legend.
   c. symbol.
   d. myth.
   e. ceremony.

_____ 26. Which statement below is correct?
   a. When the environment is dynamic, uncertainty is low.
   b. When the environment is unstable, uncertainty is low.
   c. A dynamic environment has more uncertainty than a stable environment.
   d. The stability of the environment does not determine the structure of the firm.
   e. None of the above is correct.

_____ 27. The text says that for leaders to ensure that employees understand a new culture they must
   a. overcommunicate.
   b. communicate less.
   c. ignore nonverbal signals.
   d. avoid creating excitement.
   e. none of the above.

_____ 28. The cultural leader needs to heed _____ activities that reinforce the cultural vision.
   a. special
   b. ceremonial
   c. occasional
   d. day-to-day
   e. leaderless

_____ 29. Managers must recognize a variety of _____ that work within the legal-political framework to influence companies to behave in a socially acceptable way.
   a. federal agencies
   b. quasi policemen
   c. vigilante groups
   d. impassioned minorities
   e. pressure groups

_____ 30. Organizational culture has _____ impact on performance.
   a. a significant
   b. no
   c. an unproven amount of
   d. an inverse
   e. none of the above

True/False: Please indicate whether the following statements are true or false by writing a T or an F in the blank in front of each question.

F 1. The task environment is part of an organization's internal environment.

T 2. A company that does not export will still run into competitors in its own marketplace, including some from developing countries.

T 3. The sociocultural dimension of the general environment represents the demographic characteristics.

F 4. Demography has little influence on shaping a society's norms and values.

F 5. If British Petroleum (BP) provides jet fuel for United Airlines (UAL), then BP is considered a customer for UAL.

T 6. One strategy for coping with high environmental uncertainty is to influence the environment to make it more compatible with organizational needs.

✓ _T_ 7. A clan culture operates in a flexible environment with an internal strategic focus.

✓ _T_ 8. Any company's culture can be interpreted by observing its symbols, stories, heroes, slogans, and ceremonies.

✓ _F_ 9. Managers have little to do with defining important symbols, stories, and heroes that help shape the culture.

✓ _T_ 10. The cultural leader articulates a vision for the organizational culture that employees can believe in and that generates excitement.

Short Answer: Please indicate your answer in the space provided.

1. Briefly describe the task environment and its four primary sectors.

2. Give an example of how a symbol and a ceremony you are familiar with support a corporate or organizational culture.

3. Is culture visible or invisible? Explain the justification for your answer.

4. Describe how a cultural leader influences culture and ensures that employees understand the new values.

Manager's Workbook

What is a Strong Corporate Culture? *(Also available on page 75 of text.)*

Think about an organization with which you are familiar, such as your school or a company for which you have worked. Respond to the statements below based on whether you agree that they describe the organization.

Disagree Strongly				Agree Strongly
1	2	3	4	5

1 Virtually all managers and most employees can describe the company's values, purpose, and customer importance.

| 1 | 2 | 3 | 4 | 5 |

2 There is clarity among organization members about how their jobs contribute to organizational goals.

| 1 | 2 | 3 | 4 | 5 |

3 It is very seldom that a manager will act in a way contrary to the company's espoused values.

| 1 | 2 | 3 | 4 | 5 |

4 Warmth and support of other employees is a valued norm, even across departments.

| 1 | 2 | 3 | 4 | 5 |

5 The company and its managers value what's best for the company over the long term more than short-term results.

| 1 | 2 | 3 | 4 | 5 |

6 Leaders make it a point to develop and mentor others.

| 1 | 2 | 3 | 4 | 5 |

7 Recruiting is taken very seriously, with multiple interviews in an effort to find traits that fit the culture.

| 1 | 2 | 3 | 4 | 5 |

8 Recruits are given negative as well as positive information about the company so they can freely choose whether to join.

| 1 | 2 | 3 | 4 | 5 |

9 Employees are expected to acquire real knowledge and mastery—not political alliances—before they can be promoted.

| 1 | 2 | 3 | 4 | 5 |

10 Company values emphasize what the company must do well to succeed in a changing environment.

        1   2   3   4   5

11 Conformity to company mission and values is more important than conformity to procedures and dress.

        1   2   3   4   5

12 You have heard stories about the company's leaders or "heroes" who helped make the company great.

        1   2   3   4   5

13 Ceremonies and special events are used to recognize and reward individuals who contribute to the company in significant ways.

        1   2   3   4   5

Total Score   ☐

Compute your score. If your total score is **52** or above, your organization has a strong culture, similar to a Procter & Gamble or Hewlett-Packard. A score from **26** to **51** suggests a culture of medium strength, which is positive for the organization, such as for American Airlines, Coca-Cola, and Citibank. A score of **25** or below indicates a weak culture, which is probably not helping the company adapt to the external environment or meet the needs of organization members. Discuss the pros and cons of a strong culture. Does a strong culture mean everyone has to be alike?

SOURCE: Adapted from Richard Pascale, "The Paradox of 'Corporate Culture': Reconciling Ourselves to Socialization," *California Management Review* 27, no. 2 (1985); and David A. Kolb, Joyce S. Osland, and Irwin M. Rubin, *Organizational Behavior: An Experiential Approach*, 6th ed. (Englewood Cliffs, N.J.: Prentice-Hall, 1995), 346-347.

What Economic Culture Is Your Company In?

According to *INC.* magazine, the U.S. economy is dividing into three separate worlds. These economies are the Networked, the Kluge, and the Provincial.

In the Networked economy are dense urban concentrations of companies and entrepreneurs that generate most of the country's high-wage jobs in globally competitive industries. Examples are high tech developers in Silicon Valley, the biomedical Research Triangle in North Carolina, and midwestern auto developers.

The Kluge economy consists of public bureaucracies, universities, and quasi-government industries such as defense or utilities. Kluge (pronounced "klooj") is software slang for ill assigned collection of code that is poorly matched and which forms a distressing whole.

The Networked and Kluge economies generate 45 percent (or 50 million) of the nation's non-agricultural jobs.

On the sidelines is the Provincial economy, clustered in the US's southern and intermountain western regions, which includes low-wage and low-skilled manufacturers, and back-office service providers. This economy makes up about 35 percent of the total.

The Kluge economy, though the least able to survive into the next century, nonetheless tries to attack the healthier and more formidable Networked economy.

Which economy does your company fit?

1. Think of a company. Choose either one you have worked or studied in, or else interview a friend or family member about their workplace. Fill out the questionnaire below.

2. Score the questionnaire.

3. What is the prognosis for the company you chose? How will its economic culture impact on its future survival?

Questionnaire:

1. Which does your company value most?
   a. constant interaction with other companies and individuals to define new products and services.
   b. locating in regions with the lowest wage, regulatory, and tax burdens.
   c. gaining access to key public officials.

2. Which best describes your company's staff?
   a. individuals whose responsibilities are constantly evolving and among whom lines of authority are blurred.
   b. a kingdom where the CEO's word is law.
   c. tenured senior employees administering teams of untenured underlings.

3. Which best describes the business-development activities your company would pursue?
   a. a daily diet of telephone calls, meetings and chance encounters with previous collaborators or new contacts they recommend.
   b. offering to cut the price of core products or services to stimulate sales.
   c. a detailed response to an RFP (request for proposal).

4. Which best describes what your management would most like to achieve?
   a. teaming up with other specialized businesses to develop new products no one ever thought of before.
   b. Doing big mail-order turnover from a converted barn in Kalispell, Montana.
   c. getting a 25% surcharge for your products approved by the relevant bureaucracy.

5. How would you describe your suppliers and customers?
   a. partners that change every day or week depending on the project.
   b. stable relationships governed largely by the price of what's bought or sold.
   c. organizations defined by what government agencies require.

6. How would you describe your markets?
   a. they're always changing.
   b. they closely correspond to double-digit standard industrial codes.
   c. they seem to vary only with major electoral changes.

7. Whom would your company be most likely to hire?
   a. someone who will one day function as a skilled partner in your company's business-development network.
   b. someone trustworthy and reliable, who can answer telephones in English.
   c. someone who helps meet state or federal regulatory requirements and has good political contacts.

8. Your business is being recruited to move to a new state. What's the primary concern?
   a. the depth of the businesses and the skill base in the new region.
   b. the tax breaks and incentive package the new state's willing to offer.
   c. potential long-term relations and cooperation with state and local officials.

9. Which best describes your company's view of American urban areas?
   a. a challenging environment but one offering an intellectual pulse and skill mix that is essential for maintaining a competitive edge.
   b. an anti-business, unsafe, regulatory quagmire.
   c. a public-contract heaven.

10. Which best describes your company's view of American rural areas?
    a. a great place to take ski trips and entertain clients.
    b. clean, homogenous communities perfect for building a new plant and raising the kids.
    c. an agricultural and public-power contract paradise.

11. What does "diversity" mean to your company?
    a. a gateway to world markets and an essential resource for fashioning new products or services.
    b. a complicated and contentious issue that can be avoided by moving to Idaho.
    c. a critical contract compliance requirement.

12. Which best describes your company's view of technology?
    a. whatever's exciting that can be integrated into new or existing products or services.
    b. something that comes in discrete waves and is bought when your customers demand it.
    c. something produced by a public institution named with an acronym.

13. You've come up with a new product idea. To bring it to market, your company would...
    a. start a new company, staff it with the most creative people you could find and jointly try to find as many creative applications of your ideas as possible.
    b. look for investors to back your idea, or sell out to an Asian consortium.
    c. Write a grant proposal for a feasibility study.

14. What's more attractive to your company?
    a. getting a piece of the action on a new deal.
    b. boosting margins from 4 percent to 5 percent (or maybe 5.14 percent if South Carolina is serious about that tax break).
    c. a check imprinted with the words "State of" or signed by the Secretary of the Treasury.

15. Which best describes where the CEO would probably like to be in 20 years?
   a. the respected founder of a major new industry.
   b. fishing in Utah.
   c. chair of a national technology-policy commission.

Scoring:
Give yourself 0 points for each A, 5 points for each B, and 10 points for each C.

Total Score:

0-30: Your company is a solid member of the Networked economy.

31-60: Your company has many characteristics in common with Networked companies, but it is also tending toward the low-skill, low-wage Provincial-economy model.

61-90: Your company is a solid member of the Provincial economy. Expect increasing wage and price pressures not just from businesses in other Provincial regions but from low-skill, low-wage launching platforms throughout the world.

91-120: Your company is midway between the Provincial and Kluge economies--hardly a happy mix for the 21st century, with global price competition increasing and the public sector shrinking.

121-150: Your company is a core Kluge-economy participant. You are probably in more trouble than an endangered species.

SOURCE: Adapted from David Friedman, "Are you ready for the networked economy?" *Inc.*, Feb. 1996, 62-65.

Manager's Workshop

Comparing Environments

1. Find a family member, friend, or other associate, who is at least 20 years older than you are. Fill out the left column in table below, interviewing this person to find out what the world was like when they were your age. Later, fill out the right hand-column to indicate your current world.

	Name of person interviewed	**You**
Discuss town where you lived: size, appearance, population, types of jobs for people, educational opportunities, etc.		
How did you get around, types of transportation? Did you have a car? What kind?		

What kind of house did you live in?		
How did you communicate with people—family, friends, business colleagues? How often?		
What kind of work did you do?		
Where did you travel?		
What did you expect out of life?		
What stressors did you have? Things that made you feel under a lot of stress?		
What was a dream you were never able to realize? Why?		

2. In groups of 3-5 compare your answers and come up with common themes on the differences between life 20 years ago and that of today. What can you say about the changing nature of the environment you live in? What implications does this have for your future?

3. What impact do these changes have on organizations, managers and career paths?

4. The instructor may either have a class discussion or ask your group to turn in a short paper describing answers to #2 above.

Organizational Graffiti *(Also available on page 76 of text.)*

Needed: a) 2 x 2 Post-it Notes, or blank sheets of paper (optional)
                  b) Colored sticky dots (optional)

1. Each person creates graffiti on the post-it or paper. The topics should relate to the following questions (your instructor may choose different questions): (5-10 min)

    What are the norms of behavior in most of your courses? What types of norms would you prefer instead?

2. All notes are stuck up on a large board (or pages are taped on the blackboard). (5 min)

3. The whole group works together to organize graffiti into theme categories, reducing them to the least number of categories without sacrificing substance. (5-10 min)

4. Each grouping is given a title by group. (5-10 min)

5. Each person is given three sticky dots, which are used to "vote" for most important title. If no sticky dots, each person puts three check marks by titles. Someone can use all marks or dots on one title, if desired. (5 min)

6. The top two titles are discussed as action plans. What does the group plan to do? Who will do it? When? How? How will the group know how good it is doing? What is the first step? How can this information benefit the whole school or department? (10-20 min)

7. Final discussion. What did you learn about cultures and norms? How can it be helpful to make the implicit explicit? (5-10 min)

Optional method: small groups develop their own group graffiti and present it to the entire class.

SOURCE: Adapted from Christopher Taylor, "Organizational Graffiti: A different approach to uncovering issues," *Journal of Management Education*, Vol. 23 (3), June 1999, 290-96.

Study Guide Solutions

Chapter Review

Multiple-Choice Questions

1	2	3	4	5	6	7	8	9	10
A	B	D	B	E	B	E	E	E	B

11	12	13	14	15	16	17	18	19	20
A	C	A	E	D	A	B	A	C	E

21	22	23	24	25	26	27	28	29	30
B	A	C	D	A	C	A	D	E	A

True/False Questions

1	2	3	4	5	6	7	8	9	10
F	T	T	F	F	T	T	T	F	T

Short Answer Questions

1. The task environment is the portion of the external environment that directly influences the organization's operations and performance.

   The task environment is made up of customers, competitors, suppliers, and the labor market. These sectors typically conduct day-to-day transactions with the organization.

2. One example most students would be familiar with exists within churches. A priest in a Roman Catholic Church wears a robe and other artifacts to symbolize his position and authority. Communion is a ceremony that supports the position and authority of the priest and the church.

3. Culture has both visible and invisible elements. Many artifacts such as symbols, slogans, and ceremonies are highly visible. Underlying values are invisible.

4. The cultural leader articulates a vision for the organizational change that generates excitement and that employees can believe in. He or she also heeds the day-to-day activities that reinforce the vision.

Manager's Workbook

What Is a Strong Corporate Culture?: Scoring and interpretation provided with exercise.

What Economic Culture Is Your Company In?: Scoring and interpretation provided with exercise.

Manager's Workshop

Comparing Environments: Results will vary based on environment.

Organizational Graffiti: Answers to this application will vary according to perceptions of each student.

Chapter 3

Managing in a Global Environment

Chapter Outline

Key Terms

International management: the management of business operations conducted in more than one country.

Infrastructure: a country's physical facilities that support economic activities.

Political risk: a company's risk of loss of assets, earning power, or managerial control due to politically based events or actions by host governments.

Political instability: events such as riots, revolutions, or government upheavals that affect the operations of an international company.

Most favored nation: a term describing a GATT clause that calls for member countries to grant other member countries the most favorable treatment they accord any country concerning imports and exports.

Euro: a single European currency that replaced the currencies of 11 European nations.

Culture: the shared knowledge, beliefs, values, behaviors and ways of thinking among members of a society.

Power distance: the degree to which people accept inequality in power among institutions, organizations, and people.

Uncertainty avoidance: a value characterized by people's intolerance for uncertainty and ambiguity and resulting support for beliefs that promise certainty and conformity.

Individualism: a preference for a loosely knit social framework in which individuals are expected to take care of themselves.

Collectivism: a preference for a tightly knit social framework in which individuals look after one another and organizations protect their members' interests.

Masculinity: a cultural preference for achievement, heroism, assertiveness, work centrality, and material success.

Femininity: a cultural preference for cooperation, group decision making, and quality of life.

Long-term orientation: a greater concern for the future and high value on thrift and perseverance.

Short-term orientation: a concern with the past and present and a high value on meeting social obligations.

Ethnocentrism: a cultural attitude marked by the tendency to regard one's own culture as superior to others.

Market entry strategy: an organizational strategy for entering a foreign market.

Global outsourcing: engaging in the international division of labor so as to obtain the cheapest sources of labor and supplies regardless of country; also called *global sourcing*.

Exporting: an entry strategy in which the organization maintains its production facilities within its home-country and transfers its products for sale in foreign countries.

Licensing: an entry strategy in which an organization in one country makes certain resources available to companies in another in order to participate in the production and sale of its products abroad.

Franchising: a form of licensing in which an organization provides its foreign franchisees with a complete package of materials and services.

Direct investing: an entry strategy in which the organization is involved in managing its production facilities in a foreign country.

Joint venture: a variation of direct involvement in which an organization shares costs and risks with another firm to build a manufacturing facility, develop new products, or set up a sales and distribution network.

Multinational corporation (MNC): an organization that receives more than 25 percent of its total sales revenues from operations outside the parent company's home country; also called *global corporation* or *transnational corporation*.

Culture shock: feelings of confusion, disorientation, and anxiety that result from being immersed in a foreign culture.

Learning Objectives

1.   Describe the emerging borderless world.

2.   Define international management and explain how it differs from the management of domestic business operations.

3.   Indicate how dissimilarities in the economic, sociocultural, and legal-political environments throughout the world can affect business operations.

4.   Describe market entry strategies that businesses use to develop foreign markets.

5.   Describe the characteristics of a multinational corporation.

6.   Explain the challenges of managing in a global environment.

Chapter Review

Multiple Choice: Please indicate the correct response to the following questions by writing the letter of the correct answer in the space provided.

_____   1.   The importance of international business to the study of management can best be described by which of these statements?
   a.   International business is more important than the study of management.
   b.   International business is less important than the study of management.
   c.   Since the management functions are universal, international business in not important to the study of management.
   d.   If you are not thinking international, you are not thinking business management.
   e.   International business has nothing to do with the study of management.

_____ 2. The phases of globalization are
   a. domestic, international, multinational, and global.
   b. global, multinational, international, and democratic.
   c. domestic, international, multinational, and multidomestic.
   d. cottage, domestic, international, and multinational.
   e. domestic, cottage, international, and global.

_____ 3. The management of business operations conducted in more than one country is called
   a. global management.
   b. international management.
   c. outsourcing management.
   d. planning management.
   e. domestic management.

_____ 4. The criterion for being classified as a less developed country is
   a. per capita income.
   b. lower moral standards.
   c. having more jungles.
   d. having less foreigners.
   e. having less agriculture.

_____ 5. Economic development differs widely throughout the world. Countries can be categorized as either _____ or _____.
   a. deprived, developed
   b. developing, developed
   c. disadvantaged, destitute
   d. debilitated, developed
   e. determined, destined

_____ 6. _____ generally are located in Asia, Africa and South America.
   a. MNCs
   b. EUs
   c. LDCs
   d. WTOs
   e. MFNs

_____ 7. Infrastructure refers to a country's
   a. climate.
   b. economic physical support facilities.
   c. form of government.
   d. organizational preferences.
   e. societal structure and classes.

8. Exchange rates refer to
    a. the quantity of students who study in other countries.
    b. the number of students who visit a respective country.
    c. the arrangements between airlines to have reciprocal landing rights across national boundaries.
    d. the rate at which one country's currency is exchanged for another country's.
    e. the number of foreign businesses allowed to operate within a given country.

9. Political risk may involve
    a. violent acts against a firm's property.
    b. outright seizure of a company's facilities.
    c. gradual government encroachment into management of the firm.
    d. a timetable for shift of ownership to local interests.
    e. all of the above.

10. Which of the following is/are (an) example(s) of political instability?
    a. riots
    b. revolutions
    c. civil disorders
    d. frequent changes in government
    e. all of the above

11. The GATT term for one member country agreeing to grant other member countries the most favorable treatment they accord any country is
    a. most favored nation.
    b. equal nation status.
    c. free trade.
    d. fair trade.
    e. free and fair trade.

12. The goal of the World Trade Organization (WTO) is to _____--and sometimes-- _____ the nations of the world toward free trade and open markets.
    a. recommend, force
    b. coerce, impose on
    c. discourage, dissuade
    d. guide, urge
    e. legislate, militarize

13. The European Union has expanded to a _____-nation alliance.
    a. 10
    b. 12
    c. 15
    d. 16
    e. 21

_____ 14. The _____ is the single European currency that will eventually replace up to 15 national currencies and unify a huge marketplace.
  a. mark
  b. franc
  c. mfn
  d. euro
  e. pound

_____ 15. A country that has low power distance is
  a. Malaysia.
  b. the Philippines.
  c. Sweden.
  d. Panama.
  e. all of the above.

_____ 16. NAFTA is an agreement among
  a. Canada, Mexico, and the U.S.
  b. Newly Aligned Free Trade Areas.
  c. North African Free Trade Areas.
  d. Norway and Afghanistan Free Trade Areas.
  e. none of the above.

_____ 17. Having a feminine cultural preference means that
  a. the female population is at least 10 percent greater than the male population.
  b. women are chosen as political leaders.
  c. there is a tendency to emphasize the quality of life.
  d. heroism is emphasized.
  e. mothers are honored more than fathers.

_____ 18. If members of a society feel uncomfortable with uncertainty and ambiguity, it is called
  a. cognitive dissonance.
  b. high uncertainty avoidance.
  c. collective insecurity.
  d. cultural paranoia.
  e. security backlash.

_____ 19. Germany's cultural preference is for achievement, heroism, assertiveness, and material success. This would be considered
  a. power distance.
  b. individualism.
  c. masculinity.
  d. ethnocentrism.
  e. collectivism.

_____ 20. The entry strategy of _____ provides the least amount of risk and resource costs, but also the least control.
   a. exporting
   b. licensing
   c. franchising
   d. a joint venture
   e. a wholly owned subsidiary

_____ 21. Global outsourcing means that a company decides to
   a. attempt to influence foreign governments to allow you to do business.
   b. engage in the international division of labor.
   c. hire managers from other countries to manage operations in its home country.
   d. seek a growth strategy by aggressively entering foreign markets.
   e. delete a product line by allowing existing supplies to run out.

_____ 22. An entry strategy in which the company maintains its production facilities at home and transfers its products for sale in foreign markets is called
   a. countertrade.
   b. licensing.
   c. franchising.
   d. exporting.
   e. direct investing.

_____ 23. Finding a cheaper source of supply offshore is called
   a. foreign cost minimization.
   b. maximum materials management.
   c. a joint venture.
   d. direct investment.
   e. outsourcing.

_____ 24. Global sourcing refers to
   a. the same thing as outsourcing.
   b. finding customers to buy your exports.
   c. conserving the environment worldwide.
   d. using international financing.
   e. joint ventures in a third country.

_____ 25. An arrangement in which one company provides a foreign company with a complete package of materials and services including advice and standardized operating procedures is called
   a. outsourcing.
   b. licensing.
   c. direct investment.
   d. franchising.
   e. exporting.

_____ 26. A joint venture is a type of
    a. exporting.
    b. licensing.
    c. franchising.
    d. direct investment.
    e. international division.

_____ 27. Culture shock refers to
    a. realizing that one's own culture is inferior.
    b. having to learn about the arts of a new country quickly.
    c. frustration and anxiety from being in a strange culture.
    d. being sleepy when you arrive in a foreign country due to *jet lag*.
    e. suddenly realizing that you cannot speak the local language.

_____ 28. In Asia, the Arab world, and Latin America, managers should use a _____ management approach.
    a. task-oriented
    b. macho
    c. impersonal
    d. critical
    e. warm, relationship-oriented

_____ 29. A manager in Japan should realize that Japanese are motivated
    a. by time off.
    b. by individual rewards.
    c. in groups.
    d. by money only.
    e. by public praise only.

_____ 30. One reason Japanese companies have been so successful internationally is that their culture
    a. encourages learning and adaptability.
    b. can withstand challenges from other cultures.
    c. tends to dominate other cultures.
    d. is practically nonexistent.
    e. is so complex that it encompasses all other cultures.

True/False: Please indicate whether the following statements are true or false by writing a T or an F in the blank in front of each question.

___T___ 1. The process of globalization typically passes through four distinct stages.

___F___ 2. A company in the domestic stage has its marketing and production facilities located in many countries.

___T___ 3. The basic management functions of planning, organizing, leading, and controlling are different depending on whether a company operates domestically or internationally.

F✓ 4. A country's physical facilities that support economic activities are called its development structure.

F✓ 5. Changes in the exchange rates do not affect the profitability of international operations.

F 6. Although most companies would prefer to do business in stable countries, some of the greatest growth opportunities lie in areas characterized by instability.

T✓ 7. GATT was originally signed by 23 nations, while today it has more than 100 member countries that abide by its rules.

T✓ 8. Countries like Japan which support beliefs that provide stability and conformity among its citizenry are characterized by the social value of uncertainty avoidance.

F✓ 9. An attitude called geocentric means that people have a tendency to regard their own culture as superior and to downgrade other cultures.

T✓ 10. Direct acquisition of an affiliate can provide cost savings over exporting by shortening distribution channels and reducing storage and transportation costs.

Short Answer: Please indicate your answer in the space provided.

1. What are the advantages and disadvantages of using exporting as a market entry strategy internationally?

2. Explain why anyone would oppose NAFTA.

3. List three examples of a country's infrastructure.

4. List five of the countries that make up the European Union (EU).

Manager's Workbook

State of the World Test *(Also available on page 104 of text.)*

How aware are you of the rest of the planet? If you will be working internationally, the better you know about the world, the more successful you are likely to be.

1. Six countries contain one-half the total population of the world. Which are the six countries?

    1.   4.

    2.   5.

    3.   6.

2. Which six most commonly spoken first languages account for one-third of the total world population?

    1.

    2.

    3.

    4.

    5.

    6.

3. How many living languages (those still spoken) are there in the world?
   a. 683   b. 2,600   c. 6,800

4. How many nations were there in 2001?
   a. 291
   b. 191
   c. 91

5. The proportion of people in the world over age 60 will increase ___ percent by 2050.

6. The number of people immigrating from poorer countries to developed ones will be ___ per year in coming years.

7. Between 1970 and 2000, the number of people in the world suffering from malnutrition:
   a. declined
   b. remained about the same
   c. increased

8. Between 1960 and 1987, the world spent approximately $10 trillion on health care. How much did the world spend on military?
   a. $7 trillion
   b. $10 trillion
   c. $17 trillion
   d. $25 trillion

9. According to the United Nations, what percentage of the world's work (paid and unpaid) is done by women?
   a. one-third
   b. one-half
   c. two-thirds
   d. three-fourths

10. Women make up ___ percent of the world's illiterates.

11. In some African countries, ____ percent of women have suffered female genital mutilation.

12. According to the United nations, what percentage of the world's income is earned by women?
    a. one-tenth
    b. three-tenths
    c. one-half
    d. seven-tenths

13. The nations of Africa, Asia, Latin American and the Middle East, often referred to as the Third World, contain about 78% of the world's population. What percentage of the world's monetary income do they possess?
    a. 10%
    b. 20%
    c. 30%
    d. 40%

14. Americans constitute approximately 5% of the world's population. What percentage of the world's resources do Americans consume?

    a. 15%
    b. 25%
    c. 35%
    d. 45%

15. Which city has the worst air pollution: New York, Mexico City, or Moscow?

16. The total output of the world economy was $6.3 trillion in 1950. What was it in 2000?

17. The number of host computers on the internet grew by _____ percent from 1990 to 2000.

18. Which three countries have the highest rate of HIV infection?

19. If the world were represented by 100 people, fill in the blanks below to indicate what percentage of people are the following:

_____ would be Asian

_____ would be non-White

_____ would be non-Christian

_____ would live in substandard housing

_____ would be illiterate

_____ would have a college education

_____ would own a computer

SOURCE: Reka Balu, "Please Don't Forward This E-mail!" *Fast* Company (June 2001), 58-59; World Watch Institute, *World Watch 2002,* W.W. Norton; *http://www.un-org.* 2002.

Test Your Global Potential

A global environment requires that American managers learn to deal effectively with people in other countries. The assumption that foreign business leaders behave and negotiate in the same manner as Americans is false. How well prepared are you to live with globalization? Consider the following.

Are you Guilty of:	Definitely No				Definitely Yes
	1	2	3	4	5

1. Impatience? Do you think "Time is money" or "Let's get to the point"?

     1   2   3   4   5

2. Having a short attention span, bad listening habits, or being uncomfortable with silence?

     1   2   3   4   5

3. Being somewhat argumentative, sometimes to the point of belligerence?

     1   2   3   4   5

4. Ignorance about the world beyond your borders?

     1   2   3   4   5

5. Weakness in foreign languages?

     1   2   3   4   5

6. Placing emphasis on short-term success?

     1   2   3   4   5

7. Believing that advance preparations are less important than negotiations themselves?

     1   2   3   4   5

8. Being legalistic? Of believing "A deal is a deal," regardless of changing circumstances?

     1   2   3   4   5

9. Having little interest in seminars on the subject of globalization, failing to browse through libraries or magazines on international topics, not interacting with foreign students or employees?

     1   2   3   4   5

Total Score [　　　　]

If you scored less than 27, congratulations. You have the temperament and interest to do well in a global company. If you scored more than 27, it's time to consider a change. Regardless of your score, go back over each item and make a plan of action to correct deficiencies indicated by answers of 4 or 5 to any question.

SOURCE: Reprinted by permission of the publisher from Cynthia Barmun and Netasha Wolninsky, "Why Americans Fail at Overseas Negotiations," *Management Review* (October 1989), 55-57, 1989 American Management Association, New York. All rights reserved.

Manager's Workshop

What Is the Cultural Significance of Your Name?

In cross-cultural or mixed-ethnic groups of 4-6 members, answer the following questions with one another.

The questions below are designed to help you talk with others about the cultural significance of your name. These questions should be asked of both your family name and your given name(s):

1. What does your name mean in your culture? Does it imply that you are any special type of person? (e.g., strong, wise, beautiful, etc.)

2. What nicknames if any do you have? Are they nicknames that commonly go with your name (ex: "Bob" for "Robert") or are they more unique to you personally?

3. How common is your name? Is it found mainly in your culture, or is it found in other cultures as well?

4. Does your name have any religious significance?

5. Does your name have a clear gender association, i.e., is it definitely masculine or feminine in your culture? Is there a variation of your name that is given to the opposite sex?

6. Do you have any reminders that you tell people to help them remember your name?

7. Is your name the subject of any songs or jokes in your culture? Are there children's rhymes that use your name?

8. What else would you say about your name to help someone remember it and what it means?

SOURCE: Peter Vaill, University of St. Thomas, Minneapolis, MN.

Chinese, Indian and American Values

1. To be completed prior to class: Rank order the 15 values for Chinese, Indian, and American.

2. In class break into small discussion groups of 4-6 and try to achieve consensus on the ranking of values for both Chinese and American cultures, as well as Indian, if time permits.

3. Each group presents its rankings and discusses rationale for decisions (optional).

4. As a class, discuss the differences between Chinese and American value systems; the instructor will give out the correct rankings.

Background

In the 1950s and 1960s a number of value orientation studies were conducted using university students in various countries. The data presented here come from some studies which used the Edwards Personal Preference Schedule. Groups tested included 1504 Americans, 2876 Chinese and 288 Indian students.

Value Rankings

Rank order each of the 15 values below according to what you think it is in the Chinese, Indian (from India) and American cultures. *Use "1" to be the most important value for the culture and "15" to be the least important value for that culture.*

Value	American	Chinese	Indian
Achievement			
Deference			
Order			
Exhibition			
Autonomy			
Affiliation			
Intraception (defined below)			
Succorance (defined below)			
Dominance			
Abasement (defined below)			
Nurturance			

South-Western

Change			
Endurance			
Heterosexuality			
Aggression			

Some definitions:

Succorance: willingness to come to the aid of another or to offer relief.

Abasement: to lower oneself in rank, prestige, or esteem.

Intraception: the other side of extraception, where one is governed by concrete clearly observable physical conditions. Intraception, on the other hand, is the tendency to be governed by more subjective factors, such as feelings, fantasies, speculations, and aspirations.

Internal/External Locus of Control

Considering American and Chinese groups, which would be more internal locus of control (tend to feel in control of one's destiny, that rewards come as a result of hard work, perseverance, responsibility) and which would be more external (fate, luck, or other outside forces control destiny) control?

Machiavellianism

This concept was defined by Christie and Geis as the belief one can manipulate and deceive people for their personal gain. Do you think Americans or Chinese would score higher on the Mach scale?

Discussion Questions

1. What are some main differences between the cultures? Did any patterns emerge?

2. Were you surprised by the results?

3. What behaviors could you expect in business dealings with Chinese (or Indians) based on their value system?

4. How do American values dictate Americans' behaviors in business situations?

SOURCE: Copyright 1996 and 1993 by Dorothy Marcic. Adapted from the Michael Harris Bond (ed.) book, *The Psychology of the Chinese People* (Hong Kong: Oxford University Press, 1986.) The selection used here is "Chinese Personality and its Change" by Kuo-Shu Yang, pp.106-170.

Global Economy Scavenger Hunt *(Also available on page 105 of text.)*

In order to get a perspective on the pervasiveness of the global economy, you will be asked to find a number of things and bring them back to class.

1. Divide into teams of 4-6 members.

2. Each team is to bring items to a future class from the list below.

3. On the day in class, each team will give a short, two-minute presentation on the items that were the most difficult to find or the most interesting.

4. How many countries did your team get items from? How many for the entire class?

List for scavenger hunt:

1. Find brochures or annual reports of four multi-national corporations.

2. Gather evidence from three local businesses to show they do business internationally.

3. Locate a retail store that sells only "Made in America."

4. Find 10 toys or games that originate in other countries.

5. Find five toys or games that have components from one country and were assembled in another—or show how they were otherwise developed in more than one country.

6. List food items from 25 different countries.

7. List articles of clothing from 15 different countries.

8. List books sold in your town from authors of 12 different countries. Where were the books published? Who translated them?

9. List 12 films in the past five years that starred someone from another country.

10. List five films in the past five years that had multi-national crews and locations. Include at least one that was co-produced by two or more countries.

11. Gather descriptions of interviews from five foreigners (not from your team or the class), in which they were asked to list six things that they like about the United States and six things they don't like.

12. Create a list of eight places where a language other than English is displayed (on a bulletin board, poster, etc.).

13. Find two maps of the world drawn before 1900.

14. List five items in your town that were manufactured in another country and were not being made in that country six years ago.

Adapted from: Jan Drum, Steve Hughes and George Otere, "Global Scavenger Hunt," in *Global Winners* (Yarmouth, Maine: Intercultural Press, 1994), 21-23.

Study Guide Solutions

Chapter Review

Multiple-Choice Questions

1	2	3	4	5	6	7	8	9	10
D	A	B	A	B	C	B	D	E	E

11	12	13	14	15	16	17	18	19	20
A	D	C	D	C	A	C	B	C	A

21	22	23	24	25	26	27	28	29	30
B	D	E	A	D	D	C	E	C	A

True/False Questions

1	2	3	4	5	6	7	8	9	10
T	F	F	F	F	T	T	T	F	T

Short Answer Questions

1. Exporting involves the lowest cost and risk of all the strategies. It is a neat way to get your products into other markets. However, the long distances, government regulations, and differences in currencies and cultures can often cause problems. Also, the profit is not as great as it could be with more direct involvement.

2. NAFTA is opposed by some who fear a job loss to Mexico and the potential for industrial "ghost towns." Others feel that it can also endanger the environment.

3. Transportation facilities such as railroads and airports; energy-producing facilities such as utilities and power plants; and communication facilities such as telephone lines and radio stations.

4. Choose any five of the following: Sweden, Finland, Denmark, Ireland, United Kingdom, Luxembourg, Netherlands, Germany, Belgium, France, Portugal, Spain, Austria, Italy, and Greece.

Manager's Workbook

State of the World: Answers provided on page AD-1 in the back of the textbook.

Test Your Global Potential: Scoring and interpretation provided with exercise.

Manager's Workshop

What Is the Cultural Significance of Your Name?: Answers to this application will vary from student to student.

Chinese, Indian and American Values:

Chinese, Indian, and American Values:

Value	American	Chinese	Indian
Achievement	7	3	5
Deference	12	11 (tie)	10
Order	15	8	13
Exhibition	8	13	12
Autonomy	10	11 (tie)	11
Affiliation	3	4	8
Intraception	1	2	4
Succorance	14	10	14
Dominance	5	9	7
Abasement	9	6	1
Nurturance	6	1	2
Change	2	7	3
Endurance	11	5	6
Heterosexuality	14	15	15
Aggression	13	14	9

INTERNAL/EXTERNAL LOCUS OF CONTROL

Americans tend to be more internal and Chinese more external

VALUES

In terms of the value survey, it can be seen that Chinese students tend to show a higher need than Americans for Achievement, Order, Deference, Abasement, Succorance, Nurturance and Endurance, with a lower need on Exhibition, Intraception, Dominance, Change, Heterosexuality and Aggression. It was expected that a sample of the general population, rather than students, would have shown even greater cultural differences.

The results of twenty studies done of Chinese students in Taiwan showed their predominant profile of value orientation to consist of inner development, past perspective, collectivism (lineality), and submission to nature. They choose to combine contemplation, action and enjoyment in acceptable proportions. They feel it is important to accept social constraints, to show and express sympathetic concern for others and to preserve and maintain good human traditions and achievements. Further, they are high in theoretical and aesthetic pursuits and low in economic and religious ones. They feel sensuous enjoyment, as well as silent submission to external forces are both wrong. Harmony, self-restraint and conscientiousness are rated high.

When asking Chinese students which goals were important to them, they ranked top ones as good marriage and happy family, beating one's brains out to pursue knowledge and handsome salary. Low for them were goals such as religious belief, being a leader to dominate others, exercising intensely to develop physical qualities, and being successful in social life.

Studies of Machiavellianism, or the belief that one can manipulate and deceive people for personal gain, have shown that (despite a Western stereotype otherwise) that Chinese people have a lower level of Machiavellianism than Westerners.

In another study (in 1967) of authoritarianism using the California Fascism Scale, it was found that students from India and Rhodesia (now Zimbabwe) showed highest levels, then came China and Arabia (tied), then Brazil and finally, much further down, USA.

Some researchers, though, have found that Chinese society is moving away from the traditional values and going more towards (slowly, of course) autonomy, achievement and inner-control beliefs.

Global Economy Scavenger Hunt: Results will vary.

Chapter 4

Managerial Ethics and Corporate Social Responsibility

Chapter Outline

I.   What Is Managerial Ethics?

II. Criteria for Ethical Decision Making

    A.   Utilitarian Approach

    B.   Individualism Approach

    C.   Moral Rights Approach

    D.   Justice Approach

III. Factors Affecting Ethical Choices

    A.   The Manager

    B.   The Organization

IV. What Is Social Responsibility?

V.   Organizational Stakeholders

VI. The Natural Environment

VII. Evaluating Corporate Social Performance

    A.   Economic Responsibilities

    B.   Legal Responsibilities

    C.   Ethical Responsibilities

    D.   Discretionary Responsibilities

VIII. Managing Company Ethics and Social Responsibility

    A.   Ethical Individuals

    B.   Ethical Leadership

    C.   Organizational Structures and Systems

    D.   Whistle-blowing

IX. Ethics and the New Workplace

Key Terms

Ethics: the code of moral principles and values that govern the behaviors of a person or group with respect to what is right or wrong.

Ethical dilemma: a situation that arises when all alternative choices or behaviors have been deemed undesirable because of potentially negative consequences, making it difficult to distinguish right from wrong.

Utilitarian approach: the ethical concept that moral behaviors produce the greatest good for the greatest number.

Individualism approach: the ethical concept that acts are moral when they promote the individual's best long-term interests, which ultimately leads to the greater good.

Moral-rights approach: the ethical concept that moral decisions are those that best maintain the rights of those people affected by them.

Justice approach: the ethical concept that moral decisions must be based on standards of equity, fairness, and impartiality.

Social responsibility: the obligation of organization management to make decisions and take actions that will enhance the welfare and interests of society as well as the organization.

Stakeholder: any group within or outside the organization that has a stake in the organization's performance.

Discretionary responsibility: organizational responsibility that is voluntary and guided by the organization's desire to make social contributions not mandated by economics, law, or ethics.

Code of ethics: a formal statement of the organization's values regarding ethics and social issues.

Ethics committee: a group of executives assigned to oversee the organization's ethics by ruling on questionable issues and disciplining violators.

Chief ethics officer: a company executive who oversees ethics and legal compliance.

Ethics training: training programs to help employees deal with ethical questions and values.

Whistle-blowing: the disclosure by an employee of illegal, immoral, or illegitimate practices by the organization.

Learning Objectives

1. Define ethics and explain how ethical behavior relates to behavior governed by law and free choice.

2. Explain the utilitarian, individualism, moral rights, and justice approaches for evaluating ethical behavior.

3. Describe how both individual and organizational factors shape ethical decision making.

4. Define corporate social responsibility and how to evaluate it along economic, legal, ethical, and discretionary criteria.

5. Describe four corporate responses to social demands.

6. Explain the concept of stakeholder and identify important stakeholders for organizations.

7. Discuss how ethical organizations are created through ethical leadership and organizational structures and systems.

Chapter Review

Multiple Choice: Please indicate the correct response to the following questions by writing the letter of the correct answer in the space provided.

_____ 1. In the domain of ethical behavior is
   a. obedience to unenforceable norms and standards.
   b. obedience to laws.
   c. obedience to what one personally feels is right.
   d. obedience to regulatory agencies.
   e. obedience to conscience.

_____ 2. The domain of free choice pertains to behavior
   a. dictated by the law that one may choose to obey or disobey.
   b. about which the law has no say.
   c. for which an individual does not have complete freedom.
   d. for which standards of conduct are based on shared values about moral conduct.
   e. of a sexual nature.

_____ 3. Advocates of the individualism approach claim that in the long-term employing of this approach,
   a. the greater good is served.
   b. people learn to accommodate each other.
   c. lying and cheating will cease.
   d. honesty and integrity will result.
   e. all of the above.

_____ 4. Under the utilitarian approach, a
   a. decision maker is expected to consider the effect of some decision alternatives on some of the parties and select the one that optimizes satisfaction for the some.
   b. decision maker is not expected to consider the effect of each decision alternative on all parties and selects the one that optimizes satisfaction for him or her.
   c. decision maker is expected to consider the effect of each decision alternative on all parties and select the one that optimizes satisfaction for the greatest number.
   d. decision maker is to look at each opportunity and select the one that is best for the organization.
   e. decision maker is to look at each opportunity and select the one that is best for them.

_____ 5.   The moral right of freedom of conscience says that
   a.   individuals are to be treated only as they knowingly and freely consent to be treated.
   b.   individuals have a right to live without endangerment or violation of their health and safety.
   c.   individuals may refrain from carrying out any order that violates their moral or religious norms.
   d.   individuals have a right to an impartial hearing and fair treatment.
   e.   individuals can choose to do as they please away from work.

_____ 6.   According to the _____ approach, the ethically correct decision is the one that best maintains the rights of those people affected by it.
   a.   utilitarian
   b.   individualism
   c.   moral-rights
   d.   justice
   e.   ethics

_____ 7.   _____ requires that different treatment of people not be based on arbitrary characteristics.
   a.   Ethical behavior
   b.   Distributive justice
   c.   The utilitarian approach
   d.   The ethics committee
   e.   Compensatory justice

_____ 8.   The radio payola scandal of the 1950s involved
   a.   radio stations asking for kickbacks from advertisers.
   b.   listeners giving kickbacks to stations for winning on air contests.
   c.   disc jockeys taking money to play certain songs.
   d.   legislatures giving broadcasting rights to radio stations in exchange for money.
   e.   retailers receiving payments to promote certain brands or radios they sold.

_____ 9.   The _____ approach is closest to the thinking underlying the domain of codified law.
   a.   justice
   b.   utilitarian
   c.   moral-rights
   d.   individualism
   e.   postconventional

_____ 10.   Specific _____ characteristics, such as ego strength, self-confidence, and strong sense of independence, may enable managers to make ethical decisions.
   a.   perceptual
   b.   cognitive
   c.   professional
   d.   personality
   e.   attitudinal

_____11. Which leadership style matches with the preconventional level of personal moral development?
a. Autocratic
b. Team oriented
c. Servant leadership
d. Guiding/encouraging
e. Transforming

_____ 12. The level of moral development at which internal values are more important than expectations of significant others is the _____ stage.
a. preconventional
b. conventional
c. anti-conventional
d. principled
e. self-righteous

_____ 13. When a Navy pilot disobeyed orders and risked his life to save men from the USS Indianapolis when it sank, he was operating from the _____ level of moral development.
a. invisible
b. rebellious
c. highest
d. selfish
e. social

_____ 14. At the _____ level of moral development one follows the rules to avoid physical punishment.
a. physiological
b. preconventional
c. conventional
d. postconventional
e. principled

_____ 15. Social responsibility
a. is difficult to understand.
b. means considering the interests of society and the organization.
c. considers only the welfare of society, not of the organization.
d. does not mean being a good corporate citizen.
e. does not consider managerial actions.

_____ 16. Important stakeholders include all of the following except
a. employees.
b. customers.
c. competitors.
d. creditors.
e. investors.

_____ 17.   Which of the following approaches would be considered the most "green" to indicate its commitment to environmental responsibility?
a.   legal
b.   market
c.   stakeholder
d.   activist
e.   preconventional

_____18.   The first criterion of social responsibility is
a.   discretionary responsibility.
b.   corporate greed.
c.   economic responsibility.
d.   profit-maximization.
e.   legal responsibility.

_____19.   _____ responsibility defines the ground rules, laws, and regulations that businesses are expected to follow.
a.   Economic
b.   Legal
c.   Ethical
d.   Discretionary
e.   Accommodative

_____20.   The company executive who oversees ethics and legal compliance is called the
a.   priest
b.   ethical ombudsman
c.   ethical watchman
d.   chief ethics officer
e.   wimp

_____ 21.   _____ responsibility is purely voluntary and guided by a company's desire to make social contributions.
a.   Economic
b.   Legal
c.   Ethical
d.   Discretionary
e.   Accommodative

_____ 22.   Which of the following is an element of ethical leadership?
a.   role modeling
b.   rewarding ethical behavior
c.   swift discipline of unethical behavior
d.   upholding ethical values in the organization
e.   all of the above

_____ 23. The code of ethics at Lockheed Martin
   a.   details an appropriate level of potential profits.
   b.   is printed on cards so employees can carry them.
   c.   is determined by employee vote.
   d.   violates organizational cultural norms.
   e.   reflects the theme "Setting the Standard."

_____ 24. Principle-based codes of ethics include statements about
   a.   treatment of employees.
   b.   marketing practices.
   c.   conflicts of interests.
   d.   political gifts.
   e.   observance of laws.

_____ 25. An ethics committee is responsible for
   a.   developing ethics training programs.
   b.   maintaining a corporate hot line.
   c.   avoiding taxes.
   d.   overseeing the organization's ethics by ruling on questionable issues.
   e.   pacifying outside groups.

_____ 26. The ethics committee
   a.   involves the disclosure by an employee to an outside authority of some company indiscretion.
   b.   disciplines violators.
   c.   directly violates a code of ethics.
   d.   usually conducts social audits monthly.
   e.   violates individual privacy rights.

_____ 27. Whistle-blowing refers to
   a.   inflating product benefits in advertisements.
   b.   telling the public about unethical practices of competitors.
   c.   the reporting of questionable practices by an employee.
   d.   actions by regulatory agencies in response to unethical behavior by corporations.
   e.   taking time out in ethical disputes to consider the other party's point of view.

_____ 28. Research findings indicate that good citizenship by companies
   a.   always lowers profits.
   b.   always increases financial performance.
   c.   is usually ignored by everyone.
   d.   usually hurts the company.
   e.   has a small positive relationship with financial performance.

_____ 29. Snooping on employees by companies for the sake of snooping is
   a.   a good idea.
   b.   ethically questionable.
   c.   often necessary.
   d.   weird.
   e.   in violation of legal rights.

_____ 30.   Ethics training programs
        a.   help employees deal with ethical questions and values.
        b.   have been shown to be ineffective.
        c.   are now considered illegal.
        d.   are unethical themselves.
        e.   are used as punishment for ethical lapses only.

True/False: Please indicate whether the following statements are true or false by writing a T or an F in the blank in front of each question.

_F_ 1.   Free choice lies between the domains of codified law and ethics.

_T_ 2.   When managers are accused of lying, cheating, or stealing, the blame is usually placed on the individual or on the company situation.

_T_ 3.   Justice requires that rules should be clearly stated and consistently and impartially enforced.

_F_ 4.   Individuals at the conventional level are concerned with external rewards and punishments and obey authority to avoid detrimental personal consequences.

_T_ 5.   The great majority of managers operate at level two of personal moral development, the conventional level.

_F_ 6.   Any group within or outside the organization that has a stake in the organization's performance is referred to as a shareholder.

_F_ 7.   The four criteria of corporate social responsibility are economic, legal, ethical, and mandatory responsibilities.

_F_ 8.   The activist approach responds to customers concerns only.

_F_ 9.   Management methods for helping organizations be more responsible include leadership by example, code of ethics, ethical structures, and eliminating whistle-blowers.

_T_ 10.   A code of ethics is a formal statement of the organization's values regarding moral principles and governing its response to social values.

Short Answer: Please indicate your answer in the space provided.

1. List the four criteria for ethical decision making described in the book.

2. List three examples of primary stakeholders.

3. Which choice is more difficult to make, one governed by law or ethics?

4. Explain which approach you feel is more prevalent among managers today—the utilitarian, individualism, or moral-rights approach?

Manager's Workbook

Workplace-Ethics Quiz *(Also available on page 138 of text.)*

The spread of technology into the workplace has raised a variety of new ethical questions, and many old ones still linger. Compare your answers with those of other Americans surveyed.

Office Technology

1. Is it wrong to use company e-mail for personal reasons?
   Yes   No

2. Is it wrong to use office equipment to help your children or spouse do schoolwork?
   Yes   No

3. Is it wrong to play computer games on office equipment during the workday?
   Yes   No

4. Is it wrong to use office equipment to do Internet shopping?
   Yes   No

5. Is it unethical to blame an error you made on a technological glitch?
   Yes   No

6. Is it unethical to visit pornographic Web sites using office equipment?
   Yes   No

Gifts and Entertainment

7. What's the value at which a gift from a supplier or client becomes troubling?
    $25 $50 $100

8. Is a $50 gift to a boss unacceptable?
    Yes   No

9. Is a $50 gift from the boss unacceptable?
    Yes   No

10. Of gifts from suppliers: Is it okay to take a $200 pair of football tickets?
    Yes   No

11. Is it okay to take a $120 pair of theater tickets?
    Yes   No

12. Is it okay to take a $100 holiday food basket?
    Yes   No

13. Is it okay to take a $25 gift certificate?
    Yes   No

14. Can you accept a $75 prize won at a raffle at a supplier's conference?
    Yes   No

Truth and Lies

15. Due to on-the-job pressure, have you ever abused or lied about sick days?
    Yes   No

16. Due to on-the-job pressure, have you ever taken credit for someone else's work or idea?
    Yes   No

SOURCES: Ethics Officer Association, Belmont, Mass.; Ethical Leadership Group, Wilmette, Ill.; surveys sampled a cross-section of workers at large companies and nationwide. "The Wall Street Journal Workplace-Ethics Quiz," *Wall Street Journal*, Oct. 21, 1999, pp. B1, B4.

Ethical Work Climates

Answer the following questions by circling the number that best describes an organization for which you have worked.

		Disagree				Agree
1.	What is the best for everyone in the company is the major consideration here.	1	2	3	4	5
2.	Our major concern is always what is best for the other person.	1	2	3	4	5
3.	People are expected to comply with the law and professional standards over and above other considerations.	1	2	3	4	5
4.	In this company, the first consideration is whether a decision violates any law	1	2	3	4	5

South-Western

5. It is very important to follow the company's rules and procedures here.	1	2	3	4	5
6. People in this company strictly obey the company policies.	1	2	3	4	5
7. In this company, people are mostly out for themselves.	1	2	3	4	5
8. People are expected to do anything to further the company's interests, regardless of the consequences.	1	2	3	4	5
9. In this company, people are guided by their own personal ethics.	1	2	3	4	5
10. Each person in this company decides for himself or herself what is right and wrong.	1	2	3	4	5

Total Score

Add up your score. These questions measure the dimensions of an organization's ethical climate. Questions 1 and 2 measure caring for people, questions 3 and 4 measure lawfulness, questions 5 and 6 measure rules adherence, questions 7 and 8 measure emphasis on financial and company performance, and questions 9 and 10 measure individual independence. Questions 7 and 8 are reverse scored (1 = 5; 2 = 4; 3 = 3; 4 = 2; 5 = 1). A total score above 40 indicates a very positive ethical climate. A score from 30 to 40 indicates above-average ethical climate. A score from 20 to 30 indicates a below-average ethical climate, and a score below 20 indicates a very poor ethical climate.

Go back over the questions and think about changes that you could have made to improve the ethical climate in the organization. Discuss with other students what you could do as a manager to improve ethics in future companies you work for.

SOURCE: Based on Bart Victor and John B. Cullen, "The Organizational Bases of Ethical Work Climates," *Administrative Science Quarterly* 33 (1988), 101-125.

Manager's Workshop

What Is Right? *(Also available on page 139 of text.)*

It is often hard for a manager to determine what is "right" and even more difficult to put ethical behavior into practice. A manager's ethical orientation often brings him or her into conflict with people, policies, customers, or bosses. Consider the following dilemmas. How would you handle them? In groups of 4-6 members, discuss each incident. What is the ethical thing to do?

1.   A well-liked member of your staff with an excellent record confides to you that he has Acquired Immune Deficiency Syndrome (AIDS). Although his illness has not affected his performance, you're concerned about his future health and about the reactions of his coworkers. You

   a.   tell him to keep you informed about his health and say nothing to his coworkers.
   b.   arrange for him to transfer to an area of the organization where he can work alone.
   c.   hold a staff meeting to inform his coworkers and ask them how they feel about his continued presence on your team.
   d.   consult your human resources officer on how to proceed.

2.   During a reorganization, you're told to reduce staff in the department you manage. After analyzing staffing requirements, you realize the job would be a lot easier if two professionals, who both are over age 60, would retire. You

     a.   say nothing and determine layoffs based purely on performance and length of service.
     b.   schedule a meeting with both employees and ask if they'd consider early retirement.
     c.   schedule a meeting with all staff and ask if anyone is interested in severance or early retirement.
     d.   lay off the older workers.

3.   One of your colleagues has recently experienced two personal tragedies—her husband filed for divorce and her mother died. Although you feel genuine sympathy for her, her work is suffering. A report you completed, based on inaccurate data she provided, has been criticized by management. Your manager asks you for an explanation. You

     a.   apologize for the inaccuracies and correct the data.
     b.   tell your manager that the data supplied by your colleague was the source of the problem.
     c.   say your colleague has a problem and needs support.
     d.   tell your manager that because of your work load, you didn't have time to check the figures in the report.

4.   Your firm recently hired a new manager who is at the same level you are. You do not like the man personally and consider him a rival professionally. You run into a friend who knows your rival well. You discover this man did not attend Harvard as he stated on his resume and in fact has not graduated from any college. You know his supposed Harvard background was instrumental in getting him hired. You

     a.   expose the lie to your superiors.
     b.   without naming names, consult your human resources officer on how to proceed.
     c.   say nothing. The company obviously failed to check him out, and the lie probably will surface on its own.
     d.   confront the man with the information and let him decide what to do.

5.   During a changeover in the accounting department, you discover your company has been routinely overcharging members of the public for services provided to them. Your superiors say repayment of charges would wreak havoc on company profits. Your company is federally regulated, and the oversight commission has not noticed the mistake. Your bosses say the problem will never come to light and they will take steps to correct the problem so it never happens again. You

     a.   contact the oversight commission.
     b.   take the matter public, anonymously or otherwise.
     c.   say nothing. It is now in the hands of the bosses.
     d.   work with the bosses on a plan to recognize the company's error and set up a schedule of rebates that would not unduly penalize the company.

6.   In this morning's mail, you received plans and samples for a promising new product from a competitor's disgruntled employee. You

     a.   throw the plans away.
     b.   send the samples to your research department for analysis.
     c.   notify your competitor about what is going on.
     d.   call the FBI.

Questions

1.   Use the guidelines described in the Chapter 4 Focus on Ethics Box: "Guidelines for Ethical Decision Making" (p. 116) to determine the appropriate behavior in these cases. Do you have all the information you need to make an ethical decision? How would family or friends react to each alternative if you were in these situations?

2.   Which approach to ethical decision making—utilitarian, individualism, justice, or moral-rights— seems most appropriate for handling these situations?

SOURCES: Game developed by Katherine Nelson, "Board Games," *Owen Manager*, Spring 1990, 14-16; Craig Dreilinger and Dan Rice, "Office Ethics," *Working Woman*, December 1991, 35-39; and Kevin Kelly and Joseph Weber, "When a Rival's Trade Secret Crosses Your Desk ...," *Business Week* (May 20, 1991), 48.

Gwen's Dilemma

Read the following case and discuss it in small groups. Come to a consensus in your small group and report back to the class your conclusions.

Gwen Ferguson is a Communications Management Consultant in Charlotte, North Carolina. She conducts various workshops to help persons improve communication skills. Most of the work she does is "in-house" training. She goes to the place of business of the client and conducts training sessions for the employees of the client. She is very good at what she does and stays very busy. Recently, Gwen was approached by a college executive training center to provide training for a client. She was asked to visit with the client and design a series of workshops to be provided through the executive training center.

Gwen met with the client and had a very good meeting. She and the client agreed on 12 different training sessions for Gwen to present. In the course of the discussion the client representative, Mr. Brown, said, "I wish we could just take the middleman out of this arrangement. Would it be possible for us to hire you directly rather than your going through the college's executive training center?"

1.   How would you answer this question if you were in Gwen's position?

Gwen said that she felt that she had a moral obligation to work through the college since it had provided the contact in the first place. Mr. Brown said he understood. Gwen then provided the college with the outline of proposed workshops. The director of the college executive training center said to Gwen, "You know that we will only tell you how much we will pay you for providing these workshops to the client. You will not know how much the client is paying us."

Gwen felt very uncomfortable with this arrangement. She does not want the client to be taken advantage of even if she is paid what she feels is reasonable. She is considering demanding that the college tell her how much the client is paying for this service so she will feel comfortable with the arrangement. If the college will not tell her this information or provide a price to the client that she feels is fair, she is considering withdrawing from the arrangement altogether.

2.   Do you think the college has the right to withhold this information from Gwen?

3.   Do you feel that Gwen has the right to demand to know all of the financial arrangements? Why do you think she wants to know so badly?

4.   If Gwen does end up withdrawing from the arrangement and the college finds someone else to take her place, the client could end up not liking the substitute (or the price) and decide to cancel the arrangement itself. If this happens and the client then calls Gwen directly to ask her to provide the services, should she do it? If so, should she pay the college anything?

Study Guide Solutions

Chapter Review

Multiple-Choice Questions

1	2	3	4	5	6	7	8	9	10
A	B	E	C	C	C	B	C	A	D

11	12	13	14	15	16	17	18	19	20
A	D	C	B	B	C	D	C	B	D

21	22	23	24	25	26	27	28	29	30
D	E	E	A	D	B	C	E	B	A

True/False Questions

1	2	3	4	5	6	7	8	9	10
F	T	T	F	T	F	F	F	F	T

Short Answer Questions

1. Utilitarianism, individualism, moral-rights, and justice.

2. Investors, shareholders, employees, customers, and suppliers are all examples of primary stakeholders.

3. It would seem that a choice governed by ethics would be more difficult to make than one governed by law. If the law governs the choice, then the behavior is prescribed, or at least one knows the legal consequences of a given action. For ethics the behavior is based on shared principles and values, all of which may be subject to interpretation. Another factor making the ethical decision more difficult is variations of principles and values from one group to another. If a person is a member of two different

groups having variations of principles and ethics, the ethical dilemmas result.

4. Since this question requires an opinion, answers will vary. An argument could be made for the utilitarian approach since managers should be considering the good of the organization. One would expect to see this more at upper levels of management where performance is judged based on the entire organization. One could also argue for the individualism approach, especially among lower-level managers who are anxious for career advancement. With the heightened level of morality in modern society, one could even make an argument for the moral-rights approach.

Manager's Workbook

Workplace-Ethics Quiz

Compare your answers with other Americans who were surveyed:

1. 34% said personal e-mail on company computers is wrong.
2. 37% said using office equipment for schoolwork is wrong.
3. 49% said playing computer games at work is wrong.
4. 54% said Internet shopping at work is wrong.
5. 61% said it's unethical to blame your error on technology.
6. 87% said it's unethical to visit pornographic sites at work.
7. 33% said $25 is the amount at which a gift from a supplier or client becomes troubling, while 33% said $50, and 33% said $100.
8. 35% said a $50 gift to the boss is unacceptable.
9. 12% said a $50 gift from the boss is unacceptable.
10. 70% said it's unacceptable to take the $200 football tickets.
11. 70% said it's unacceptable to take the $120 theater tickets.
12. 35% said it's unacceptable to take the $100 food basket.
13. 45% said it's unacceptable to take the $25 gift certificate.
14. 40% said it's unacceptable to take the $75 raffle prize.
15. 11% reported they lie about sick days.
16. 4% reported they take credit for the work or ideas of others.

SOURCE: "The Wall Street Journal workplace-ethics quiz," *Wall Street Journal*; Oct 21, 1999, B1 +B4.

Ethical Work Climates: Scoring and interpretation provided with exercise.

Manager's Workshop

What Is Right?
1. In a true ethical dilemma, more information can be acquired than the limited data available in a case presentation. Moreover, knowing that family or friends may learn about real-life actions sometimes causes people to undertake different behavior. The first and the third ethical dilemmas are probably the most difficult to resolve. Suggested alternatives are as follows: 1 (d); 2 (c); 3 (c); 4 (d); 5 (d); 6 (c).

2. Since this question asks for an opinion, the answers will vary. Opinions may be divided between individualism and the justice approach for the first question regarding the employee with AIDS, taking into account either the individual's best long-term interest or the argument for equity, fairness, and impartiality. Because question two affects everyone in the department, some may easily select the utilitarian approach as the appropriate response. In situation three, concerns for the tragic personal

circumstances of the employee will lead most students to select individualism. Question four may lean many toward individualism in order to assist a coworker in facing the truth. Number five again addresses concerns for the greatest good for the greatest number, but some may argue for the moral rights approach because individual rate payers have rights which can't be taken away or ignored by company actions. Situation six may be the most difficult because two companies are involved, although fairness (the justice approach) may carry the argument.

Gwen's Dilemma

1. Your answer will depend on your own value system. The standard practice in this type of situation is not to delete the middleman since he was the one who made this contact possible in the first place. He has provided both the client and Gwen with something of value and deserves to be compensated for it.

2. Certainly, the college has the right to withhold this information from Gwen. It has no legal obligation to tell her how much it is charging the client.

3. Legally, Gwen probably does not have the right to demand to know all of this information. She probably wants to know so that she can be sure that the client is not being overcharged for the service she provides. The argument could be made that if the client is willing to pay and Gwen is receiving a fee she feels good about, it is none of her business what the client pays.

4. This last question is very tough. The argument might be made that since the college provided the initial contact that resulted in Gwen's ultimately being asked to do the job, that it still deserves to receive remuneration. Gwen might argue that since the college was not willing to meet her terms, her contract with the college is null and void and that she then has the right to do business with whomever she wishes.

Chapter 5

Organizational Planning and Goal Setting

Chapter Outline

I.   Overview of Goals and Plans

II.   Purpose of Goals and Plans

III.   Goals in Organizations

    A. Organizational Mission

    B. Goals and Plans

    C. Hierarchy of Goals

IV.   Criteria for Effective Goals

V.   Planning Types and Performance

    A. Management by Objectives

    B. Single-Use and Standing Plans

    C. Contingency Plans

    D. Crisis Management Planning

VI.   Planning in the New Workplace

    A. Traditional Approaches to Planning

    B. New Workplace Approaches to Planning

VII.   Thinking Strategically

    A. What is Strategic Management?

    B. Purpose of Strategy

VIII. The Strategic Management Process

    A. Strategy Formulation Versus Implementation

    B. Situation Analysis

IX.   Formulating Business-Level Strategy

    A. Porter's Competitive Forces and Strategies

    B. Partnership Strategies

X.   Putting Strategy into Action

    A. Leadership

    B. Human Resources

Key Terms

Goal: a desired future state that the organization attempts to realize.

Plan: a blueprint specifying the resource allocations, schedules, and other actions necessary for attaining goals.

Planning: the act of determining the organization's goals and the means for achieving them.

Mission: the organization's reason for existence.

Mission statement: a broadly stated definition of the organization's basic business scope and operations that distinguishes it from similar types of organizations.

Strategic goals: broad statements of where the organization wants to be in the future; pertain to the organization as a whole rather than to specific divisions or departments.

Strategic plans: the action steps by which an organization intends to attain strategic goals.

Tactical goals: goals that define the outcomes that major divisions and departments must achieve in order for the organization to reach its overall goals.

Tactical plans: plans designed to help execute major strategic plans and to accomplish a specific part of the company's strategy.

Operational goals: specific measurable results expected from departments, work groups, and individuals within the organization.

Operational plans: plans developed at the organization's lower levels that specify action steps toward achieving operational goals and that support tactical planning activities.

Management by objectives: a method of management whereby managers and employees define goals for every department, project, and person and use them to monitor subsequent performance.

Contingency plans: plans that define company responses to specific situations, such as emergencies, setbacks, or unexpected conditions.

Central planning department: a group of planning specialists who develop plans for the organization as a whole and its major divisions and departments and typically report directly to the president or CEO.

Decentralized planning: managers work with planning experts to develop their own goals and plans.

Planning task force: a group of managers and employees who develop a strategic plan.

Strategic management: the set of decisions and actions used to formulate and implement strategies that will provide a competitively superior fit between the organization and its environment so as to achieve organizational goals.

Grand strategy: the general plan of major action by which an organization intends to achieve its long-term goals.

Strategy: the plan of action that prescribes resource allocation and other activities for dealing with the environment and helping the organization attain its goals.

Core competence: a business activity that an organization does particularly well in comparison to competitors.

Synergy: the condition that exists when the organization's parts interact to produce a joint effect that is greater than the sum of the parts action alone.

Strategy formulation: the stage of strategic management that involves the planning and decision making that lead to the establishment of the organization's goals and of a specific strategic plan.

Strategy implementation: the stage of strategic management that involves the use of managerial and organizational tools to direct resources toward achieving strategic outcomes.

Situation analysis: analysis of the strengths, weaknesses, opportunities, and threats (SWOT) that affect organizational performance.

Differentiation: a type of competitive strategy with which the organization seeks to distinguish its products or services from competitors'.

Cost leadership: a type of competitive strategy with which the organization seeks efficient facilities, cuts costs, and employs tight cost controls to be more efficient than competitors.

Focus: a type of competitive strategy that emphasizes concentration on a specific regional market or buyer group.

Learning Objectives

1. Define goals and plans and explain the relationship between them.

2. Explain the concept of organizational mission and how it influences goal setting and planning.

3. Describe the types of goals an organization should have and why they resemble a hierarchy.

4. Define the characteristics of effective goals.

5. Describe the four essential steps in the MBO process.

6. Describe and explain the importance of the three stages of crisis management planning.

7. Discuss how planning in the new workplace differs from traditional approaches to planning.

8. Define the components of strategic management.

9. Describe the strategic planning process and SWOT analysis.

10. Describe business-level strategies, including Porter's competitive forces and strategies and partnership strategies.

11. Explain the major considerations in formulating functional strategies.

12. Enumerate the considerations used for implementing strategy.

Chapter Review

Multiple Choice: Please indicate the correct response to the following questions by writing the letter of the correct answer in the space provided.

_____   1.   What does a plan specify?
- a.   resource allocations
- b.   schedules
- c.   future ends
- d.   actions
- e.   all of the above

_____   2.   Which of the management functions is considered the most fundamental?
- a.   planning
- b.   organizing
- c.   leading
- d.   controlling
- e.   coordinating

_____   3.   At which of the following levels may an organization's goals and plans exist?
- a.   strategic
- b.   tactical
- c.   department
- d.   operational
- e.   all of the above

_____   4.   Operational objectives lead to the achievement of
- a.   profits.
- b.   rules.
- c.   procedures.
- d.   tactical goals.
- e.   high morale.

_____   5.   An organization's _____ describes what the organization stands for and its reason for existence, symbolizing the legitimacy of the organization to external audiences.
- a.   goal
- b.   plan
- c.   structure
- d.   strategy
- e.   mission

_____   6.   Which of these is/are primarily responsible for operational goals/plans?
- a.   Middle management
- b.   Board of directors
- c.   Consultants
- d.   Senior management
- e.   Lower management

_____ 7. Mission statements describe
   a. corporate values.
   b. company philosophy.
   c. company purpose.
   d. all of the above.
   e. a and b only.

_____ 8. Which of these represent the broad statements of where the organization wants to be in the future?
   a. Operational goals
   b. Tactical goals
   c. Strategic goals
   d. Operational goals
   e. Tactical plans

_____ 9. Broad statements of where the organization is going as a whole are called
   a. mission statements.
   b. strategic goals.
   c. strategic plans.
   d. organizational objectives.
   e. strategic objectives.

_____ 10. A marketing vice-president has said that he is committed to introducing two new product lines this year. This is an example of
   a. a mission statement.
   b. a strategic goal.
   c. a tactical goal.
   d. an operational goal.
   e. a strategic plan.

_____ 11. Effective goals should
   a. be left somewhat vague to allow flexibility.
   b. not specify key areas of responsibility to permit innovation in new areas.
   c. "reach for the stars" regardless of abilities so employees will always be required to do better.
   d. have defined time limits on their accomplishment so their achievement cannot be put off.
   e. not be linked to rewards because so many things outside the control of the individual can cause goals not to be met.

_____ 12. Which of the following goals is stated best?
   a. Be the best convenience market in town.
   b. Trim the work force by 50 persons by December 31.
   c. Become the best teacher in the school.
   d. Find a job where I will be a success.
   e. Achieve job satisfaction by the end of five years.

_____ 13. Which of the following is not one of the characteristics of effective goal setting?
    a. Specific and measurable
    b. Challenging but realistic
    c. Linked to rewards
    d. Defined time period
    e. Covers every aspect of employee behavior

_____ 14. What is the appropriate sequence of the MBO activities?
    a. Setting goals, developing action plans, reviewing progress, and appraising overall performance
    b. Developing action plans, setting goals, reviewing progress, and appraising overall performance
    c. Setting goals, developing action plans, appraising overall performance, and reviewing progress
    d. Developing action plan, setting goals, appraising overall performance, and reviewing progress
    e. None of the above

_____ 15. Miabili Co. has used MBO for the past year. Top management just finished evaluating overall performance. The next step in the MBO process should be
    a. to develop new action plans.
    b. to develop new objectives based on the review of last year's performance.
    c. to begin a new MBO "cycle" using the same objectives as last year.
    d. to wait several months to allow information to be digested.
    e. none of the above.

_____ 16. In the MBO process individual objectives are
    a. mutually derived by the supervisor and the subordinate.
    b. developed by the subordinate.
    c. assigned by the supervisor.
    d. independent of departmental objectives.
    e. not translated into action plans.

_____ 17. Action plans are made for
    a. departments.
    b. individuals.
    c. both departments and individuals.
    d. only the company as a whole.
    e. none of the above.

_____ 18. One major problem with MBO is
    a. it discourages individual creativity.
    b. it does not work well in constantly changing environments.
    c. it decreases employee motivation.
    d. it does not work well in non-profit organizations.
    e. none of the above.

_____ 19. Single-use plans are
    a.   plans that are developed to achieve a set of goals that are unlikely to be repeated in the future.
    b.   plans that are used to provide guidance for tasks performed repeatedly within the organization.
    c.   plans that define company responses to specific situations, such as emergencies or setbacks.
    d.   most important in the organizations.
    e.   none of the above.

_____ 20. Standing plans are
    a.   plans that are developed to achieve a set of goals that are unlikely to be repeated in the future.
    b.   plans that are used to provide guidance for tasks performed repeatedly within the organization.
    c.   plans that define company responses to specific situations, such as emergencies or setbacks.
    d.   most important in the organizations.
    e.   none of the above.

_____ 21. Which of the following is an example of standing plans?
    a.   Policy
    b.   Rule
    c.   Procedures
    d.   All of the above
    e.   None of the above

_____ 22. Which of these define boundaries within which to make a decision?
    a.   Programs
    b.   Policies
    c.   Rules
    d.   Procedures
    e.   Project

_____ 23. A group of planning specialists assigned to major departments and divisions to help managers develop their own strategic plans is known as a
    a.   planning task force.
    b.   decentralized planning staff.
    c.   centralized planning department.
    d.   schewhart planning group.
    e.   total quality management group.

_____ 24. _____ is the set of decisions and actions used to formulate and implement strategies that will provide a competitively superior fit between the organization and its environment.
   a. Contingency plan
   b. Supervisory level strategy
   c. Strategic management
   d. Middle level strategy
   e. A mission statement

_____ 25. A business activity that an organization does especially well relative to its competition is known as
   a. a strategy.
   b. a synergy.
   c. a cash cow.
   d. a core competence.
   e. retrenchment.

_____ 26. _____ are characteristics of the external environment that have the potential to help the organization achieve or exceed its strategic goals.
   a. Strengths
   b. Threats
   c. Opportunities
   d. Weaknesses
   e. SWOT

_____ 27. When looking at strategy formulation, two models for formulating are competitive strategies and the product life cycle. Who formulated the competitive model?
   a. Frederick Taylor
   b. Wm. Edwards Deming
   c. Michael E. Porter
   d. Michael Hammer
   e. Stephen R. Covey

_____ 28. The _____ strategy can be profitable for an organization because customers are loyal and willing to pay high prices.
   a. focus
   b. globalization
   c. overall cost leadership
   d. differentiation
   e. liquidation

_____ 29. Sunset Cruises concentrates its efforts on its target market of 55 to 70 year olds. It is using a(n) _____ strategy.
   a. focus
   b. differentiation
   c. overall cost leadership
   d. multidomestic
   e. universal strategy

_____ 30. Persuasion, motivation, and changes in cultures and values are examples of which of the dimensions used to implement strategy?
    a. Leadership
    b. Structural design
    c. Human resources
    d. Information and control systems
    e. Compensation

True/False: Please indicate whether the following statements are true or false by writing a T or an F in the blank in front of each question.

_T_ 1. Goals specify future ends; plans specify today's means.

_F_ 2. A plan provides the "why" of an organization's or subunit's existence; whereas, a goal tells "how" to achieve the goal.

_F_ 3. The strategic plan is the department manager's tool for daily and weekly operations.

_F_ 4. Operational goals are typically developed by top management.

_F_ 5. The easiest step in the MBO process is setting goals.

_F_ 6. Tactical plans are also referred to as scenarios.

_T_ 7. The interaction of Production and Sales working together to produce profit greater than the total of both working separately is an example of synergy.

_T_ 8. Bargaining power of customers is one of Porter's five competitive forces.

_F_ _T_ 9. Differentiation, cost leadership, and cooperation are Porter's competitive strategies.

_T_ 10. Opportunities are characteristics of the external environment that have the potential to help the organization achieve or exceed its strategic goals.

Short Answer: Please indicate your answer in the space provided.

1. What is a mission statement and why is it important?

2. Why must a goal be specific and measurable?

3. Why is it important to use participation in setting goals?

4. List the four components of a situation analysis.

Manager's Workbook

Goal Setting *(Also available on page 180 of text.)*

Consider goals for yourself regarding doing well in this course. What do you need to do in order to get a good grade? Goals should be according the "Criteria for Effective Goals" in the chapter on pp. 153-154. In addition, you need a system to monitor your progress, such as the table below, which shows the types of goals you may choose to select for yourself.

Goals	Class Week			
	First Week (from now)	Second Week	Third Week	Fourth Week
1. 100% attendance				
2. Class notes				
3. Read assigned chapters				
4. Outline chapters				
5. Define vocabulary words				
6. Answer end of chapter questions.				
7. Complete "Workbook" assignments				
8. Class participation				
9.				
10.				

Your instructor may ask you to turn in your monitor sheets at the end of the course.

1. According to goal-setting theory, using and monitoring goals is supposed to help performance. Did do you better as a result of your goals?

2. What did you learn from this that could help you in other classes?

Copyright 1996 by Dorothy Marcic.

Personal Strategy

1. In one or two sentences write out your personal mission statement. Your statement should answer these two questions: What is your purpose in life? And what do you want to accomplish in the next ten years?

2. Do a SWOT analysis on yourself, as shown below.

	Qualities within yourself	Characteristics of the environment
Positive qualities, strengths	Strengths	Opportunities
Negative qualities, weaknesses	Weaknesses	Threats

Consider your positive qualities, your strengths, with the positive qualities of the environment that matches your strengths. What are these? These are the opportunities for you. For example, if you have abilities in computer programming, are diligent and the environment needs hard-working computer-skilled people, that is your opportunity.

What have you learned about yourself from this exercise?

Manager's Workshop

Company Crime Wave

Senior managers in your organization are concerned about internal theft. Your department has been assigned the task of writing an ethics policy that defines employee theft and prescribes penalties. Stealing goods is easily classified as theft, but other activities are more ambiguous. Before writing the policy, go through the following list and decide which behaviors should be defined as stealing and whether penalties should apply. Discuss the items with your department members until agreement is reached. Classify each item as an example of (1) theft, (2) acceptable behavior, or (3) in between with respect to written policy. Is it theft when an employee:

_____ Gets paid for overtime not worked?

_____ Takes a longer lunch or coffee break than authorized?

_____ Punches a time card for another?

_____ Comes in late or leaves early?

_____ Takes care of personal business on company time?

_____ Occasionally uses company copying machines or makes long-distance telephone calls for personal purposes?

_____ Takes a few stamps, pens, or other supplies for personal use?

_____ Takes money from the petty cash drawer?

_____ Uses company vehicles or tools for own purposes but returns them?

_____ Damages merchandise so a cohort can purchase it at a discount?

_____ Accepts a gift from a supplier?

Now consider those items rated "in between." Do these items represent ethical issues as defined in Chapter 5? How should these items be handled in the company's written policy?

In groups of 3-6 members, discuss your answers. What assumptions does each member have to come up with the individual responses?

Developing Strategy for a Small Business *(Also available on page 181 of text.)*

Instructions:

1. Divide into groups of 4-6 members. Select a local business with which your group members are familiar.

2. Complete the following activities.

Activity 1 Perform a SWOT analysis for the business.

SWOT Analysis for _____ (name of company)

	Internal (within company)	**External (outside company)**
Positive	**Strengths:**	**Opportunities:**
Negative	**Weaknesses:**	**Threats:**

Activity 2 Write a statement of the business's current strategy.

Activity 3 Decide on a goal you would like the business to achieve in two years, and write a statement of proposed strategy for achieving that goal.

Activity 4 Write a statement describing how the proposed strategy will be implemented.

Activity 5 What have you learned from this exercise?

Study Guide Solutions

Chapter Review

Multiple-Choice Questions

1	2	3	4	5	6	7	8	9	10
E	A	E	D	E	E	D	C	B	C
11	**12**	**13**	**14**	**15**	**16**	**17**	**18**	**19**	**20**
D	B	E	A	B	A	C	B	A	B
21	**22**	**23**	**24**	**25**	**26**	**27**	**28**	**29**	**30**
D	B	B	C	D	C	C	D	A	B

True/False Questions

1	2	3	4	5	6	7	8	9	10
T	F	F	F	F	F	T	T	F	T

Short Answer Questions

1. A mission statement is a broadly stated definition of the organization's scope of operations that distinguishes it from similar organizations. It is important because it defines what the entire organization is all about and leads to the development of goals and plans.

2. A goal must be specific and measurable to be motivating for employees. Otherwise, it is too vague and one cannot tell when enough is enough and the goal has been met.

3. Participation should be used in goal setting so that all employees adopt the goals as their own. They will then be more motivated to reach those goals.

4. A situation analysis includes a search for SWOT—strengths, weaknesses, opportunities, and threats.

Manager's Workbook

Goal Setting: Goals will vary based on each student's perceptions of what they must do in order to get a good grade.

Personal Strategy: Each student will have unique mission statements and SWOT analyses.

Manager's Workshop

Company Crime Wave: This exercise should generate some interesting discussion.

Developing Strategy for a Small Business: Results will vary depending on the company selected.

Chapter 6

Managerial Decision Making

Chapter Outline

I.   Types of Decisions and Problems

    A. Programmed and Nonprogrammed Decisions

II.   Decision-Making Models

    A. Classical Model

    B. Administrative Model

    C. Political Model

III. Decision-Making Steps

IV.   Personal Decision Framework

V.   Increasing Participation in Decision Making

    A.   The Vroom-Jago Model

    B.   New Decision Approaches for the New Workplace

VI.   Using Information Technology for Decision Making

VII. Information Technology

    A. Data versus Information

    B. Characteristics of Useful Information

VIII. Types of Information Systems

    A. Operations Information Systems

    B. Management Information Systems

IX.   The Internet and E-business

    A.   E-business Strategies and E-marketplaces

    B.   Customer Relationship Management

X.   Management Implications of Information Technology

XI.   IT Trends in the New Workplace

    A.   Instant Messaging, Wireless Internet, and Peer-to-Peer File Sharing

Key Terms

Decision: a choice made from available alternatives.

Decision making: the process of identifying problems and opportunities and then resolving them.

Programmed decision: a decision made in response to a situation that has occurred often enough to enable decision rules to be developed and applied in the future.

Nonprogrammed decision: a decision made in response to a situation that is unique, is poorly defined and largely unstructured, and has important consequences for the organization.

Certainty: all the information the decision maker needs is fully available.

Risk: a decision has clear-cut goals and good information is available, but the future outcomes associated with each alternative are subject to chance.

Uncertainty: managers know which goal they wish to achieve, but information about alternatives and future events is incomplete.

Ambiguity: the goals to be achieved or the problem to be solved is unclear, alternatives are difficult to define, and information about outcomes is unavailable.

Classical model: a decision-making model based on the assumption that managers should make logical decisions that will be in the organization's best economic interests.

Normative: an approach that defines how a decision maker should make decisions and provides guidelines for reaching an ideal outcome for the organization.

Administrative model: a decision-making model that describes how managers actually make decisions in situations characterized by nonprogrammed decisions, uncertainty, and ambiguity.

Bounded rationality; the concept that people have the time and cognitive ability to process only a limited amount of information on which to base decisions.

Satisficing; to choose the first solution alternative that satisfies minimal decision criteria regardless of whether better solutions are presumed to exist.

Descriptive: an approach that describes how managers actually make decisions rather than how they should.

Intuition: the immediate comprehension of a decision situation based on past experience but without conscious thought.

Coalition: an informal alliance among managers who support a specific goal.

Problem: a situation in which organizational accomplishments have failed to meet established goals.

Opportunity: a situation in which managers see potential organizational accomplishments that exceed current goals.

Diagnosis: the step in the decision-making process in which managers analyze underlying causal factors associated with the decision situation.

Risk propensity: the willingness to undertake risk with the opportunity of gaining an increased payoff.

Implementation: the step in the decision-making process that involves using managerial, administrative, and persuasive abilities to translate the chosen alternative into action.

Decision style: differences among people with respect to how they perceive problems and make decisions.

Vroom-Jago model: a model designed to help managers gauge the amount of subordinate participation in decision making.

Escalating commitment: continuing to invest time and resources in a failing decision.

Devil's advocate: a decision-making technique in which an individual is assigned the role of challenging the assumptions and assertions made by the group to prevent premature consensus.

Point-counterpoint: a decision-making technique in which people are assigned to express competing points of view.

Information technology: the hardware, software, telecommunications, database management, and other technologies used to store, process, and distribute information.

Data: raw, unsummarized, and unanalyzed facts and figures.

Information: data that have been converted into a meaningful and useful context for the receiver.

Operations information system: a computer-based information system that supports a company's day-to-day operations.

Transaction-processing system: a type of operations information system that records and processes data resulting from routine business transaction such as sales, purchases, and payroll.

Office automation systems: systems that combine modern hardware and software to handle the tasks of publishing and distributing information.

Management information system (MIS): a computer-based system that provides information and support for effective managerial decision making.

Internet: a global collection of computer networks linked together for the exchange of data and information.

World Wide Web (WWW): a collection of central servers for accessing information on the Internet.

e-business: any business that takes place by digital processes over a computer network rather than in physical space.

e-commerce: business exchanges that occur electronically.

Intranet: an internal communications system that uses the technology and standards of the Internet but is accessible only to people within the organization.

Electronic Data Interchange (EDI): a network that links the computer systems of buyers and sellers to allow the transmission of structured data primarily for ordering, distribution, and payables and receivables.

Extranet: an external communications system that uses the Internet and is shared by two or more organizations.

B2B marketplace: an electronic marketplace set up by an intermediary where buyers and sellers meet.

Customer relationship management (CRM) systems: systems that help companies track customers' interactions with the firm and allow employees to call up information on past transactions.

Instant messaging: technology that provides a way to send quick notes from PC to PC over the Internet so two people who are online at the same time communicate instantly.

Peer-to-peer (P2P) file sharing: file sharing that allows PCs to communicate directly with one another over the Internet, by passing central database servers, control points, and Web pages.

Learning Objectives

1. Explain why decision making is an important component of good management.

2. Explain the difference between programmed and nonprogrammed decisions and the decision characteristics of risk, uncertainty, and ambiguity.

3. Describe the classical, administrative, and political models of decision making and their applications.

4. Identify the six steps used in managerial decision making.

5. Explain four personal decision styles used by managers.

6. Discuss the advantages and disadvantages of participative decision making.

7. Identify techniques for improving decision-making in today's fast-moving and uncertain environment.

8. To describe the importance of information technology for organizations and the attributes of quality information.

Chapter Review

Multiple Choice: Please indicate the correct response to the following questions by writing the letter of the correct answer in the space provided.

_____ 1. Which of the following is an example of a nonprogrammed decision?
  a. reordering office supplies
  b. developing a new product
  c. deciding which motor oil to put in the company car
  d. responding to a customer request for a sales demonstration
  e. deciding when to hold the office Christmas party

_____ 2. Nonprogrammed decisions usually
  a. involve routine situations.
  b. are well defined.
  c. are largely structured.
  d. have important consequences for the organization.
  e. have occurred several times before.

_____ 3. If you knew in advance that a horse race had been fixed so that "Whirlaway" was going to win, you would be operating under a condition of
  a. risk.
  b. uncertainty.
  c. ambiguity.
  d. certainty.
  e. intuitiveness.

_____ 4.   _____ is the most difficult decision situation.
    a.   Ambiguity
    b.   Risk
    c.   Certainty
    d.   Uncertainty
    e.   None of the above

_____ 5.   According to the classical model of decision making,
    a.   objectives are not known or agreed upon.
    b.   the decision maker operates under conditions of risk.
    c.   criteria for evaluating alternatives are known.
    d.   the decision maker is often irrational.
    e.   we often make decisions which do not maximize our payoff.

_____ 6.   An assumption underlying the classical model is that
    a.   problems are precisely formulated and defined.
    b.   only some alternatives need to be considered.
    c.   the alternative that will minimize economic return is the best.
    d.   the decision maker should not order preferences.
    e.   the decision maker strives for conditions of risk.

_____ 7.   If you are satisficing, when you graduate from college you will
    a.   hunt until you find the ultimate job meeting all your expectations.
    b.   take the first job offer that meets your minimal criteria.
    c.   ask for a raise within the first six months of taking a job.
    d.   look for a job that gives you the most personal satisfaction.
    e.   give up on some of your criteria for a good job to have other criteria met.

_____ 8.   Administrative decision-making procedures are most appropriate for _____ situations and problems.
    a.   clear-cut, programmed
    b.   rational
    c.   vague
    d.   difficult, nonprogrammed
    e.   slow-moving

_____ 9.   According to the administrative model
    a.   managers are always aware of problems that exist in the organization.
    b.   rational procedures are always used.
    c.   managers always strive for maximizing.
    d.   managers' search for alternatives is limited.
    e.   decision objectives are clear-cut.

_____ 10. When you use intuition to make a decision, you are
   a. basing your decision on past experience.
   b. being arbitrary.
   c. being irrational.
   d. being foolish.
   e. All of the above except a are correct.

_____ 11. When you ask the question, "How is the state of disequilibrium affecting us?" you are trying to
   a. be vague to buy time to make a better decision later.
   b. develop effective alternatives.
   c. use intuition to make the decision.
   d. discover the underlying causes of the problem.
   e. decide how to implement the solution.

_____ 12. If you were the coach of a football team that is one point behind and you chose a play which would result in a tie rather than a win, you could be said to have
   a. a low propensity for risk.
   b. a high propensity for risk.
   c. an intuitive approach to decision making.
   d. low ethical standards.
   e. a fear of making decisions.

_____ 13. Implementation of an alternative may require
   a. discussion with those affected.
   b. communication.
   c. motivation.
   d. leadership skills.
   e. all of the above.

_____ 14. The directive style is used by managers who
   a. like to consider complex solutions.
   b. prefer to gather as much data as they can.
   c. are very concerned about the impact of the decision on others.
   d. prefer simple, clear-cut solutions.
   e. want to understand the feelings of others before making the decision.

_____ 15. The behavioral style is used by managers who
   a. like to consider complex solutions.
   b. prefer to gather as much data as they can.
   c. are very concerned about the impact of the decision on others.
   d. prefer simple, clear-cut solutions.
   e. search for the best possible decision based on the information available.

16. Which of the following is considered the most highly democratic?
   a. You make the decision yourself with the available information.
   b. You share the problem with subordinates as a group, try not to influence the group, and are willing to go along with the decision of the group.
   c. You obtain information from subordinates and then decide yourself.
   d. You share the problem with subordinates as a group, get their ideas, and then you make the decision.
   e. You share the problem with subordinates individually and then make the decision.

17. The diagnostic questions of the Vroom-Jago model
   a. cannot be answered with a "yes" or "no" answer.
   b. help the manager decide which leader decision style to use.
   c. are not able to consider the type of problem.
   d. consider the problem, but not the required level of decision quality.
   e. ignore the importance of having subordinates accept the decision.

18. When an organization continues to invest time and money in a solution despite strong evidence that it is not appropriate, it is called
   a. plain stupidity.
   b. groupthink.
   c. an escalating commitment.
   d. diminished returns.
   e. reverse practicality.

19. A communication system using Internet technology, shared by two or more organizations
   a. Intranet.
   b. Extranet.
   c. electronic data interchange.
   d. e-business facilitator.
   e. Local Wide Web.

20. A devil's advocate is supposed to
   a. challenge the assumptions and assertions made by the group.
   b. point out the evil side of the alternative being considered.
   c. try to get the group to make an immoral decision.
   d. speak on behalf of the competition.
   e. try to disrupt the decision-making process.

21. A decision-making technique in which people are assigned to express competing points of view is
   a. devil's advocate.
   b. point-counterpoint.
   c. corporate debate.
   d. collective intuition.
   e. conflicted collaboration.

_____ 22. _____ comes from the combined knowledge, experience, and understanding of the group.
    a.   Point-counterpoint
    b.   Combined intuition
    c.   Factual forecasting
    d.   Groupthink
    e.   Political decision-making

_____ 23. What are the important attributes of useful information?
    a.   Time, content, and form
    b.   Quality, timeliness, and relevance
    c.   Space, completeness, and relevance
    d.   Price, quality, timeliness, and completeness
    e.   Product, price, place, and promotion

_____ 24. _____ are systems that link people and departments within or among organizations for the purpose of sharing information resources.
    a.   Electronic data interchange
    b.   Networks
    c.   Electronic bulletin boards
    d.   Computer meetings
    e.   EIS

_____ 25. A computer network that uses Internet technology but limits access to all or some of the organization's employees is called a(n)
    a.   extranet.
    b.   middleware
    c.   groupware.
    d.   intranet.
    e.   GDSS.

_____ 26. A type of information system that supervisors routinely use to help with their recordkeeping is called a(n)
    a.   management information system.
    b.   transaction processing system.
    c.   executive information system.
    d.   recordkeeping system.
    e.   GDSS.

_____ 27. Tony is a production manager at a local food processing plant. He needs data on the anticipated number of orders and the current inventory. He is using a computer-based information system to help him make production decisions. What type of system is he using?
    a.   A transaction processing system
    b.   An executive information system
    c.   A production information system
    d.   A management information system
    e.   None of these

_____ 28. Management information systems facilitate
    a. effective management decision making.
    b. programmed decisions.
    c. routine decisions.
    d. distant mapping decisions.
    e. none of the above.

_____ 29. Technology that provides a way to send quick notes from PC to PC over the Internet is called
    a. An expert system.
    b. A collaborative work system.
    c. Instant messaging.
    d. communication information system.
    e. GIS.

_____ 30. Peer-to-peer file sharing allows PCs to communicate
    a. over the Internet.
    b. while bypassing central databases.
    c. without the use of Webpages.
    d. directly with one another.
    e. all of the above.

True/False: Please indicate whether the following statements are true or false by writing a T or an F in the blank in front of each question.

_F_ 1. Decisions that are made for situations that have occurred often in the past and allow decision rules to be developed to guide future decisions are called nonprogrammed decisions.

_F_ 2. The administrative decision-making model assumes that the decision-maker is rational, and makes the optimal decision each time.

_F_ 3. The use of computerized information systems and databases has decreased the power of the classical approach of decision making.

_T_ 4. A coalition is an informal alliance among managers who support a specific goal.

_T_ 5. Managers confront a decision requirement in the form of either a problem or an opportunity.

_T_ 6. The advantages of participative decision making include enriched problem diagnoses, member satisfaction, and support for decision.

_F_ 7. Facts that are raw, unsummarized, and unanalyzed are called information.

_T_ 8. Blending traditional operations with an Internet initiative is called integrating *bricks and clicks.*

_T_ 9. B2B means a business to business transaction.

_T_ 10. Because of advances in information technology, time and place are becoming less important communication variables.

Short Answer: Please indicate your answer in the space provided.

1. What are the six steps in the managerial decision-making process?

2. Explain why recognition of decision requirement is the *first* step in the decision-making process.

3. Why is timeliness an important characteristic of information for a manager?

4. How will a devil's advocate improve decision making?

Manager's Workbook

What's Your Personal Decision Style? *(Also available on page 225 of the text.)*
Read each of the following questions and circle the answer that best describes you. Think about how you typically act in a work or school situation and mark the answer that first comes to your mind. There are no right or wrong answers.

1. In performing my job or class work, I look for:
   a. practical results.
   b. the best solution.
   c. creative approaches or ideas.
   d. good working conditions.

2. I enjoy jobs that:
   a. are technical and well-defined.
   b. have a lot of variety.
   c. allow me to be independent and creative.
   d. involve working closely with others.

3. The people I most enjoy working with are:
   a. energetic and ambitious.
   b. capable and organized.
   c. open to new ideas.
   d. agreeable and trusting.

4. When I have a problem, I usually:
   a. rely on what has worked in the past.
   b. apply careful analysis.
   c. consider a variety of creative approaches.
   d. seek consensus with others.

5. I am especially good at:
   a. remembering dates and facts.
   b. solving complex problems.
   c. seeing many possible solutions.
   d. getting along with others.

6. When I don't have much time, I:
   a. make decisions and act quickly.
   b. follow established plans or priorities.
   c. take my time and refuse to be pressured.
   d. ask others for guidance and support.

7. In social situations, I generally:
   a. talk to others.
   b. think about what's being discussed.
   c. observe.
   d. listen to the conversation.

8. Other people consider me:
   a. aggressive.
   b. disciplined.
   c. creative.
   d. supportive.

9. What I dislike most is:
   a. not being in control.
   b. doing boring work.
   c. following rules.
   d. being rejected by others.

10. The decisions I make are usually:
    a. direct and practical.
    b. systematic or abstract.
    c. broad and flexible.
    d. sensitive to others' needs.

Scoring:

Count the number of **a** answers. This is your directive score:_____
Count the number of **b** answers for your analytical score: _____
The number of **c** answers is your conceptual score: _____
The number of **d** answers is your behavioral score: _____

What is your dominant decision style? Are you surprised, or does this reflect the style you thought you used most often?

SOURCE: Adapted from Alan J. Rowe and Richard O. Mason, *Managing with Style: A Guide to Understanding, Assessing, and Improving Decision Making* (San Francisco: Jossey-Bass, 1987), 40-41.

What Is Your MIS Style?

Following are 14 statements. Circle the number that indicates how much you agree that each statement is characteristic of you. The questions refer to how you use information and make decisions.

	Disagree Strongly				Agree Strongly
1. I like to wait until all relevant information is examined before deciding something.	1	2	3	4	5
2. I prefer information that can be interpreted in several ways and leads to different but acceptable solutions.	1	2	3	4	5
3. I like to keep gathering data until an excellent solution emerges.	1	2	3	4	5
4. To make decisions, I often use information that means different things to different people.	1	2	3	4	5
5. I want just enough data to make a decision quickly.	1	2	3	4	5
6. I act on logical analysis of the situation rather than on my "gut feelings" about the best alternative.	1	2	3	4	5
7. I seek information sources or people that will provide me with many ideas and details.	1	2	3	4	5
8. I try to generate more than one satisfactory solution for the problem faced.	1	2	3	4	5
9. When reading something, I confine my thoughts to what is written rather than search for additional understanding.	5	4	3	2	1
10. When working on a project, I try to narrow, not broaden, the scope so it is clearly defined.	5	4	3	2	1
11. I typically acquire all possible information before making a final decision.	1	2	3	4	5
12. I like to work on something I've done before rather than take on a complicated problem.	5	4	3	2	1
13. I prefer clear, precise data.	5	4	3	2	1
14. When working on a project, I like to explore various options rather than maintain a narrow focus.	1	2	3	4	5

Total Score on even-numbered statements _____

Total Score on even-numbered statements _____

Your information-processing style determines the extent to which you will benefit from computer-based information systems.

The odd-numbered questions pertain to the "amount of information" you like to use. A score of 28 or more suggests you prefer a large amount. A score of 14 or less indicates you like a small amount of information.

The even-numbered questions pertain to the "focus of information" you prefer. A score of 28 or more suggests you are comfortable with ambiguous, multifocused information, while a score of 14 or less suggests you like clear, unifocused data.

If you are a person who likes a large amount of information and clear, focused data, you will tend to make effective use of management information systems. You could be expected to benefit greatly from an EIS or MIS in your company. If you are a person who prefers a small amount of data and data that are multifocused, you would probably not get the information you need to make decisions through formal information systems. You probably won't utilize EIS or MIS to a great extent, preferring instead to get decision data from other convenient sources, including face-to-face discussions.

SOURCES: This questionnaire is adapted from Richard L. Daft and Norman B. Macintosh, "A Tentative Exploration into the Amount and Equivocality of Information Processing in Organizational Work Units," *Administrative Science Quarterly* 26 (1981), 207–224; and Dorothy Marcic, *Organizational Behavior: Experiences and Cases*, 4th ed. (St. Paul, Minn.: West, 1995).

Manager's Workshop

Whom Do You Choose *(Also available on page 226 of text.)*

1. You are the member of a medical selection committee. Take five minutes to individually fill out the table below with your rank orderings. Dilemma: A group of well-know people have all applied for a liver transplant. Without the transplant, they can expect to die in anywhere from six months to two years, depending on other factors. A number of donor livers are expected in the next few weeks. You are on the medical selection committee that decides who gets the transplants. Of course, you cannot know who will match up with the livers that arrive. So your job is just to choose the five who you recommend, then ran-order those five people below in terms of whom you think is most deserving of the transplant. Give "1" as the first one to get it, "2" as the next, and so on. List your reasons in the appropriate box.
2. Form groups of four to six. Using the classical and administrative models of decision-making, answer the following dilemma by rank ordering in the table below. You will first need to choose your top five as a group, then rank-order those five.
3. Each group shares its top five and the rankings with the whole class. Describe how and when you used the classical or administrative models in your decision making.

People who applied for liver transplant: Michael Jackson, Britney Spears, Allicia Keyes, Justin Timberlake, Nelson Mandela, Dale Earnhart, Jr., Julia Roberts, Brad Pitt, Stephen Spielberg, President Bush, Jennifer Lopez, Reese Witherspoon, Monica Lewinsky, Halle Berry, President Clinton, Bill Gates, Denzel Washington, Elton John, Harry Potter author J.K. Rowling, Oprah Winfrey, TV Producer David E. Kelley, the Pope, Mark McGuire, Madonna, Shaquille O'Neil, Michael Jordan, Michelle Kwan.

Name	Rank order you assigned	Group ranking	Classical or administrative model? Why?	Reason for your ranking

Discussion Questions

1. How can a decision model help in the process of making a decision?

2. Did the models help explain any of the conflict you had? Did they help to deal with the conflict?

3. Did the models help you understand how difficult decision making can sometimes be?

The Desert Survival Situation

The situation described in this exercise is based on more than 2,000 actual cases in which men and women lived or died depending on the survival decisions they made. Your "life" or "death" will depend on how well your group can share its present knowledge of a relatively unfamiliar problem so that the team can make decisions that will lead to your survival.

This exercise will challenge your ability to take advantage of a participative approach to decision making and to apply decision steps such as developing alternatives and selecting the correct alternative. When instructed, read about the situation and do Step 1 without discussing it with the rest of the group.

The Situation

It is approximately 10:00 AM in mid-August, and you have just crash-landed in the Sonora Desert in the southwestern United States. The light twin-engine plane, containing the bodies of the pilot and the copilot, has completely burned. Only the airframe remains. None of the rest of you have been injured.

The pilot was unable to notify anyone of your position before the crash. However, he had indicated before impact that you were 70 miles south-southwest from a mining camp that is the nearest known habitation and that you were approximately 65 miles off the course that was filed in your VFR Flight Plan.

The immediate area is quite flat and, except for occasional barrel and saguaro cacti, appears to be rather barren. The last weather report indicated the temperature would reach 110° that day, which means that the temperature at ground level will be 130°. You are dressed in lightweight clothing: short-sleeved shirts, pants, socks, and street shoes. Everyone has a handkerchief. Collectively, your pockets contain $2.83 in change, $85 in bills, a pack of cigarettes, and a ballpoint pen.

Your Task

Before the plane caught fire, your group was able to salvage the 15 items listed in the following table. Your task is to rank these items according to their importance to your survival, starting with 1 as the most important, to 15 as the least important.

You may assume the following:

1 The number of survivors is the same as the number on your team.
2 You are the actual people in the situation.
3 The team has agreed to stick together.
4 All items are in good condition.

Step 1 Each member of the team is to individually rank each item. Do not discuss the situation or problem until each member has finished the individual ranking.

Step 2 After everyone has finished the individual ranking, rank order the 15 items as a team. Once discussion begins, do not change your individual ranking. Your instructor will inform you of how much time you have to complete this step.

	Step 1: Your Individual Ranking	Step 2: The Team's Ranking	Step 3: Survival Expert's Ranking*	Step 4: Difference Between Step 1 and Step 3	Step 5: Difference Between Step 2 and Step 3
Items					
Flashlight (4-battery size)					
Jackknife					
Sectional air map of the area					
Plastic raincoat (large size)					
Magnetic compass					
Compress kit with gauze					
.45 caliber pistol (loaded)					
Parachute (red and white)					
Bottle of salt tablets (1,000 tablets)					
1 quart of water per person					
A book titled *Edible Animals of the Desert*					
A pair of sunglasses per person					
2 quarts of 180-proof vodka					
1 topcoat per person					
A cosmetic mirror					
Totals (the lower the score, the better)					
				Your Score, Step 4	Team Score, Step 5

Team Number

Please complete the following steps and insert the scores under your team's number	1	2	3	4	5	6

Step 6: Average Individual Score

Add up all the individual scores (Step 4) on the team, and divide by the number on the team.

_____

Step 7: Team Score

_____

Step 8: Gain Score – the difference between the Team Score and the Average Individual Score. If the Team Score is lower than Average Individual Score, then gain is "1." If Team Score is higher than Average Individual Score, then gain is "2."

_____

Step 9: Lowest Score on the Team

_____

Step 10: Number of Individual Scores Lower than the Team Score

_____

SOURCE: L. Clayton Lafferty, Patrick M. Eady, and Alonzo W. Pond, "The Desert Survival Situation: A Group Decision Making Experience for Examining and Increasing Individual and Team Effectiveness," 8th ed. Copyright © 1974 by Experiential Learning Methods, Inc., 15200 E. Jefferson, Suite 107, Grosse Pointe Park, MI 48230. (313)-823-4400.

Study Guide Solutions

Chapter Review

Multiple-Choice Questions

1	2	3	4	5	6	7	8	9	10
B	D	D	A	C	A	B	D	D	A

11	12	13	14	15	16	17	18	19	20
D	A	E	D	C	B	B	C	B	A

21	22	23	24	25	26	27	28	29	30
B	B	A	B	D	B	D	A	C	E

True/False Questions

1	2	3	4	5	6	7	8	9	10
F	F	F	T	T	T	F	T	T	T

Short Answer Questions

1. The six steps are (a) recognize the decision requirement; (b) diagnose and analyze the causes; (c) develop alternatives; (d) select the desired alternative; (e) implement the chosen alternative; and (f) evaluate and determine feedback.

2. If one does not recognize that a problem exists, no search will be made for a solution. If the problem is not defined accurately, the chosen alternative may not solve the problem.

3. If the information is slow in coming to a manager, it may be too late to take appropriate action. To find out that a competitive price change has occurred *after* losing one's customers does not help a manager, for example.

4. A devil's advocate will improve decision making by pointing out opposing viewpoints and weaknesses in the assumptions of alternatives being presented. Groupthink will then be avoided.

South-Western

Manager's Workbook

What's Your Personal Decision Style?: Scoring and interpretation provided with exercise.

What Is Your MIS Style?: Scoring and interpretation provided with exercise.

Manager's Workshop

Whom Do You Chose?: Answers will vary.

The Desert Survival Situation: Solutions to the exercise can be obtained through your instructor.

Scoring the Decision

The Expert: Alonzo W. Pond, M. A., is the desert survival expert who has contributed the basis for the item ranking. He is the former Chief of the Desert Branch of the Arctic Desert Tropic Information Center of the Air Force University at Maxwell Air Force Base. Two of the several books Mr. Pond has written are *Survival*, an excellent reference if you would like to do more reading on this subject, and *Peoples of the Desert*, written after Mr. Pond had spent years living with people of every desert in the world except the Australian. During World War II, Mr. Pond spent much of his time working with the Allied forces in the Sahara on desert survival problems. While there as Chief of the Desert Branch, he encountered the countless survival cases that serve as a basis of the rationale for these rankings.

The Expert Ranking and Rationales

No. 1---COSMETIC MIRROR. Of all the items, the mirror is absolutely critical. It is the most powerful tool you have for communicating your presence. In sunlight a simple mirror can generate 5 to 7 million candle power of light. The reflected sunbeam can even be seen beyond the horizon. If you had no other items you would still have better than an 80 percent chance of being spotted and picked up within the first 24 hours.

No. 2---TOP COAT PER PERSON. Once you have a communication system to tell people where you are, your next problem is to slow down dehydration. Forty percent of the body moisture that is lost through dehydration is lost through respiration and perspiration. Moisture lost through respiration can be cut significantly by remaining calm. Moisture lost through perspiration can be cut by preventing the hot dry air from circulating next to the skin. The top coats, ironic as it may seem, are the best available means for doing this. Without them, survival time would be cut by at least a day.

No. 3---QUART OF WATER PER PERSON. You could probably survive three days with just the first two items. Although the quart of water would not significantly extend the survival time, it would help to hold off the effects of dehydration. It would be best to drink the water as you become thirsty, so that you can remain as clear-headed as possible during the first day when important decisions have to be made and a shelter erected. Once dehydration begins, it would be impossible to reverse it with the amount of water available in this situation. Therefore, rationing it would do no good at all.

No. 4---FLASHLIGHT (4-BATTERY SIZE). The only quick reliable night signaling device is the flashlight. With it and the mirror, you have 24-hour signaling capacity. It is also a multiple-use item during the day. The reflector and lens could be used as an auxiliary signal device or for starting a fire. The battery container could be used for digging or as a water container in the distillation process (see plastic raincoat).

No. 5---PARACHUTE (RED AND WHITE). The parachute can serve as both shelter and signaling device. The saguaro cactus could serve as a tent pole and the parachute shrouds as tent ropes. Double or triple folding the parachute would give shade dark enough to reduce the temperature underneath it by as much as 20 percent.

No. 6---JACKKNIFE. Although not as crucial as the first five items, the jackknife would be useful for rigging the shelter and for cutting up the very rough barrel cactus for moisture. Its innumerable other uses give it the high ranking.

No. 7---PLASTIC RAINCOAT. (LARGE SIZE) In recent years the development of plastic, nonporous materials have made it possible to build a solar still. By digging a hole and placing the raincoat over it the temperature differential will extract some moisture from urine-soaked sand and pieces of barrel cactus and produce condensation on the underside of the plastic. By placing a small stone in the center of the plastic, a cone shape can be formed and cause moisture to drip into the flashlight container buried in the center of the hole. Up to a quart a day could be obtained in this way. This would be helpful, but not enough to make any significant difference. The physical activity required to extract the water is likely to use up about twice as much body water as could be gained.

No. 8---45-CALIBER PISTOL (LOADED). By the end of the second week, speech would be seriously impaired and you might be unable to walk (6 to 10 percent dehydration). The pistol would be useful as a sound signaling device and the bullets a quick fire starter. The international distress signal is three shots in rapid succession. There have been numerous cases of survivors going undetected because they couldn't make any loud sounds. The butt of the pistol might also be used as a hammer.

The pistol's advantages are counterbalanced by its very dangerous disadvantages. Impatience, irritability, and irrationality would all occur as dehydration set in. Under the circumstances, the availability of so lethal a tool constitutes a real danger to the team. Assuming it was not used against humans, it might be used for hunting, which would be a complete waste of effort. Even if someone were able to shoot an animal with it, which is very unlikely, eating the meat would increase dehydration enormously as the body uses its water to process the food.

No. 9—A PAIR OF SUNGLASSES PER PERSON. In the intense sunlight of the desert photothermia and solar retinituos (both similar to the effects of snowblindness) could be serious problems, especially by the second day. However, the dark shade of the parachute shelter would reduce the problem, as would darkening the area around the eyes with soot from the wreckage. Using a handkerchief or compress material as a veil with eye slits cut into it would eliminate the vision problem. But sunglasses would make things more comfortable.

No. 10---COMPRESS KIT WITH GAUZE. Because of the desert's low humidity, it is considered one of the healthiest (least infectious) places in the world. Due to the fact that blood thickens with dehydration, there is little danger from bleeding unless a vein is severed. In one well-documented case, a man, lost and without water, who had torn off all of his clothes and fallen among sharp cactus and rocks until his body was covered with cuts, didn't bleed until he was rescued and given water.

The kit materials might be used as rope, or for wrapping legs, ankles, and head, including face, as further protection against dehydration and sunlight.

South-Western

No. 11---MAGNETIC COMPASS. Aside from the possibility of using its reflective surfaces as an auxiliary signaling device, the compass is of little use. It could even be dangerous to have around once the effects of dehydration take hold. It might give someone the notion of walking out.

No. 12---SECTIONAL AIR MAP OF THE AREA. Might be helpful for starting a fire or for toilet paper. One might use it for a head cover or eye shade. It might have entertainment value. But it is essentially useless and perhaps dangerous because it too might encourage walking out.

No. 13---A BOOK ENTITLED *EDIBLE ANIMALS OF THE DESERT*. The problem confronting the group is dehydration, not starvation. Any energy expended in hunting would be costly in terms of potential water loss. Desert animals, while plentiful, are seldom seen. They survive by lying as low, as should the survivors. If the hunt were successful, the intake of protein would cause an increase in the amount of water used to process the protein in the body. General rule of thumb—if you have lots of water, eat, otherwise, don't consume anything. Although the book might contain useful information, it would be difficult to adjust your eyes to reading and remain attentive as dehydration increases.

No. 14.---2 QUARTS OF 180 PROOF VODKA. When severe alcoholism kills someone, he or she usually dies of dehydration. Alcohol absorbs water. The body loses an enormous amount of water trying to throw off the alcohol. We estimate a loss of 2 to 3 ounces of water per ounce of alcohol. The vodka consumed could be lethal in this situation. Its presence could cause someone in a dehydrated state to increase his problem. The vodka would be helpful for a fire or a temporary coolant for the body. The bottle might also be helpful. All in all, the vodka represents more dangers than help.

No. 15---BOTTLE OF SALT TABLETS (1,000 TABLETS). Widespread myths about salt tablets exist. The first problem is that with dehydration and loss of water, blood salinity increases. Sweat contains less salt than extracellular fluids. Without lots of water, the salt tablets would require body water to get rid of the increased salinity. The effect would be like drinking sea water. Even the man who developed salt tablets now maintains they are of questionable value except in geographical areas where there are salt deficiencies.

Team Performance Data

These figures are based on 4,116 participants (802 trams):

Average Individual Score	63.2*
On winning teams	60.5*
On losing teams	67.5*
Average Team Score	54.3*
On winning teams	42.0*
Average Gain Score	8.9*
On winning teams	18.5*
On losing teams	-1.1*
Percent of Individuals that Scored Better Than Their Teams	26.0*
On winning teams	13.1*
On losing teams	45.6*
Average Lowest (Best Score)	48.1*
On winning teams	44.2*
On losing teams	52.4*
Difference Between Lowest and Team Score	- 6.2*

On winning teams 2.2*
On losing teams 15.7*
Total Number of Teams Improving over Individual Average 650 (81%)
Total Number Whose Performance Was Poorer 152 (19%)

*These findings were statistically significant when completed within the grouping at greater than the 0.001 level.

Group	Average of Individual Teams	Average of Team Scores	Average Scores	Gain
Top Management	106	59.9	48.5	11.4
Michigan Education Association	24	63.4	49.7	13.7
Boy Scout Executives	3	66.4	59.7	15.7
School Principals	29	64.0	51.3	12.7
Mixed Management	219	61.1	51.7	9.4
Supervisors	39	63.3	54.7	8.6
Junior High School Students	19	67.9	55.7	12.1
Teachers	195	63.6	56.3	7.3
Plant Superintendents	27	65.7	57.7	8.0
Police	6	65.5	58.0	7.5
College Students	68	67.7	59.6	8.1
High School Students	12	71.8	64.6	7.2
Campfire Girls	5	76.6	65.6	11.0
Inner City People (paid to attend)	5	73.6	71.6	2.0
Greek Executives	6	74.7	78.0	-3.3
Inner City Government Poverty Program	4	67.7	85.0	-17.3

(Nonsupervisory)

Results of Three Best Teams to Date

Junior High School Students	1	81	10	71
Multi Company	1	41	14	27
General Motors	1	66	22	44

South-Western

Chapter 7

Fundamentals of Organizing

Chapter Outline

I. Organizing the Vertical Structure

    A. Work Specialization

    B. Chain of Command

    C. Span of Management

    D. Centralization and Decentralization

II. Departmentalization

    A. Team Approach

    B. Network Approach

    C. The Virtual Organization Approach

    D. The Horizontal Organization

    E. The Need for Coordination

    F. Task Forces, Teams, and Project Management

    G. Reengineering

III. Traditional Organization versus the New Workplace

    A. Horizontal Structure

    B. Open Information

    C. Decentralized Decision Making and Participative Strategy

    D. Empowered Employees and Shared Responsibility

    E. Strong, Adaptive Culture

    F. Factors Affecting Structure

    G. Structure Follows Strategy

    H. Structure Reflects the Environment

    I. Structure Fits the Technology

Key Terms

Organizing: the deployment of organizational resources to achieve strategic goals.

Organization structure: the framework in which the organization defines how tasks are divided, resources are deployed, and departments are coordinated.

Organization chart: the visual representation of an organization's structure.

Work specialization: the degree to which organizational tasks are subdivided into individual jobs; also called division of labor.

Chain of command: an unbroken line of authority that links all individuals in the organization and specifies who reports to whom.

Authority: the formal and legitimate right of a manager to make decisions, issue orders, and allocate resources to achieve organizationally desired outcomes.

Responsibility: the duty to perform the task or activity an employee has been assigned.

Accountability: the fact that the people with authority and responsibility are subject to reporting and justifying task outcomes to those above them in the chain of command.

Delegation: the process managers use to transfer authority and responsibility to positions below them in the hierarchy.

Line authority: a form of authority in which individuals in management positions have the formal power to direct and control immediate subordinates.

Staff authority: a form of authority granted to staff specialists in their area of expertise.

Span of management: the number of employees who report to a supervisor; also called span of control.

Tall structure: a management structure characterized by an overall narrow span of management and a relatively large number of hierarchical levels.

Flat structure: a management structure characterized by an overall broad narrow span of management and a relatively few of hierarchical levels.

Centralization: the location of decision authority near top organizational levels.

Decentralization: the location of decision authority near lower organization levels.

Departmentalization: the basis on which individuals are grouped into departments and departments into the total organization.

Cross-functional team: a group of employees from various departments that meets as a team to resolve mutual problems.

Permanent team: a group of participants from several functions who are permanently assigned to solve ongoing problems of common interest.

Team-based structure: structure in which the entire organization is made up of teams that coordinate their work and work directly with customers to accomplish the organization's goals.

Network structure: an organization structure that disaggregates major functions into separate companies that are brokered by a small headquarters organization.

Modular approach: a manufacturing company uses outside suppliers to provide large components of the product, which are then assembled into a final product by a few workers.

Virtual organization: an organization that has few on-site employees and does most of its interactions online.

Coordination: the quality of collaboration across departments.

Task force: a temporary team or committee formed to solve a specific short-term problem involving several departments.

Team: a group of participants from several departments who meet regularly to solve ongoing problems of common interest.

Project manager: a person responsible for coordinating the activities of several departments on a full-time basis for the completion of a specific project.

Reengineering: the radical redesign of business processes to achieve dramatic improvements in cost, quality, service, and speed.

Process: an organized group of related tasks and activities that work together to transform inputs into outputs and create value.

Learning organization: an organization in which everyone is engaged in identifying and solving problems, enabling the organization to continuously experiment, improve, and increase its capability.

Technology: the knowledge, tools, techniques, and activities used to transform the organization's inputs into outputs.

Small-batch production: a type of technology that involves the production of goods in batches of one or a few products designed to customer specifications.

Mass production: a type of technology characterized by the production of a large volume of products with the same specifications.

Continuous process production: a type of technology involving mechanization of the entire work flow and nonstop production.

Technical complexity: the degree to which complex machinery is involved in the production process to the exclusion of people.

Service technology: technology characterized by intangible outputs and direct contact between employees and customers.

Digital technology: technology characterized by use of the Internet and other digital processes to conduct or support business operations.

Learning Objectives

1. Discuss the fundamental characteristics of organizing including such concepts as work specialization, chain of command, line and staff, centralization, and span of management.

2. Explain the contemporary team and network structures and why they are being adopted by organizations.

3. Discuss the advantages and disadvantages of the new virtual approach to organizing.

4. Describe mechanisms for achieving coordination and where they may be applied.

5. Explain the major differences between traditional vertical organizations and the new workplace learning organization.

6. Describe how organization structure can be designed to fit environmental uncertainty.

7. Define production technology (manufacturing, service, and digital) and explain how it influences organization structure.

Chapter Review

Multiple Choice: Please indicate the correct response to the following questions by writing the letter of the correct answer in the space provided.

_____ 1. Although work specialization has many advantages, _____ is a disadvantage of specialization.
a. the development of boring jobs
b. inherent inefficiency
c. lack of development of expertise by workers
d. lack of standardization
e. not being able to select employees with proper abilities

_____ 2. Which of the following is true of authority?
a. It is vested in people, not their positions.
b. A manager has authority only if subordinates choose to accept his or her commands.
c. Positions at the bottom of the hierarchy are vested with more formal authority than are those at the top.
d. A subordinate will obey an order outside his or her zone of acceptance.
e. Authority cannot be illustrated by the organizational chart.

_____ 3. _____ is the duty to perform the task or activity an employee has been assigned.
a. Authority
b. Accountability
c. Power
d. Responsibility
e. Span of management

_____ 4. Accountability means that the people with authority and responsibility are subject to _____ those above them in the chain of command.
a. reporting and justifying task outcomes to
b. the whims of
c. the mercy of
d. the span of management of
e. the decentralization of

_____ 5. The process whereby managers transfer authority and responsibility to lower positions is called
    a. accountability.
    b. responsibility sharing.
    c. departmentalization.
    d. creation of span of management.
    e. delegation.

_____ 6. A department that performs tasks reflecting the organization's primary goal and mission is called a _____ department.
    a. Line
    b. Staff
    c. Functional
    d. Product
    e. Production

_____ 7. The trend in recent years has been toward _____ spans of control.
    a. Narrower
    b. No
    c. Wider
    d. Equalized
    e. Managerial

_____ 8. A larger span of control is called for when
    a. work performed by subordinates is unstable and changing.
    b. subordinates perform dissimilar tasks.
    c. subordinates are spread out geographically.
    d. subordinates are highly training and need little direction in performing tasks.
    e. there are no support systems available for the manager.

_____ 9. Johnson & Johnson gives almost complete authority to its 180 operating companies to develop and market their own products. This is an example of
    a. loss of control.
    b. spreading oneself too thinly.
    c. authoritarianism.
    d. decentralization.
    e. centralization.

_____ 10. The most widespread trend in departmentalization has been the effort to implement the _____ approach.
    a. vertical functional
    b. Divisional
    c. horizontal matrix
    d. Team
    e. Network

_____ 11. Reengineering
     a.   is inexpensive to implement.
     b.   is implemented in a relatively short time.
     c.   is often painful.
     d.   does not involve management.
     e.   does not involve rank and file workers.

_____ 12. The structural design approaches that reflect different uses of chain of command in departmentalization are
     a.   functional, divisional, matrix, teams, and networks.
     b.   functional, departmental, minimal, teams, and networks.
     c.   fundamental, divisional, matrix, teams, and organizational.
     d.   divisional, matrix, teams, and networks.
     e.   functional, matrix, teams, and networks.

_____ 13. The _____ means that the organization desegregates major functions into separate companies that are coordinated by smaller headquarters organizations.
     a.   geographical approach
     b.   network structure
     c.   divisional approach
     d.   matrix approach
     e.   organizational approach

_____ 14. An advantage of team structure is
     a.   increased barriers among departments.
     b.   unplanned decentralization.
     c.   time and resources spent on meetings.
     d.   less response time, quicker decisions.
     e.   all of the above.

_____ 15. The question, "Where is the organization?" is most likely to be asked concerning the _____ approach.
     a.   vertical functional
     b.   divisional
     c.   horizontal matrix
     d.   team
     e.   network

_____ 16. Which of the following is an advantage of the network structure?
     a.   less hands-on control, providing autonomy
     b.   less employee loyalty, meaning more motivation
     c.   more administrative tasks
     d.   global competitiveness
     e.   easy to understand

17. Turnover tends to be higher in a _____ organization.
    a. vertical functional
    b. divisional
    c. horizontal matrix
    d. team
    e. Network

18. Which of these represent the ultimate in horizontal coordination?
    a. The learning organization
    b. Reengineering
    c. Switching to a functional structure
    d. Increasing the number of hierarchical levels in the organization
    e. Narrow span of management

19. Typically, project managers have authority over _____ but not over _____ assigned to it.
    a. people, the project
    b. the project, people
    c. resources, the project
    d. people, other resources
    e. finances, products

20. Which of these can be defined as one in which everyone is engaged in identifying and solving problems, enabling the organization to continually experiment, change, and improve?
    a. Learning organization
    b. Traditional organization
    c. Functional organization
    d. Vertical organization
    e. Centralized organization

21. Which of these means giving employees the power, freedom, knowledge, and skills to make decisions and perform effectively?
    a. Egalitarianism
    b. Corporate culture
    c. Empowerment
    d. Adaptation
    e. Boundaryless organization

22. Which of the following is NOT a contingency factor that influences an organization's structure?
    a. Strategy
    b. Environment
    c. Interdependence
    d. Production technology
    e. Competitor's structure

_____ 23. Which of the following structures works best in an uncertain organizational environment?
a. A tight structure
b. A mechanistic structure
c. A horizontal structure
d. A functional structure
e. A vertical structure

_____ 24. A type of technology characterized by the production of a large volume of products with the same specifications is referred to as
a. unit production.
b. flexible manufacturing.
c. mass production.
d. continuous process production.
e. service technology production.

_____ 25. Which of the following structures works best in a stable organizational environment?
a. A loose organizational structure
b. A vertical structure
c. An organic structure
d. A horizontal structure
e. a and c only

_____ 26. Which of the following structures is an incorrect fit in an unstable organizational environment?
a. A horizontal structure
b. A vertical structure
c. A loose organizational structure
d. An organic structure
e. All of the above

_____ 27. The most sophisticated and complex form of production technology, according to Woodward, is
a. continuous process production.
b. mass production.
c. small batch production.
d. routine production.
e. unit production.

_____ 28. The technology associated with use of the Internet is
a. digital.
b. service.
c. continuous production.
d. small batch
e. none of the above.

_____ 29. Structure _____ strategy.
   a.   dictates
   b.   follows
   c.   is not related to
   d.   is the opposite of
   e.   has an inverse relationship to

_____ 30. _____ technology is characterized by intangible outputs and direct contact between employees and customers.
   a.   Flexible
   b.   Large batch
   c.   Continuous process
   d.   Service
   e.   Unit batch

True/False: Please indicate whether the following statements are true or false by writing a T or an F in the blank in front of each question.

1. The deployment of organizational resources to achieve strategic goals is known as organizing.

2. The organizational chart can never be changed.

3. The matrix approach to organizational structure is the only structure that uses both functional and divisional chains of command simultaneously.

4. A temporary team designed to solve short-term problems is called a task force.

5. Self-directed teams are the fundamental unit in a learning organization.

6. Learning organizations de-emphasize the importance of getting people communicating face-to-face.

7. The culture of a learning organization is egalitarian.

8. The vertical functional structure is appropriate when the primary goal is innovation and flexibility.

9. Technology includes the knowledge, tools, techniques, and activities used to transform organizational inputs into outputs.

10. Law firms, airlines, advertising firms, and amusement parks are examples of service firms.

Short Answer: Please indicate your answer in the space provided.

1. List the five approaches to departmentalization.

2. List the four contingency factors that influence organization structure.

3. Should an organization maintain flexibility in an uncertain environment? Explain your answer.

4. What advantages does decentralization have over centralization?

Manager's Workbook

Family Business

You are the parent of ten children and have just used your inheritance to acquire a medium-sized pharmaceutical company. Last year's sales were down 18 percent from the previous year. In fact, the last three years have been real losers. You want to clean house of current managers over the next ten years and bring your children into the business. Being a loving parent, you agree to send your children to college to educate each of them in one functional specialty. The ten children are actually five sets of twins exactly one year apart. The first set will begin college this fall, followed by the remaining sets the next four years. The big decision is which specialty each child should study. You want to have the most important functions taken over by your children as soon as possible, so you will ask the older children to study the most important areas.

Your task right now is to rank in order of priority the functions to which your children will be assigned and develop reasons for your ranking.

The ten functions follow:

	Distribution
	Manufacturing
	Market Research
	New-Product Development
	Human Resources
	Product Promotion
	Quality Assurance
	Sales
	Legal and Governmental Affairs
	Office of the Controller

Analyze your reasons for how functional priority relates to the company's environmental/ strategic needs. Now rank the functions as part of a group. Discuss the problem until group members agree on a single ranking. How does the group's reasoning and ranking differ from your original thinking?

Loose versus Tight Organization Structure *(Also available on page 269 of text.)*

Interview an employee at your university, such as a department head or secretary. Have the employee answer the following thirteen questions about his or her job and organizational conditions.

		Disagree Strongly				**Agree Strongly**
1	Your work would be considered routine.	5	4	3	2	1
2	There is a clearly known way to do the major tasks you encounter.	5	4	3	2	1
3	Your work has high variety and frequent exceptions.	1	2	3	4	5
4	Communications from above consist of information and advice rather than instructions and directions.	1	2	3	4	5
5	You have the support of peers and supervisors to do your job well.	1	2	3	4	5
6	You seldom exchange ideas or information with people doing other kinds of jobs.	5	4	3	2	1
7	Decisions relevant to your work are made above you and passed down.	5	4	3	2	1
8	People at your level frequently have to figure out for themselves what their jobs are for the day.	1	2	3	4	5
9	Lines of authority are clear and precisely defined.	5	4	3	2	1
10	Leadership tends to be democratic rather than autocratic in style.	1	2	3	4	5
11	Job descriptions are written and up-to-date for each job.	5	4	3	2	1
12	People understand each other's jobs and often do different tasks.	1	2	3	4	5
13	A manual of policies and procedures is available to use when a problem arises.	5	4	3	2	1

Total Score

A score of **52** or above suggests that the employee is working in a "loosely structured" organization. The score reflects a flexible structure that is often associated with uncertain environments and small-batch technology. People working in this structure feel empowered. Many organizations today are moving in the direction of flexible structures and empowerment.

A score of **26** or below suggests a "tight structure." This structure utilizes traditional control and functional specialization, which often occurs in a certain environment, a stable organization, and routine or mass-production technology. People in this structure may feel controlled and constrained.

Discuss the pros and cons of loose versus tight structure. Does the structure of the employee you interviewed fit the nature of the organization's environment, strategic goals, and technology? How might you redesign the structure to make the work organization more effective?

Manager's Workshop

Bistro Technology (*Also available on page 270 of text.*)

You will be analyzing the technology used in three different restaurants—McDonald's, Burger King, and a typical family restaurant. Your instructor will tell you whether to do this assignment as individuals or in a group.

You must visit all three restaurants and infer how the work is done, according to the criteria below. However, you are not allowed to "interview" any employees, but instead be an observer. Take lots of notes when you are there.

	McDonald's	Burger King	Family restaurant
Organization goals: speed, service, atmosphere, etc.			
Authority structure			
Type of technology using Woodward's model			
Organization structure: mechanistic or organic			
Team vs. individual- do people work together or alone?			

Tasks: routine vs. non-routine			
Specialization of tasks by employees (division of labor)			
Expertise required: technical vs. social			
Decision making: centralized vs. decentralized			

1. Is the technology used the best one for each restaurant, considering its goals and environment?

2. From the data above, determine if the structure and other characteristics fit the technology.

3. If you were part of a consulting team assigned to improve the operations of each organization, what recommendations would you make?

Making Rules

As a way of figuring out what rules and policies make sense for your organization, you might start by deciding how your group would handle each of these scenarios. Based on your discussion, you will be able to formulate a good working rule.

In groups of 4-7 members, discuss the following questions. Your assignment is to develop your group's list of policies and rules, which you will turn in to the instructor. Be prepared to defend your choices to the rest of the class.

1. Your team agreed to meet at 1 p.m. Wednesday for two hours to work on the project. Jane doesn't show up until 1:20.

2. Your team divided up the tasks of the project and set up a meeting for each person to report on his or her progress. When it's Fred's turn to present, he says that he didn't have time to complete his part.

3. When decisions need to be made during your team's meetings, Chris often says, "It doesn't matter what we do. Let's just hurry up and get it done and turn it in."

4. Your team members reported on the work each had been doing, but it was clear that Frank had not put much effort into his part.

5. The teams are given the next class period to work on their project. Sandy doesn't show up for class; she has all of your team's materials.

6. Phil frequently interrupts other team members during meetings.

7. Once Connie has an idea in her head, she won't listen to anyone else's opinions.

8. Bob takes over team meetings. Others rarely get a chance to talk.

9. Sarah is a popular student. It seems that other team members agree with what she says regardless of the quality of her idea.

10. Tom comes to all the team's meetings but rarely says anything.

11. During your meeting, Carolyn starts talking about things unrelated to the project, like what's happening in other classes and upcoming parties.

12. Stan and Beth have very different opinions of how your team's work should progress. They seem to be at odds with each other most of the time. They argue during team meetings.

13. In your group, half the members are Asian, half-Caucasian. The Asian students don't say very much, and the Caucasian students dominate the group.

14. In your group, three members belong to the same sorority. They arrive and leave together, take breaks together, and spend time in the group talking about sorority activities.

Developed by Karen Harlos, University of British Columbia.

Study Guide Solutions

Chapter Review

Multiple-Choice Questions

1	2	3	4	5	6	7	8	9	10
A	B	D	A	E	A	C	D	D	D

11	12	13	14	15	16	17	18	19	20
C	A	B	D	E	D	E	A	B	A

21	22	23	24	25	26	27	28	29	30
C	E	C	C	B	B	A	A	B	D

True/False Questions

1	2	3	4	5	6	7	8	9	10
T	F	T	T	T	F	T	F	T	T

Short Answer Questions

1. Vertical functional, divisional, horizontal matrix, team-based, and network.

2. Strategy, environment, technology, and interdependence.

3. Yes, an organization in an uncertain environment should maintain a high degree of flexibility. An uncertain environment often changes, which requires the organization to change also. Flexibility must be present so the organization can adapt to the change.

4. Decentralization provides greater use of human resources, unburdens top managers, ensures that decisions are made close to the action by well-informed people, and permits more rapid response to external changes. However, there will be less control by top management, less standardization, and the loss of economies of scale.

Manager's Workbook

Family Business: There is no one right answer here. First the group needs to decide on what their strategy is and what kind of environment they are in. If they want to make the *best* product, then new-product development and manufacturing will be important, followed by market research, distribution and sales. If the strategy is to be the largest market share, then market research and product promotion will be most important followed by distribution and new-product development. If being seen as a quality company with environmental concerns is important, then quality assurance and new product development will be important. If a long-term view is taken of being the best product with a high market share, over the next ten years, then Human Resources would be very important, for it is only with good and competent people that such long-term goals can be met. If one of the main strategies is to be competitive on price, then the Controller's position would be important. If good relations with government because the industry is heavily regulated, or could become too heavily regulated, then Legal and Governmental Affairs is crucial.

Justify rankings with data, not merely opinions. Keep answering the question: "What evidence do you have that such a ranking will lead to success in your strategy?"

Loose versus Tight Organization Structure: Scoring and interpretation provided with exercise.

Manager's Workshop

Bistro Technology: Answers to this application will vary.

Making Rules: Answers to this application will vary.

Chapter 8

Change and Development

Chapter Outline

I.   Change and the New Workplace

II. Model of Planned Organizational Change

   A.   Forces for Change

   B.   Need for Change

III. Initiating Change

   A.   Search

   B.   Creativity

   C.   Idea Champions and New-Venture Teams

IV. Implementing Change

   A.   Resistance to Change

   B.   Force Field Analysis

   C.   Implementation Tactics

V.   Types of Planned Change

   A.   Technology Changes

   B.   New-Product Changes

   C.   Structural Changes

VI. Culture/People Changes

   A.   Training and Development

   B.   Organizational Development

Key Terms

Organizational change: the adoption of a new idea or behavior by an organization.

Performance gap: a disparity between existing and desired performance levels.

Search: the process of learning about current developments inside or outside the organization that can be used to meet a perceived need for change.

Creativity: the generation of novel ideas that may meet perceived needs or offer opportunities for the organization.

Idea champion: a person who sees the need for and champions productive change within the organization.

New-venture team: a unit separate from the mainstream of the organization that is responsible for developing and initiating innovations.

Skunkworks: a separate small, informal, highly autonomous, and often secretive group that focuses on breakthrough ideas for the business.

Idea incubator: an in-house program that provides a safe harbor where ideas from employees throughout the organization can be developed without interference from company bureaucracy or politics.

Force-field analysis: the process of determining which forces drive and which resist a proposed change.

Technology change: a change that pertains to the organization's production process.

Process change: a change in the organization's product or service output.

Time-based competition: a strategy of competition based on the ability to deliver products and services faster than competitors.

Structural changes: any changes in the way in which the organization is designed and managed.

Culture/people change: a change in employees' values, norms, attitudes, beliefs, and behavior.

Organizational development (OD): the application of behavioral science techniques to improve an organization's health and effectiveness through its ability to cope with environmental changes, improve internal relationships, and increase problem-solving capabilities.

Team building: a type of OD intervention that enhances the cohesiveness of departments by helping members learn to function as a team.

Survey feedback: a type of OD intervention in which questionnaires on organizational climate and other factors are distributed among employees and the results reported back to them by a change agent.

Large-group intervention: an approach that brings together participants from all parts of the organization (and may include key outside stakeholders as well) to discuss problems or opportunities and plan for major change.

Unfreezing: the stage of organizational development in which participants are made aware of problems in order to increase their willingness to change their behavior.

Change agent: an OD specialist who contracts with an organization to facilitate change.

Changing: the intervention stage of organizational development in which individuals experiment with new workplace behavior.

Refreezing: the reinforcement stage of organizational development in which individuals acquire a desired new skill or attitude and are rewarded for it by the organization.

Learning Objectives

1. Define organizational change and explain the forces for change.

2. Describe the sequence of four change activities that must be performed in order for change to be successful.

3. Explain the techniques managers can use to facilitate the initiation of change in organizations, including idea champions, new venture teams, and idea incubators.

4. Define sources of resistance to change.

5. Explain force field analysis and other implementation tactics that can be used to overcome resistance to change.

6. Explain the difference among technology, product, structure, and culture/people changes.

7. Explain the change process—bottom up, top down, horizontal—associated with each type of change.

8. Define organizational development and large-group interventions.

Chapter Review

Multiple Choice: Please indicate the correct response to the following questions by writing the letter of the correct answer in the space provided.

_____ 1. The current trend is toward development of the _____, which engages everyone in problem solving and continuous improvement based on the lessons of experience.
   a.   international organization
   b.   learning organization
   c.   unified organization
   d.   lean organization
   e.   vertical organization

_____ 2. The change sequence includes
   a.   internal and external forces for change.
   b.   managers becoming aware of a need for change.
   c.   the initiation of change.
   d.   the implementation of change.
   e.   all of the above.

_____ 3. Which of the following is/are an internal force for change?
   a.   customers
   b.   competitors
   c.   the setting of a higher growth rate goal
   d.   a depressed economy
   e.   an international political incident

_____ 4.   Which of these indicate a disparity between existing and desired performance levels?
    a.   Environmental opportunity
    b.   Performance gap
    c.   Behavioral occurrence
    d.   Critical incident
    e.   Organizational structural imbalance

_____ 5.   _____ typically uncovers existing knowledge that can be applied or adopted within the organization.
    a.   Search
    b.   Creativity
    c.   Intrapreneurship
    d.   A venture team
    e.   A skunkworks

_____ 6.   A creative person is usually
    a.   more authoritarian.
    b.   highly disciplined.
    c.   not very persistent.
    d.   open-minded.
    e.   less playful.

_____ 7.   The most creative organizations encourage employees to
    a.   always make sure they are right before proceeding.
    b.   make mistakes.
    c.   avoid taking risks.
    d.   follow procedures for research and development.
    e.   put ideas into suggestion boxes.

_____ 8.   The _____ is a person who sees the need for and champions productive change in an organization.
    a.   idea challenger
    b.   critic
    c.   idea champion
    d.   skunkworks leader
    e.   change agent

_____ 9.   New venture teams should
    a.   be relatively large groups to facilitate more ideas.
    b.   report through the normal organizational structure.
    c.   give free reign to members' creativity.
    d.   be subject to all organizational rules and procedures.
    e.   develop a bureaucratic structure as rapidly as possible.

_____ 10.   A(n) _____ is an in-house program that provides a safe harbor where ideas from employees throughout the organization can be developed without interference.
    a.   skunkworks
    b.   idea incubator
    c.   invention room
    d.   venture department
    e.   invention sponsor

_____ 11. A creative organization would
    a. have contacts with outside sources.
    b. hire people who make it uncomfortable.
    c. encourage people to defy their bosses.
    d. run a loose ship.
    e. all of the above.

_____ 12. Which of the following is not a reason for employee resistance to change?
    a. Self-interest
    b. Lack of understanding and trust
    c. Uncertainty
    d. Opportunity for advancement
    e. Different assessment of goals

_____ 13. The biggest barrier to organizational change is usually
    a. disagreements about the benefits.
    b. uncertainty about the future.
    c. a lack of understanding and trust.
    d. fear of personal loss.
    e. too much trust.

_____ 14. Kurt Lewin proposed that change was the result of the competition between _____ and _____ forces.
    a. driving; flying
    b. real; imagined
    c. abstract; materialistic
    d. driving; restraining
    e. coercive; restrictive

_____ 15. To use the results of a force field analysis, a manager should
    a. force the employees to accept the change.
    b. analyze the field of workers to find the resistance and then threaten these workers if they do not accept the change.
    c. selectively remove forces that restrain change.
    d. selectively remove the driving forces.
    e. do any or all of the above.

_____ 16. Just-in-time inventory control systems schedule material to arrive at the company _____ on the production line.
    a. just after they are needed
    b. way before they are needed
    c. just as they are needed
    d. irrespective of when needed because of finished goods
    e. as the finished goods are completed

_____ 17.   Which approach to change implementation should be used when users have power to resist?
   a.   Education
   b.   Participation
   c.   Coercion
   d.   Top management support
   e.   Domination

_____ 18.   Top management support for a change
   a.   symbolizes to employees that it is important.
   b.   is not necessary if the change involves multiple departments.
   c.   usually causes changes to get bogged down since most people naturally resist authority figures.
   d.   often undercuts that very change.
   e.   all of the above.

_____ 19.   If a manager uses coercion to implement a change
   a.   he is using formal power to force the employees to change.
   b.   resisters are told to accept the change or lose rewards.
   c.   employees can be made to feel like victims.
   d.   anger may result on the part of the employees.
   e.   all of the above.

_____ 20.   A technology change is related to
   a.   the organization's production process.
   b.   the way people relate to each other.
   c.   the products the company makes.
   d.   the organizational structure of the company.
   e.   none of the above.

_____ 21.   _____ means that ideas are initiated at lower organizational levels and channeled upward for approval.
   a.   Bottom-up approach
   b.   Top-down approach
   c.   Horizontal-linkage approach
   d.   Diagonal approach
   e.   None of the above

_____ 22.   What is the term that is associated with a strategy of competition based on the ability to deliver products and services faster than the competitors?
   a.   Service competition
   b.   Time-based competition
   c.   Parallel competition
   d.   All of the above
   e.   None of the above

_____ 23.   A product change
     a.   may define a new market.
     b.   does not usually involve a new technology.
     c.   need not consider customers' needs.
     d.   is successful 9 times out of 10.
     e.   must be restricted to one department.

_____ 24.   Which of these changes may involve hierarchy, goals, and procedures?
     a.   New product
     b.   Technological
     c.   Structural
     d.   Culture/people
     e.   Customer

_____ 25.   Changes in culture and people pertain to
     a.   technology.
     b.   structure.
     c.   products.
     d.   how employees think.
     e.   how refined the employees are.

_____ 26.   Which of the following problems can OD help managers address?
     a.   mergers/acquisitions
     b.   organizational decline
     c.   conflict management
     d.   organizational revitalization
     e.   all of the above

_____ 27.   In the survey-feedback method of OD
     a.   the employees receive feedback on the results of a questionnaire regarding values, climate, participation, leadership, and group cohesion in the organization.
     b.   employees are allowed to give feedback on the questions that should be asked on a survey.
     c.   the OD specialist receives feedback on his survey to help refine and improve the questionnaire.
     d.   similar organizations are surveyed to determine problems in the current organization.
     e.   communication style is classified as parent, child, or adult.

_____ 28.   The first step in the change process of OD is
     a.   unfreezing, which makes the participants aware of problems and helps them become willing to change.
     b.   changing behaviors so that attitudes will follow.
     c.   refreezing on the desired attitude.
     d.   intervention in the problem at hand.
     e.   survey of the organization to discover who is willing to change.

_____ 29.   The second step for achieving behavioral and attitudinal change is
   a.   refreezing.
   b.   thawing.
   c.   changing.
   d.   unfreezing.
   e.   vaporizing.

_____ 30.   _____ occurs when individuals acquire new attitudes and are rewarded for
   them by the organization.
   a.   Refreezing
   b.   Changing
   c.   Symbolizing
   d.   Unfreezing
   e.   Metamorphosis

True/False: Please indicate whether the following statements are true or false by writing a T or an F in the blank in front of each question.

_____ 1.   The adoption of a new idea or behavior by an organization is called organizational change.

_____ 2.   The learning organization simultaneously embraces two types of planned change: operational change and nonoperational change.

_____ 3.   The disparity between existing and desired performance levels is the performance gap.

_____ 4.   Most creative companies do not tolerate employee mistakes.

_____ 5.   Uncertainty is the lack of information about past events.

_____ 6.   Resistance to change may be overcome by educating employees or inviting them to participate in implementing the change.

_____ 7.   Top management support is unnecessary for successful implementation of change.

_____ 8.   Two possible tactics for overcoming resistance to change are coercion and negotiation.

_____ 9.   Technology change involves the hierarchy of authority, goals, administrative procedures, and managerial systems.

_____ 10.   Conflicts should occur only within unhealthy organizations.

Short Answer: Please indicate your answer in the space provided.

1. List the four reasons why employees tend to resist change.

2. List the five specific tactics that can be used to overcome employee resistance to change.

3. List the three distinct steps for achieving behavioral and attitudinal change.

4. What are idea champions and why are they important to organizations?

Manager's Workbook

Personal Change

Think of a situation (a) where you wanted to (or had to) change and successfully executed the change, and (b) when your attempt to change was unsuccessful. Referring to Exhibit 8.1 on p. 278 of the text, answer the following questions:

	When change was successful	When change was not successful
1. Describe the situation		
2. What was the motive or need to change?		
3. How did you feel initially about the change?		
4. What were sources of resistance?		
5. How did you get beyond the resistance? What worked in the process of changing?		
6. What did you learn about yourself in the process of change?		
7. What have you learned about change? About motivating others to change?		

Innovation Climate *(Also available on page 299 of text.)*

In order to examine differences in level of innovation encouragement in organizations, you will be asked to rate two different organizations. You may choose one in which you have worked or the university. The other should be someone else's workplace, a family member, friend, or acquaintance. Therefore, you will have to interview that person to answer the questions below. You should put your own answers in column A, your interviewee's answers in column B, and finally, what you think would be the "ideal" in column c.

Use the following scale of 1-5: *1 = don't agree at all to 5 = agree completely*

Innovation Measures

Item of Measure	Column A Your org.	Column B Other org.	Column C Your ideal
1. Creativity is encouraged here.*			
2. People are allowed to solve the same problems in different ways.*			
3. I get free time to pursue creative ideas.#			
4. The organization publicly recognizes and also rewards those who are innovative.#			
5. Our organization is flexible and always open to change.*			
Below score items on the opposite scale: *1=agree completely* through *5=don't agree at all*			
6. The primary job of people here is to follow orders that come from the top.*			
7. The best way to get along here is to think and act like the others.*			
8. This place seems to be more concerned with the status quo than with change.*			
9. People are rewarded more if they don't rock the boat.#			
10. New ideas are great, but we don't have enough people or money to carry them out.#			
Add up Total Score for all three columns			

Note: * starred items indicate the organization's innovation climate
  # pound sign items show "resource support"

Scoring: Higher scores indicate more innovation in that organization. Compare the two organizations with your ideal, seeing which has a higher innovation score.

1. What comparisons about innovative climates can you make from these organizations?

2. How might productivity differ when there is either a climate that supports vs. a climate that does not support innovation?

3. Which type of place would you rather work? Why?

Adapted from Susanne G. Scott and Reginald A. Bruce, "Determinants of innovative behavior: A path model of individual innovation in the workplace," *Academy of Management Journal*, 37 (3), 1994, 580-607.

Act Like Managers

When Mr. Nichols became president of Associated Grocers of Arizona, he implemented several changes. One change that was noticed by many managers was his policy of having all persons above a certain level dress appropriately. All the managers were to wear a tie. Another change was implemented regarding smoking. The only authorized place to smoke was in the lunchroom. When managers arrived each morning, they were to sign in. Each time they left the office, they were to sign out. He felt the company needed to be made more professional.

Since the company was located in Arizona, many managers started wearing the western "bolo" tie. This met with the letter of the new policy, but not the spirit. Other managers started closing their doors, which were previously left open, so they could "sneak a smoke." Managers often "forgot" to sign in or out.

1. Why did some persons resist this change?

2. How could Mr. Nichols have approached this change differently to get more acceptance?

Manager's Workshop

Research for Sale (*also available on page 301 in the text*)

Lucinda Jackson walked slowly back to R&D Laboratory 4 at Reed Pharmaceuticals. She was stunned. Top management was planning to sell her entire team project to Trichem Industries in an effort to raise the capital Reed needed to buy a small, competing drug company. Two years ago, when she was named project administrator for the cancer treatment program, Jackson was assured that the program was the highest priority at Reed. She was allowed to recruit the best and the brightest in the research center in their hunt for an effective drug to treat lung cancer. There had been press releases and personal appearances at stockholder meetings.

When she first approached a colleague, Len Rosen, to become head chemist on the project, he asked her whether Reed was in cancer research for the long haul or if they were just grabbing headlines. Based on what she had been told by the vice president in charge of R&D, Jackson assured him that their project was protected for as long as it took. Now, a short two years later, she learned that not only was Reed backing out but also that the project was being sold as a package to an out-of-state firm. There were no jobs at Reed being offered as alternatives for the team. They were only guaranteed jobs if they moved with the project to Trichem.

Jackson felt betrayed, but she knew it was nothing compared to what the other team members would feel. Rosen was a ten-year veteran at Reed, and his wife and family had deep roots in the local community. A move would be devastating to them. Jackson had a few friends in top management, but she didn't know if any would back her if she fought the planned sale.

What Do You Do?

In groups of 3-6 members, discuss the following options:

1.   Approach top management with the alternative of selling the project and sending the team temporarily to train staff at Trichem but allowing them to return to different projects at Reed after the transition. After all, they promised a commitment to the project.

2.   Wait for the announcement of the sale of the project and then try to secure as much support as possible for the staff and families in their relocation: moving expense reimbursement, job placement for spouses, etc.

3.   Tell a few people, such as Rosen, and then combine forces with them and threaten to quit if the project is sold. Make attempts to scuttle the sale to Trichem before it happens, and perhaps even leak the news to the press. Perhaps the threat of negative publicity will cause top management to reconsider.

SOURCE: Adapted from Doug Wallace, "Promises Made, Promises Broken," What Would You Do? *Business Ethics* 1 (March-April 1990), 16-18. Reprinted with permission from Business Ethics, P.O. Box 8439, Minneapolis, MN 55408, (612) 879-0695.

An Ancient Tale *(Also available on page 300 of text.)*

1.   Read the introduction and case study and answer the questions.

2.   In groups of 3-4 discuss your answers.

3.   Groups report to the whole class and the instructor leads a discussion on the issues raised.

Introduction
To understand, analyze, and improve organizations, we must carefully think through the issue of who is responsible for what activities in different organizational settings. Often we hold someone responsible who has no control over the outcome, or we fail to teach or train someone who could make the vital difference.

To explore this issue, the following exercise could be conducted on either an individual or group basis. It provides an opportunity to see how different individuals assign responsibility for an event. It is also a good opportunity to discuss the concept of organizational boundaries (what is the organization, who is in or out, etc.)

Case Study
You should read the short story and respond quickly to the first three questions. Then take a little more time on questions four through six. The results, criteria, and implications could then be discussed in groups.

Long ago in an ancient kingdom there lived a princess who was very young and very beautiful. The princess, recently married, lived in a large and luxurious castle with her husband, a powerful and wealthy lord. The young princess was not content, however, to sit and eat strawberries by herself while her husband took frequent and long journeys to neighboring kingdoms.   She felt neglected and soon became quite unhappy. One day, while she was alone in the castle gardens, a handsome vagabond rode out of the forest bordering the castle. He spied the beautiful princess, quickly won her heart, and carried her away with him.

Following a day of dalliance, the young princess found herself ruthlessly abandoned by the vagabond. She then discovered that the only way back to the castle led through the bewitched forest of the wicked sorcerer. Fearing to venture into the forest alone, she sought out her kind and wise godfather. She explained her plight, begged forgiveness of the godfather, and asked his assistance in returning home before her husband returned. The godfather, however, surprised and shocked at her behavior, refused forgiveness and denied her any assistance. Discouraged but still determined, the princess disguised her identity and sought the help of the most noble of the entire kingdom's knights. After hearing the sad story, the knight pledged his unfailing aid—for a modest fee. But alas, the princess had no money and the knight rode away to save other damsels.

The beautiful princess had no one else from whom she might seek help, and decided to brave the great peril alone. She followed the safest path she knew, but when she was almost through the forest, the wicked sorcerer spied her and caused her to be devoured by the fire-breathing dragon.

1. Who was inside the organization and who was outside? Where were the boundaries?

2. Who is most responsible for the death of the beautiful princess?

3. Who is next most responsible? Least responsible?

4. What is your criterion for the above decisions?

5. What interventions would you suggest to prevent a recurrence?

6. What are the implications for organizational development and change?

Character	Most Responsible	Next Most Responsible	Least Responsible
Princess			
Husband			
Vagabond			
Godfather			
Knight			
Sorcerer			

Check one character in each column.

Adapted from J. B. Ritchie and Paul Thompson. Reprinted with permission from *Organization and People: Readings, Cases and Exercises in Organizational Behavior.* (West, 1980), 68-70. All rights reserved, in Dorothy Marcic, *Organizational Behavior: Experiences and Cases*, 4/e, pp. 378-79.

Study Guide Solutions

Chapter Review

Multiple-Choice Questions

1	2	3	4	5	6	7	8	9	10
B	E	C	B	A	D	B	C	C	B

11	12	13	14	15	16	17	18	19	20
E	D	D	D	C	C	B	A	E	A

21	22	23	24	25	26	27	28	29	30
A	B	A	C	D	E	A	A	C	A

True/False Questions

1	2	3	4	5	6	7	8	9	10
T	F	T	F	F	T	F	T	F	F

Short Answer Questions

1. Self-interest, lack of understanding and trust, uncertainty, and different assessments and goals.

2. Communication and education, participation, negotiation, coercion, and top management support.

3. Unfreezing, changing, and refreezing.

4. An idea champion is a person who sees the need for and champions productive change within the organization. This person is important as an impetus to change and in overcoming resistance to change.

Manager's Workbook

Personal Change: Answers will vary based on individual experiences with change.

Innovation Climate: Scoring and interpretation provided with exercise.

Act Like Managers

1. Change was likely resisted by some out of self-interest. They felt they were losing something of value, i.e., the right to dress comfortably, the right to smoke, the right to not punch a time clock. Others may not have understood the reasons for the change or have felt uncertain about what changes might come next. Some probably felt that the desired outcome of being more professional would not be realized by these changes.

2. This is the type of change that needed more participation by those affected. If they could have devised their own means of meeting the goals, they would more likely have been committed to these changes.

Manager's Workshop

Research for Sale: Reed Pharmaceuticals made a commitment to the project, and Jackson has a right to ask them to at least honor their commitment to employees by allowing them to return to other projects at the company after the cancer research project is sold (Option 1). If Jackson chooses Option 2, she is not honoring her own commitments to those she recruited for the team. She has assured team members that Reed is committed to the project and she owes it to them to try to make sure they still have alternative jobs if they do not want to move to Trichem. Option 3 is risky, and might only mean that team members end up with no jobs at all. The sale is probably going to happen, and the project will be moved to Trichem with or without the team members moving with it.

An Ancient Tale: Answers will vary.

Chapter 9

Human Resource Management

Chapter Outline

I. The Strategic Role of HRM

II. Environmental Influences on HRM

    A. Competitive Strategy

    B. Federal Legislation

III. The Changing Nature of Careers

    A. The Changing Social Contract

    B. The New Workplace

    C. Attracting an Effective Workforce

    D. Human Resource Planning

    E. Recruiting

    F. Selecting

IV. Developing an Effective Workforce

    A. Training and Development

    B. Performance Appraisal

V. Maintaining an Effective Workforce

    A. Compensation

    B. Benefits

    C. Termination

Key Terms

Human resource management (HRM): activities undertaken to attract, develop, and maintain an effective workforce within an organization.

Human capital: the economic value of the knowledge, experience, skills, and capabilities of employees.

Human resource information system: an integrated computer system designed to provide data and information used in HR planning and decision making.

Discrimination: the hiring or promoting of applicants based on criteria that are not job relevant.

Affirmative action: a policy requiring employers to take positive steps to guarantee equal employment opportunities for people within protected groups.

Contingent workers: people who work for an organization, but not on a permanent or full-time basis, including temporary placements, contracted professionals, or leased employees.

Telecommuting: using computers and telecommunications equipment to perform work from home or another remote location.

Matching model: an employee selection approach in which the organization and the applicant attempt to match each other's needs, interests, and values.

Human resource planning: the forecasting of human resource needs and the projected matching of individuals with expected job vacancies.

Recruiting: the activities or practices that define the desired characteristics of applicants for specific jobs.

Job analysis: the systematic process of gathering and interpreting information about the essential duties, tasks, and responsibilities of a job.

Job description: a concise summary of the specific tasks and responsibilities of a particular job.

Job specification: an outline of the knowledge, skills, education, and physical abilities needed to adequately perform a job.

Realistic job preview (RJP): a recruiting approach that gives applicants all pertinent

Selection: the process of determining the skills, abilities, and other attributes a person needs to perform a particular job.

Validity: the relationship between an applicant's score on a selection device and his or her future job performance.

Application form: a device for collecting information about an applicant's education, previous job experience, and other background characteristics.

Employment test: a written or computer-based test designed to measure a particular attribute such as intelligence or aptitude.

Assessment center: a technique for selecting individuals with high managerial potential based on their performance on a series of simulate managerial tasks.

On-the-job training (OJT): a type of training in which an experienced employee "adopts" a new employee to teach him or her how to perform job duties.

Corporate university: an in-house training and education facility that offers broad learning opportunities for employees.

Performance appraisal: the process of observing and evaluating an employee's performance, recording the assessment, and providing feedback to the employee.

360-degree feedback: a process that uses multiple raters, including self-rating, to appraise employee performance and guide development.

Stereotyping: placing an employee into a class or category based on one or a few traits or characteristics.

Halo effect: a type of rating error that occurs when an employee receives the same rating on all dimensions regardless of his or her performance on individual ones.

Behaviorally anchored rating scale(BARS): a rating technique that relates an employee's performance to specific job-related incidents.

Compensation: monetary payments (wages, salaries) and nonmonetary goods/commodities (benefits, vacations) used to reward employees.

Job evaluation: the process of determining the value of jobs within an organization through an examination of job content.

Wage and salary surveys: surveys that show what other organizations pay incumbents in jobs that match a sample of "key" jobs selected by the organization.

Pay-for-performance: incentive pay that ties at least part of compensation to employee effort and performance.

Exit interview: an interview conducted with departing employees to determine the reasons for their termination.

Learning Objectives

1. Explain the role of human resource management in organizational strategic planning.

2. Describe federal legislation and societal trends that influence human resource management.

3. Explain what the changing social contract between organizations and employees means for workers and human resource managers.

4. Explain how organizations determine their future staffing needs through human resource planning.

5. Describe the tools managers use to recruit and select employees.

6. Describe how organizations develop an effective work force through training and performance appraisal.

7. Explain how organizations maintain a work force through the administration of wages and salaries, benefits, and terminations.

Chapter Review

Multiple Choice: Please indicate the correct response to the following questions by writing the letter of the correct answer in the space provided.

_____ 1.　Over the last decade human resource management (HRM)
a.　has lost some power due to downsizing.
b.　has gained recognition as a vital player in corporate strategy.
c.　has been given a diminished role in strategic planning.
d.　has been viewed as a non-strategic element.
e.　was virtually nonexistent in corporate America.

_____ 2.　HRM planning, recruiting, and selecting, are involved in
a.　attracting an effective work force.
b.　developing an effective work force.
c.　maintaining an effective work force.
d.　controlling an effective work force.
e.　human resource needs assessment.

_____ 3.　The purpose of the HRM goals is to
a.　run a fun place within which to work.
b.　attract an effective workforce to the organization, develop the workforce to its potential, and maintain the workforce over the long term.
c.　attract competition, develop markets, and design products that will last for a long period.
d.　develop a competitive organization that is profitable.
e.　create jobs, make a good product, and be a good neighbor.

_____ 4.　_____ refers to the economic value of the knowledge, experience, skills, and capabilities of employees.
a.　Intuition
b.　Human capital
c.　The economic man
d.　Employee value
e.　People worth

_____ 5.　A policy requiring employers to take positive steps to guarantee equal employment opportunities for people within protected groups is known as
a.　Employer flexibility.
b.　EEOC.
c.　Discrimination enhancement policy.
d.　Employment-at-will policy.
e.　Affirmative action.

_____ 6.　The point of EEO legislation and Executive Orders is to
a.　provide jobs for countless numbers of bureaucrats.
b.　give minorities an advantage for a change.
c.　stop discriminatory practices that are unfair to specific groups.
d.　provide for a more liberal society.
e.　undermine morality in the United States.

_____ 7.	Discrimination occurs when some applicants are hired or promoted based on
   a.	sexual preference.
   b.	job ability alone.
   c.	criteria which are not job relevant.
   d.	favorable impressions.
   e.	job skill tests.

_____ 8.	_____ requires that an employer take positive steps to guarantee equal employment opportunities for people within protected groups.
   a.	The Gay Rights Act of 1990
   b.	Affirmative action
   c.	The Civil Rights Act of 1964
   d.	The Equal Pay Act
   e.	The Pregnancy Discrimination Act

_____ 9.	The _____ initiates investigations in response to complaints concerning discrimination.
   a.	Justice Department
   b.	Center for Non-discrimination
   c.	Equal Employment Opportunity Commission
   d.	local sheriff
   e.	FBI

_____ 10.	The Equal Pay Act
   a.	prohibits sex differences in pay for substantially equal work.
   b.	guarantees equal pay for all employees of the same company.
   c.	prohibits unequal pay for noncomparable jobs.
   d.	provides for the same pay in the public sector as in the private sector.
   e.	was passed in 1979 as a substitute for the failed ERA movement.

_____ 11.	The legislation which prohibits discrimination of qualified individuals on the basis of disability and demands that reasonable accommodations be made for the disabled in the workplace is the
   a.	Occupational Safety and Health Act.
   b.	Vocational Rehabilitation Act.
   c.	Americans with Disabilities Act.
   d.	Executive Order 11246.
   e.	Civil Rights Act of 1991.

_____ 12.	Which of these is a policy requiring employers to be proactive in being certain that equal opportunity exists for all within their organization?
   a.	Equal employment opportunity
   b.	Discrimination
   c.	Reverse discrimination
   d.	Affirmative action
   e.	Employment-at-will

_____ 13.   Which of these means using computers and telecommunications equipment to do work without going to an office?
   a.   Telecommuting
   b.   Social Loafing
   c.   New social contract
   d.   Outsourcing
   e.   Realistic Job Preview

_____ 14.   The forecasting of human resource needs and the projected matching of individuals with expected job vacancies is referred to as
   a.   human resource development.
   b.   human resource organizing.
   c.   human resource planning.
   d.   human resource selection.
   e.   human resources downsizing.

_____ 15.   Within the context of changes of trends in society, human resource managers must achieve the three primary goals of _____, _____, and _____ an effective workforce for the organization.
   a.   planning; organizing; controlling
   b.   attracting; developing; maintaining
   c.   staffing; organizing; controlling
   d.   maintaining; planning; developing
   e.   organizing; staffing; and planning

_____ 16.   The outside source for job applicants sometimes referred to as headhunters is
   a.   a newspaper ad with reference to headlines of the paper.
   b.   private employment agencies.
   c.   employee referrals.
   d.   state employee services who count heads to maintain federal funds.
   e.   colleges and universities because the company seeks management trainees there.

_____ 17.   One advantage of internal recruiting is
   a.   it is less costly.
   b.   it generates higher employee commitment.
   c.   it provides chances for advancement.
   d.   it engenders employee satisfaction.
   e.   all of the above.

_____ 18.   Which of these is a listing of job duties and desirable qualifications for a particular job?
   a.   A job analysis
   b.   A job listing
   c.   A job requirement
   d.   A job description
   e.   A realistic job previews

_____ 19. While interviews are _____, they are generally_____ predictors of subsequent job performance.
   a. rarely used; not valid
   b. widely used; not valid
   c. rarely used; excellent
   d. widely used; valid
   e. painful; excellent

_____ 20. Which of the following selection devices is now illegal?
   a. application form
   b. interview
   c. paper-and-pencil test
   d. assessment center
   e. None of the above is illegal per se.

_____ 21. A selection procedure that has _____ is one that *seems* to be valid and makes sense.
   a. face validity
   b. no internal bias
   c. surface reliability
   d. apparent reliability
   e. none of the above

_____ 22. Assessment centers were first developed by psychologists at _____ and are used to select individuals with job potential for management careers.
   a. IBM
   b. General Electric
   c. JC Penney
   d. AT&T
   e. Kimberly-Clark

_____ 23. A training method that attempts to introduce newcomers to the organization's culture is called
   a. on-the-job training.
   b. classroom training.
   c. orientation training.
   d. developmental training.
   e. external training.

_____ 24. The process of observing and evaluating an employee's performance, recording the assessment, and providing feedback to the employee is referred to as
   a. orientation training.
   b. classroom training.
   c. a paper-and-pencil test.
   d. performance appraisal.
   e. None of the above.

_____ 25.   The training method is used most frequently.
  a.   on-the-job
  b.   classroom
  c.   computer-assisted
  d.   orientation
  e.   case discussion groups

_____ 26.   The term 360-degree feedback refers to
  a.   giving feedback to all those around you.
  b.   being rated by multiple raters—above you, on your level, and below you.
  c.   providing feedback with circular logic.
  d.   being well-rounded or balanced in your feedback as a manager.
  e.   giving feedback all year long.

_____ 27.   The term compensation refers to
  a.   all goods and services the employee takes from the employer with or without permission.
  b.   cash only rewarded to employees.
  c.   all goods and commodities used in lieu of money to reward employees.
  d.   (1) all money payments; (2) all goods or commodities used in lieu of money to reward employees.
  e.   (1) cash; (2) stolen goods; (3) all other goods and commodities used instead of money to reward employees.

_____ 28.   A job evaluation is used to
  a.   determine the value of a job holder.
  b.   define the job requirements.
  c.   develop the job description.
  d.   determine the value of a job.
  e.   eliminate job discrimination practices.

_____ 29.   According to the text, benefits in general make up _____ of the U.S. labor costs.
  a.   20 percent
  b.   30 percent
  c.   40 percent
  d.   50 percent
  e.   60 percent

_____ 30.   Which of the following can uncover pockets of dissatisfaction that usually remain hidden in an organization?
  a.   job analysis
  b.   job evaluation
  c.   performance appraisal interview
  d.   selection interview
  e.   exit interview

True/False: Please indicate whether the following statements are true or false by writing a T or an F in the blank in front of each question.

_____ 1.   People who work for an organization, but not on a permanent or full-time basis are called contingent workers.

_____ 2.   The Vocational Rehabilitation Act created the Equal Employment Opportunity Commission.

_____ 3.   The Civil Rights Act of 1964 prohibits discrimination in employment on the basis of skills and abilities.

_____ 4.   It is okay to ask a person's age during a job interview.

_____ 5.   There are no advantages to external recruiting.

_____ 6.   A corporate university is an in-house training and education facility.

_____ 7.   When using the BARS method for evaluating a production supervisor, the job can be broken down into several dimensions, such as equipment maintenance, employee training, or work scheduling.

_____ 8.   Stereotyping is a type of rating error that occurs when an employee receives the same rating on all dimensions regardless of performance.

_____ 9.   Skill-based pay systems are also called competency-based pay systems.

_____ 10.   It is not a good idea to interview an exiting employee because they will be so mad that anything they say will be biased.

Short Answer: Please indicate your answer in the space provided.

1. What are the three primary goals of human resource management (HRM)?

2. Explain why a realistic job preview is so important?

3. What are the advantages of on-the-job training (OJT)?

4. How can compensation be used as a strategy?

Manager's Workbook

Test Your Human Resources Knowledge (*also found on page 334 in text*)

This quiz will test your knowledge of human resources issues affecting today's workplace. The quiz was designed by the Council on Education in Management, a Walnut Creek, California firm that conducts human resources and employment law seminars worldwide. Please indicate whether the following statements are true or false by writing a T or an F in the blank in front of each question.

_____ 1. If you receive an unsolicited résumé in the mail, you must keep it for two years.

_____ 2. Time-management principles are pretty much the same in any administrative job.

_____ 3. Regardless of the type of business or the various laws that may apply, there is a core of common practices for keeping personnel records and files that makes sense for almost any organization.

_____ 4. Every employer must have an affirmative action plan.

_____ 5. An employer must investigate an allegation of sexual harassment even if the victim asks to remain anonymous.

_____ 6. An employer is not obligated to pay overtime to a nonexempt employee who works more than 40 hours in a week after being asked not to put in overtime.

_____ 7. If your company is found guilty of discrimination, the Equal Employment Opportunity Commission will be more lenient if your records show that the violation was unintentional.

_____ 8. Americans with Disabilities Act regulations require companies to maintain written job descriptions.

_____ 9. Reference checking is an important procedure despite the fact that many companies won't release this information.

_____ 10. Your employee orientation and handbook should help assure new employees that they will be a part of the team as long as they do a good job.

Bad Attitude Billy

Even though you have only been the supervisor of the loading dock for three weeks, it is time for you to conduct annual performance appraisal review. As you are preparing for these by reading employee records, you come across Billy's file. Below are some of the things you read:

"Billy seems to have an attitude problem."

"Today Billy refused to load another box into a truck, which just reflects his bad attitude."

"Billy complained about the pay rate at the company. He is such a complainer."

"Several employees met with representatives of a union today about the possibility of forming a union. Of course, Billy took his bad attitude and went to the meeting."

Based on the above comments you are to conduct an appraisal review interview with Billy. Answer the following questions about your strategy.

1.   What additional information about Billy would you want before conducting the review?

2.   How well doe these comments agree with the BARS method?

Manager's Workshop

Hiring and Evaluating Using Core Competencies *(Also available on page 334 of text.)*
Form groups of 4-7 members. Develop a list of "core competencies" for the job of student in this course. (Or alternately, you may choose a job in one of the group members' organizations).

A.   List the core competencies below.

       1.   5.

       2.   6

       3.   7.

       4.   8.

B.   Which of the above are the most important four?

       1.   3.

       2.   4.

C.   What questions would you ask a potential employee/student to determine if that person could be successful in this class, based on the four most important core competencies? (interviewing)

       1.

       2.

       3.

       4.

D.   What learning experiences would you develop to enhance those core competencies? (training and development)

       1.

       2.

       3.

       4.

E. How would you evaluate or measure the success of a student in this class, based on the four core competencies? (performance evaluation)

    1.

    2.

    3.

    4.

Can I Ask This?

According to EEOC guidelines, you should not ask a prospective employee any questions that are not job related and which might have adverse impact on a protected group. You have been called in as a consultant to a restaurant that is planning on hiring many new employees. It wants to know if some of the questions it plans to ask on either application blanks or during job interviews are within the EEOC guidelines.

Look at the questions below and indicate if they are "okay" or "taboo" in the space provided. If they are "taboo," indicate the reason why. Discuss the answers in your group and put them in underneath each answer. Be ready to defend them to the entire class.

		Okay	Taboo
1.	Are you married?	____	____
2.	Do you own a car?	____	____
3.	Can you work evenings and weekends?	____	____

		Okay	Taboo
4.	When did you graduate from high school?	_____	_____
5.	Are you a homosexual?	_____	_____
6.	Do you have any communicable diseases?	_____	_____
7.	Do you have any small children at home?	_____	_____
8.	Are you willing to follow our dress code?	_____	_____
9.	What hobbies do you have?	_____	_____
10.	Are you handicapped?	_____	_____

Study Guide Solutions

Chapter Review

Multiple-Choice Questions

1	2	3	4	5	6	7	8	9	10
B	A	B	B	E	C	C	B	C	A

11	12	13	14	15	16	17	18	19	20
C	D	A	C	B	B	E	D	B	E

21	22	23	24	25	26	27	28	29	30
A	D	C	D	A	B	D	D	C	E

True/False Questions

1	2	3	4	5	6	7	8	9	10
T	F	F	F	F	T	T	F	T	F

Short Answer Questions

1. The first goal is to attract an effective workforce to the organization. The second goal is to train and develop the workforce to reach its potential. The third goal is to maintain the effectiveness of the workforce over the long run.

2. A realistic job preview tells the prospective employee both the positive and negative aspects of the job. It allows people to refuse a job that does not fit them and also helps them to adjust more easily to the job once it is accepted.

3. OJT has fewer out-of-pocket costs for items such as training facilities, materials, or instructors. It is also easier to transfer skills learned to the actual job than with classroom training because the training takes place on the job site.

4. If an organization has a strategic goal of improving profitability, it may need to improve employee performance. One way to do this is through a compensation incentive plan.

Manager's Workbook

Test Your Human Resources Knowledge
1. F; 2. F; 3. T; 4. F; 5. T; 6. F; 7. F; 8. F; 9. T; 10. F.

Bad Attitude Billy

1.   Before conducting the performance appraisal it would be important to know Billy's job performance record. It would also be important to know all of the circumstances surrounding the incidents mentioned in the quotations in the case.

2.   The statements presented do not link ratings to behaviors as called for in the BARS method. Concentration on his observable behaviors, which are objective, rather than making assumptions about his attitude, which is objective, is probably wise in this case.

Manager's Workshop

Hiring and Evaluating Using Core Competencies: Answers will vary.

Can I Ask This?

1.   Taboo. This question has adverse impact on women (sexual discrimination) because it is seen as a negative employment factor for women and a positive employment factor for men.

2.   Taboo. This is not job related.

3.   Okay. It is job related in this type of business. It is a legitimate requirement of the job.

4.   Taboo. This question is a sneaky way of determining one's age and could therefore indicate age discrimination. It is also not job related.

5.   Taboo, probably. Taboo because it is not job related only. However, homosexuals are not a protected group.

6.   Okay. This is job related because food handlers often pass communicable diseases. Health regulations apply here.

7.   Taboo. It has adverse impact on women because it is assumed they will miss work when the children are sick. For men it is considered a positive factor because it shows they are mature and settled down.

8.   Okay. This is job related.

9.   Taboo. This is not job related and may reveal things such as religious or ethnic background.

10. Taboo. It would be better to ask if the applicant has any physical handicap that would impair ability to do the job.   However, the employer must be willing to make "reasonable accommodations for the handicapped."

Chapter 10

Managing Diverse Employees

Chapter Outline

Key Terms

Workforce diversity: hiring people with different human qualities who belong to various cultural groups.

Ethnocentrism: the belief that one's own group or subculture is inherently superior to other groups or cultures.

Monoculture: a culture that accepts only one way of doing things and one set of values and beliefs.

Ethnorelativism: the belief that groups and subcultures are inherently equal.

Pluralism: the organization accommodates several subcultures, including employees who would otherwise feel isolated and ignored.

Biculturalism: the sociocultural skills and attitudes used by racial minorities to move back and forth between the dominant culture and their own ethnic or racial culture.

Glass ceiling: invisible barrier that separates women and minorities from top management positions.

Mentor: a higher-ranking, senior organizational member who is committed to providing upward mobility and support to a protégé's professional career.

Diversity awareness training: special training designed to make people aware of their own prejudices and stereotypes.

Expatriates: employees who live and work in a country other than their own.

High-context culture: a culture in which communication is used to enhance personal relationships.

Low-context culture: a culture in which communication is used to exchange facts and information.

Multicultural teams: teams made up of members from diverse national, racial, ethnic, and cultural backgrounds.

Learning Objectives

1. Explain the dimensions of employee diversity and why ethnorelativism is the appropriate attitude for today's corporations.

2. Discuss the changing workplace and the management activities required for a culturally diverse workforce.

3. Understand the challenges minority employees face on a daily basis.

4. Explain affirmative action and why factors such as the glass ceiling have kept it from being more successful.

5. Describe how to change the corporate culture, structure, and policies and how to use diversity awareness training to meet the needs of diverse employees.

6. Explain the importance of addressing sexual harassment in the workplace.

7. Define the importance of multicultural teams and employee networks groups for today's globally divers organizations.

Chapter Review

Multiple Choice: Please indicate the correct response to the following questions by writing the letter of the correct answer in the space provided.

_____ 1. Primary dimensions of diversity include
a. religious beliefs.
b. age.
c. income.
d. work background.
e. education.

_____ 2. A secondary dimension of diversity is one that
a. is inborn.
b. has ongoing impact throughout one's life.
c. has no impact on one's life.
d. can be acquired or changed throughout one's life.
e. all of the above.

_____ 3. _____ refers to the belief that one's own group and subculture are inherently superior.
a. Ethnocentrism
b. Monoculturism
c. Egoism
d. Unitarianism
e. Geocentrism

_____ 4. A monoculture is one in which
a. everyone has only one spouse.
b. there is only one way of doing things and one set of values and beliefs.
c. there is only one political part.
d. people who are different are readily accepted.
e. a worldview of values dominates.

_____ 5. Ethnorelativism is the belief that
a. one's culture is superior to other cultures.
b. groups and cultures are inherently equal.
c. hiring of relatives in a organization is a good idea.
d. all ethnic groups are somehow related to each other.
e. groups are superior to individuals.

_____ 6. The workforce today is different in that
a. the average worker is now younger.
b. fewer women are working, with a return to family values.
c. more people of color are working.
d. fewer immigrants are entering the workforce.
e. white males make up more than 50 percent of the workforce.

_____ 7.   According to the text, minorities will constitute _____ percent of the people entering the workforce during the first decade of the twenty-first century.
   a.   8
   b.   15
   c.   21
   d.   40
   e.   48

_____ 8.   Which of these can be defined as the sociocultural skills and attitudes used by racial minorities as they move back and forth between the dominant culture and their own ethnic or racial culture?
   a.   Ethnocentrism
   b.   Monoculture
   c.   Undecided
   d.   Biculturalism
   e.   Geocentrism

_____ 9.   By the year 2020, it is estimated that _____ the full-time U.S. workforce will be women.
   a.   one-third
   b.   one-half
   c.   two-thirds
   d.   three-fourths
   e.   eighty percent

_____ 10.   In the firm of McKinsey & Company, by 1999 about _____ of consultants were American born
   a.   20 percent
   b.   30 percent
   c.   40 percent
   d.   50 percent
   e.   60 percent

_____ 11.   Affirmative action, according to your textbook, has
   a.   been a great success.
   b.   been a limited success.
   c.   been a complete failure.
   d.   great promise for the future.
   e.   never been supported by the government.

_____ 12.   A glass ceiling refers to
   a.   an invisible barrier to important lateral movement within the organization.
   b.   the ability to see through false beliefs of other cultures.
   c.   seeing the potential of those who are different than we are.
   d.   an invisible barrier to top management positions for women and minorities.
   e.   legal remedies to discrimination.

_____ 13. Which of the following terms implies women's commitment to their children limits their commitment to the company or their ability to handle the rigors of corporate management?
   a. Balancing family priorities
   b. Invisible minorities
   c. Mommy track
   d. Family commitment
   e. Cost of diversity

_____ 14. Which of these is the most common explanation for the glass ceiling effect?
   a. The number of women in top management positions
   b. The relative lack of skills possessed by women and minorities
   c. The dominance of ethnorelativism throughout corporate America
   d. The monoculture at top levels of management in this country
   e. The pluralism at top levels of management

_____ 15. As part of the recommended response to cultural diversity, the text advises that
   a. affirmative action programs be de-emphasized since they do not work.
   b. the current culture be accepted and not be assessed.
   c. a vision for diverse workplace be created.
   d. individuals who are different be trained to fit the corporate culture.
   e. a cultural police force be established.

_____ 16. The text recommends that in the area of recruitment the company should
   a. be aware of employee demographics.
   b. ignore community demographics.
   c. ignore customer demographics.
   d. look exclusively at the dimensions of race and gender.
   e. avoid considering sexual orientation.

_____ 17. One reason fewer women enter into mentoring relationships with higher-level executives is that
   a. the women believe job competency is enough to succeed.
   b. the women fear that others may view the relationship as romantic.
   c. male mentors feel more comfortable with male protégés.
   d. male mentors do not view many women as executive material.
   e. all of the above.

_____ 18. Many companies provide for families in which both parents work which of the following?
   a. child care
   b. maternity or paternity leave
   c. flexible work schedules
   d. part-time employment
   e. all of the above

_____ 19. Diversity awareness training is intended to
    a.   help people become aware of prejudices and stereotypes.
    b.   help minorities integrate into organizations.
    c.   develop monocultural organizations.
    d.   facilitate ethnocentrism.
    e.   help organizations compete better with diverse firms.

_____ 20. Nonromantic love relationships between men and women
    a.   are impossible to achieve.
    b.   still have negative impact on the organization.
    c.   involve sex, but no divorce.
    d.   are possible only for gays and lesbians.
    e.   are now viewed as possible and positive.

_____ 21. A romance that arises between a supervisor and a subordinate
    a.   is desirable because each will work harder to impress the other person.
    b.   is often encouraged by companies.
    c.   always means that sexual harassment is occurring.
    d.   require the most attention from companies.
    e.   is called a "glass ceiling."

_____ 22. The case of the Jenny Craig Eight indicates that
    a.   Sexual harassment can be suffered by men as well as women.
    b.   Women feel pressure to lose weight if they are working.
    c.   Women in female dominate cultures can still be sexually harassed.
    d.   Lesbians can also be sexual harassers.
    e.   none of the above.

_____ 23. If a manager does something that is not sexually threatening, but still causes discomfort in another person to the extent that the subordinate has his or her freedom and ability to function in the workplace limited, this is which form of sexual harassment?
    a.   generalized
    b.   inappropriate/offensive
    c.   solicitation with promise of reward
    d.   coercion with threat of punishment
    e.   sexual crime or misdemeanor

_____ 24. The two significant aspects of global diversity programs involve
    a.   employee selection and training and the understanding of communication context.
    b.   employee pay and motivation.
    c.   employee selection and recruitment and the understanding of communication context.
    d.   employee benefits and motivation and the understanding of communication context.
    e.   employee promotion and payment.

_____ 25. Expatriates are
    a.   persons who give up their citizenship to become citizens of another country.
    b.   persons who relinquish their citizenship and wish to become citizens of no country.
    c.   employees who live and work in a country other than their own.
    d.   employees who used to be patriotic, but now consider themselves global citizens.
    e.   none of the above.

_____ 26. When selecting persons to work abroad one should consider
    a.   support of the spouse.
    b.   ability to initiate social contacts in a foreign culture.
    c.   ability to adjust to different living environments.
    d.   ability to maintain networks to the job market back home.
    e.   all of the above.

_____ 27. A(n) _____ culture is sensitive to circumstances surrounding social exchanges.
    a.   low-context
    b.   moderate-context
    c.   high-context
    d.   ethnocentric
    e.   ethnorelative

_____ 28. A multicultural team is one in which
    a.   more than one language is spoken.
    b.   you have members from diverse national, racial, ethnic, and cultural backgrounds.
    c.   travels from one country to another.
    d.   advertising campaigns are developed in Spanish.
    e.   all of the above.

_____ 29. Employee network groups are based on things such as
    a.   computer awareness.
    b.   gender or race.
    c.   geographic proximity.
    d.   all of the above
    e.   none of the above

_____ 30. An important characteristic of network groups is that they are formed by
    a.   management.
    b.   outside consultants.
    c.   activist groups.
    d.   employees voluntarily.
    e.   the human resources department.

True/False: Please indicate whether the following statements are true or false by writing a T or an F in the blank in front of each question.

_____   1.   Many managers are ill-prepared to handle diversity issues.

_____   2.   Biculturalism means that a person accepts only two cultures as legitimate.

_____   3.   The Civil Rights Act of 1991 weakened the Civil Rights Act of 1964.

_____   4.   For sexual harassment to be proven, evidence of the harasser's intentions must be provided.

_____   5.   In a low-context culture, people use communication primarily to exchange facts and information.

_____   6.   The challenge of companies today is to recognize the cultural differences and to value the use of unique strengths each person brings to the workplace.

_____   7.   Most organizations do not need to undertake any conscious effort to shift from a monoculture to one of pluralism.

_____   8.   High-context cultures include Asian and Arab countries.

_____   9.   A good way to revitalize the recruiting process is for the company to examine employee demographics, the composition of the labor pool in the area, and the composition of the customer base.

_____   10.   According to the U.S. Supreme Court, sexual harassment does not include harassment by the same sex.

Short Answer: Please indicate your answer in the space provided.

1.   Explain what is meant by primary dimensions of diversity and give examples.

2.   What is meant by the *glass ceiling*? What can companies do about it?

3. What is meant by biculturalism?

4. What are the types of sexual harassment? Give an example of each.

Manager's Workbook

How Tolerant Are You?

For each of the following questions circle the answer that best describes you.

1. Most of your friends
    a. are very similar to you.
    b. are very different from you and from each other.
    c. are like you in some respects but different in others.

2. When someone does something you disapprove of, you
    a. break off the relationship.
    b. tell how you feel but keep in touch.
    c. tell yourself it matters little and behave as you always have.

3. Which virtue is most important to you?
    a. kindness
    b. objectivity
    c. obedience

4. When it comes to beliefs, you
    a. do all you can to make others see things the same way you do.
    b. actively advance your point of view but stop short of argument.
    c. keep your feelings to yourself.

5. Would you hire a person who has had emotional problems?
   a. no
   b. yes, provided there is evidence of complete recovery
   c. yes, if the person is suitable for the job

6. Do you voluntarily read material that supports views different from your own?
   a. never
   b. sometimes
   c. often

7. You react to old people with
   a. patience.
   b. annoyance.
   c. sometimes a, sometimes b.

8. Do you agree with the statement, "What is right and wrong depends upon the time, place, and circumstance?"
   a. strongly agree
   b. agree to a point
   c. strongly disagree

9. Would you marry someone from a different race?
   a. yes
   b. no
   c. probably not

10. If someone in your family were homosexual, you would
    a. view this as a problem and try to change the person to a heterosexual orientation.
    b. accept the person as a homosexual with no change in feelings or treatment.
    c. avoid or reject the person.

11. You react to little children with
    a. patience.
    b. annoyance.
    c. sometimes a, sometimes b.

12. Other people's personal habits annoy you
    a. often.
    b. not at all.
    c. only if extreme.

13. If you stay in a household run differently from yours (cleanliness, manners, meals, and other customs), you
    a. adapt readily.
    b. quickly become uncomfortable and irritated.
    c. adjust for a while, but not for long.

14. Which statement do you agree with most?
    a. We should avoid judging others because no one can fully understand the motives of another person.
    b. People are responsible for their actions and have to accept the consequences.
    c. Both motives and actions are important when considering questions of right and wrong.

Circle your score for each of the answers below and total the scores:

1.	a = 4;	b = 0;	c = 2
2.	a = 4;	b = 2;	c = 0
3.	a = 0;	b = 2;	c = 4
4.	a = 4;	b = 2;	c = 0
5.	a = 4;	b = 2;	c = 0
6.	a = 4;	b = 2;	c = 0
7.	a = 0;	b = 4;	c = 2
8.	a = 0;	b = 2;	c = 4
9.	a = 0;	b = 4;	c = 2
10.	a = 2;	b = 0;	c = 4
11.	a = 0;	b = 4;	c = 2
12.	a = 4;	b = 0;	c = 2
13.	a = 0;	b = 4;	c = 2
14.	a = 0;	b = 4;	c = 2

Total Score: _____

0–14: If you score 14 or below, you are a very tolerant person and dealing with diversity comes easily to you.

15–28: You are basically a tolerant person and others think of you as tolerant. In general, diversity presents few problems for you, but you may be broad-minded in some areas and have less tolerant ideas in other areas of life, such as attitudes toward older people or male-female social roles.

29–42: You are less tolerant than most people and should work on developing greater tolerance of people different from you. Your low tolerance level could affect your business or personal relationships.

43–56: You have a very low tolerance for diversity. The only people you are likely to respect are those with beliefs similar to your own. You reflect a level of intolerance that could cause difficulties in today's multicultural business environment.

SOURCE: Adapted from the Tolerance Scale by Maria Heiselman, Naomi Miller, and Bob Schlorman, Northern Kentucky University, 1982, in George Manning, Kent Curtis, and Steve McMillen, Building Community: The Human Side of Work, (Cincinnati, Ohio: Thomson Executive Press, 1996), 272–277.

Diversity and Work Quiz *(Also available on page 367 of text.)*

How well do you know the status of women in the workplace? Test yourself below:

	True	False
1. Women account for 46 percent of the total US workforce.	T	F
2. By 2006, women will account for 50 percent of the total growth in the labor force.	T	F
3. Of divorced women, 75 percent are in the labor force, while 52 percent of married women work.	T	F
4. The largest occupational group for women is secretaries, while the second largest is cashiers.	T	F
5. About four million women hold more than one job.	T	F
6. Women's 1999 median earnings working full-time, year-round: $28,324.	T	F
7. In families with a working wife, the median income is $68,000, while a family without a wife in the paid labor force is $40,000.		
8. Over the age of 65, 14 percent of women live below the poverty line, while only 7 percent of men do.	T	F
9. The number of working women has doubled since 1970—from 30 million to 60 million.	T	F
10. Women earn 80 cents on the dollar compared to men.	T	F
11. The highest weekly earnings for women come from which group: Lawyers, engineers or physicians?	T	F

12. The highest weekly earnings for women come from which group? Lawyers, engineers, or physicians? _____

13. By the year 2050, what percentage of the total U.S. population will be Asians, Hispanics, blacks, or other non-whites? _____

14. Of the 43 million people in the U.S. with disabilities, how many are of working age (16-64)? ____ How many are employed? _____ How many unemployed want to work? _____

15. What percentage of the total U.S. population speaks a language other than English at home? ___ What percentage of those speaks Spanish? ___

16. Of the 8.7 million immigrants who arrived in the U.S. between 1980-1990, what percentage has college degrees? _____ What percentage of male versus female? _____ women age 25 and older? _____ men age 25 and older? _____

17. According to a recent *Newsweek* poll, what percentage of U.S. people believes gays and lesbians should be given equal rights and opportunities in the workplace? _____

18. What are the two most racially and ethnically diverse states in the U.S.? _____ The two least? _____ By 2020, what percentage of the U.s. population will be 65 or older? _____ Between 1998-2008, what is the percentage increase of workers 55 and older? _____

Manager's Workshop

Globian Exercise *(also found on page 367 in text)*

Background

In another galaxy, far, far away, there is a planet called "Globe." The inhabitants on this planet are physically very similar to the people on Earth and differ from one another, just as Earthlings do. There is one major difference, however, between Globians and Earthlings: on Globe there is no conflict.

Word has spread to Globe that Earth is a planet on which there is conflict that pervades relationships between individuals groups, nations, and many other aspects of life. So the Globian Governing Council has decided to send a team of anthropologists/sociologists to Earth to learn about conflict. Their instructions are to determine whether it would be advantageous to bring conflict, whatever it is, back to their home planet.

The Globians work in pairs as they meet with small groups of Earthlings to carry out their study

1. Selection of Globians and Earthlings
The class is divided into small groups of 6-8, from which two persons will be identified as Globians and one to two as observers, and with the rest as Earthlings.
2. Each group of Earthlings and pair of Globians meets separately to discuss their assignment and get into role. Role assignments are below. Read only the roles for your group.
3. Meetings between Groups of Earthlings (3-4 people) and Globian Pairs (2 people)
Purpose: to explore the nature and purpose of conflict.
Come up with (1) a definition of conflict and (2) what the purpose of conflict is. Make sure both sides agree with these. Write them down on a sheet of paper.
4. Debriefing in Groups
Each Earthling group and Globian pair meets separately to discuss what happened during the preceding meeting.
5. Fishbowl with Globians in the Center
Meeting in the center of the fishbowl, Globians report on what happened in their meetings with Earthlings, discuss what they learned about conflict, and explore the pros and cons of taking conflict back home to Globe.
6. Total class discussion on cultural differences, cross-cultural communication, and assumption sets.

ROLES

Instructions for Globians

You have been sent to Earth by the governing council of the planet Globe to study the Earthly phenomenon known as "conflict." You do not understand what is meant by the term and are completely ignorant about conflict in any form. The behavior known on Earth as conflict does not exist on Globe. The term "conflict" is not in the vocabulary or language of Globe. Other terms associated with conflict on Earth are also unfamiliar to you. Peace and harmony is the norm on your planet; difference and diversity are accepted and treated with appreciation. The concept of conflict is like a totally unfamiliar foreign language to you.

You are to function with a sincere attitude of inquiry. You have a serious job to perform and much depends on your ability to carry out this assignment. You enter into contact with Earthlings with a genuine curiosity about this unfamiliar phenomenon. You are prepared to ask questions, seek explanations, gather information, make observations, and in everyway possible to determine what "conflict" is and to be prepared to take this information back to your planet.

It is entirely possible that, despite the Earthlings' best efforts to help you, it will turn out that "conflict" makes no sense to you. No matter; you remain within your accustomed state of peace and harmony even though you cannot make sense of what the Earthlings say or do in their efforts to explain.

Instructions for Earthlings

As representatives of Earth, you have agreed to help the Globians. You are experts on conflict, having experienced, observed, and lived with it all your lives. Your visitors want to know what conflict is and what purposes it serves, if any. Your job is to do whatever you can to educate the Globians about conflict. Because you take conflict for granted and probably experience it almost on a daily basis, it may be difficult for you to understand how any society of intelligent, thinking beings can exist without experiencing conflict or understanding what is meant by the term. Using your skills in conflict, which you have been developing throughout your lives, you want to provide the Globians with the unique opportunity to learn and understand as much about this Earthly phenomenon as possible.

You may use whatever methods you deem appropriate to convey this concept to your guests. It is important, however, to keep in mind that it is not part of your job to persuade the Globians that conflict already exists on their planet. Their question is whether or not conflict is worth importing into their home planet. Do your best to help them understand what conflict is and what purposes it serves on Earth.

Instructions for Observers

The task of the observer is to watch the behavior of group members and note how the group works together. Guidelines on what to look for include, but aren't limited to, the following:

1. Who speaks most and least? In what order do people talk?
2. Does everyone contribute? What happens to the contributions of different members?
3. What occurs when the Globians arrive? To what extent does the group stick to its original plan for interacting with the visitors? Does the plan change? If so, how does the change occur?
4. What is the level of tension in the group: before the Globians arrive? after they join the group?
5. What kinds of emotions are expressed by group members and exhibited in their posture, facial expressions, and actions?

SOURCE: By Carole Parker and Donald Klein. The original version of the Globe Exercise was created by Donald Klein in June 1984 for use in the Beyond Conflict Training Laboratory in Bethel, Maine, conducted by NTL Institute for Applied Behavioral Science.

Stereotypes

1. Individually complete the questions below in column A:

	A	B
Questions	Your own answers	Group responses
a. List some common stereotypes you are familiar with (*you do not have to agree with the stereotypes*) regarding ethnic, racial, social class, sexual preference, religious, gender or other differences.		
b. Describe one or two situations where you were the target of a stereotype. What happened and how did you feel?		
c. List some of your own prejudices. Where do you think they came from? Do other family members share these prejudices?		
d. What effects do prejudices have in the workplace?		

2. Divide into groups of 4-6 members and discuss each question, coming up with some "group responses" for column B.

3. The instructor will lead a discussion on the origins of prejudice and its effects. How can you change yourself and others to remove prejudices?

SOURCE: Adapted from: Anne McKee and Susan Schorr, "Confronting prejudice and stereotypes: A teaching model," *Journal of Management Education*, Vol 18, no. 4, (November 1994), pp. 447-467.

South-Western

Study Guide Solutions

Chapter Review

Multiple-Choice Questions

1	2	3	4	5	6	7	8	9	10
B	D	A	B	B	C	D	D	B	C

11	12	13	14	15	16	17	18	19	20
B	D	C	D	C	A	E	E	A	E

21	22	23	24	25	26	27	28	29	30
D	A	B	A	C	E	C	B	B	D

True/False Questions

1	2	3	4	5	6	7	8	9	10
T	F	F	F	T	T	F	T	T	F

Short Answer Questions

1. Primary dimensions of diversity are the inborn differences that have ongoing impact throughout one's life. These include age, ethnicity, gender, physical abilities, race, and sexual orientation.

2. Glass ceilings refer to invisible barriers to top management positions that confront women and minorities. Companies must define a vision for a diverse workplace, assess the current culture, develop a willingness to change, alter policies and systems to support diversity, and provide diversity awareness training.

3. Biculturalism refers to the sociocultural skills and attitudes used by racial minorities to move back and forth between the dominant culture at work and their own ethnic or racial culture at home.

4. The first type of sexual harassment is generalized. It means making comments that reflect on the gender as a group, such as saying, "Women use their sexuality when they want to get their way." The second type is behavior inappropriate or offensive to the victims. An example would be displaying nude

pictures in the office. Solicitation with promise of reward is illustrated by a boss who says, "If you will sleep with me, I'll give you that raise." Coercion with threat of punishment might be a boss saying, "If you don't sleep with me, I'll see you don't get promoted, or that you get fired." A sexual crime or misdemeanor would be any illegal activity such as sexual assault.

Manager's Workbook

How Tolerant Are You?: Scoring and interpretation provided with exercise.

Diversity and Work Quiz: Answers on page AD-1 in Appendix D of text.

Manager's Workshop

Globian Exercise: Answers will vary, but should lead to interesting discussion.

Stereotypes: Answers to this application will vary.

Chapter 11

Foundations of Behavior in Organizations

Chapter Outline

I. Organizational Behavior

    A. Attitudes

    B. Components of Attitudes

    C. Work-Related Attitudes

    D. Conflicts Among Attitudes

II. Perception

    A. Perceptual Selectivity

    B. Perceptual Distortions

    C. Attributions

III. Personality and Behavior

    A. Personality Traits

    B. Emotional Intelligence

    C. Attitudes and Behaviors Influenced by Personality

    D. Person-Job Fit

IV. Learning

    A. The Learning Process

    B. Learning Styles

    C. Continuous Learning

V. Stress and Stress Management

    A. Type A and Type B Behavior

    B. Causes of Work Stress

    C. Stress Management

Key Terms

Organizational behavior: an interdisciplinary field dedicated to the study of how individuals and groups tend to act in organizations.

Organizational citizenship: work behavior that goes beyond job requirements and contributes as needed to the organization's success.

Attitude: a cognitive and affective evaluation that predisposes a person to act in a certain way.

Job satisfaction: a positive attitude toward one's job.

Organizational commitment: loyalty to and heavy involvement in one's organization.

Cognitive dissonance: a condition in which two attitudes or a behavior and an attitude conflict.

Perception: the cognitive process people use to make sense out of the environment by selecting, organizing, and interpreting information.

Perceptual selectivity: the process by which individuals screen and select the various stimuli that vie for their attention.

Perceptual distortions: errors in perceptual judgment that arise from inaccuracies in any part of the perception process.

Stereotyping: the tendency to assign an individual to a group or broad category and then attribute generalizations about the group to the individual.

Halo effect: an overall impression of a person or situation based on one attribute, either favorable or unfavorable.

Projection: the tendency to see one's own personal traits in other people.

Perceptual defense: the tendency of perceivers to protect themselves by disregarding ideas, objects, or people that are threatening to them.

Attributions: judgments about what caused a person's behavior—either characteristics of the person or of the situation.

Fundamental attribution error: the tendency to underestimate the influence of external factors on another's behavior and to overestimate the influence of internal factors.

Self-serving bias: the tendency to overestimate the contribution of internal factors to one's successes and the contribution of external factor's to one's failure.

Personality: the set of characteristics that underlie a relatively stable pattern of behavior in response to ideas, objects, or people in the environment.

Big Five personality factors: dimensions that describe an individual's extroversion, agreeableness, conscientiousness, emotional stability, and openness to experience.

Locus of control: the tendency to place the primary responsibility for one's success or failure either within oneself (internally) or on outside forces (externally).

Authoritarianism: the belief that power and status differences should exist within the organization.

Machiavellianism: the tendency to direct much of one's behavior toward the acquisition of power and the manipulation of others for personal gain.

Person-job fit: the extent to which a person's ability and personality match the requirements of a job.

Learning: a change in behavior or performance that occurs as a result of experience.

Stress: a physiological and emotional response to stimuli that place physical or psychological demands on an individual.

General adaptation syndrome (GAS): the physiological response to a stressor, beginning with an alarm response, continuing to resistance, and sometimes ending in exhaustion if the stressor continues beyond the person's ability to cope.

Type A behavior: behavior pattern characterized by extreme competitiveness, impatience, aggressiveness, and devotion to work.

Type B behavior: behavior pattern that lacks Type A characteristics and includes a more balanced, relaxed lifestyle.

Role ambiguity: uncertainty about what behaviors are expected of a person in a particular role.

Role conflict: incompatible demands of different roles.

Learning Objectives

1. Define attitudes, including their major components, and explain their relationship to behavior.

2. Discuss the importance of work-related attitudes.

3. Identify major personality traits and describe how personality can influence workplace attitudes and behaviors.

4. Define the five components of emotional intelligence and explain why they are important for managers in today's organizations.

5. Explain how people learn in general and in terms of individual learning styles.

6. To discuss the effects of stress and how individuals differ in their responses to stress.

7. Discuss the effects of stress and identify ways organizations and individuals can manage stress to improve employee health, satisfaction, and productivity.

Chapter Review

Multiple Choice: Please indicate the correct response to the following questions by writing the letter of the correct answer in the space provided.

_____ 1. An evaluation that predisposes a person to act in a certain way is called a(n)
   a. attitude.
   b. authoritarianism.
   c. perception.
   d. projection.
   e. personality.

_____ 2. Organizational behavior is dedicated to the study of everything *except*
   a. attitudes.
   b. behavior.
   c. performance in the organization.
   d. production efficiencies.
   e. both a and b.

_____ 3. When an employee does work that goes beyond job requirements we call it
   a. stupid.
   b. "brown nosing."
   c. organizational citizenship.
   d. organizational behavior.
   e. cognitive dissonance.

_____ 4. When an employee says, "I love this job," he is exhibiting the _____ component of an attitude.
   a. cognitive
   b. affective
   c. behavioral
   d. rational
   e. opinion

_____ 5. The beliefs, opinions, and information a person has about the object of an attitude is called
   a. the affective component.
   b. the feeling component.
   c. the cognitive component.
   d. the behavioral component.
   e. the dissonance aspect of attitude.

_____ 6. An employee is likely to experience high job satisfaction when
   a. personal needs are met more than organizational needs.
   b. he or she likes his or her coworkers.
   c. working conditions are challenging.
   d. pay is not equitable, thus providing motivation.
   e. the work is not interesting, thereby allowing time to daydream.

_____ 7. Which statement indicates loyalty and heavy commitment to the organization?
   a. "We are the best restaurant in town."
   b. "This is a nice place to work."
   c. "I try hard to do my job."
   d. "Management tries to keep us happy."
   e. "I'd rather be fishing."

_____ 8. When your boss asks you to work on the weekend and you have a family camping trip planned and you cancel the trip to work, you will probably experience
   a.   cognitive dissonance.
   b.   a personality disorder.
   c.   a mental breakdown.
   d.   emotional dysentery.
   e.   a divorce.

_____ 9. Which of the five is NOT one of the big five personality traits?
   a.   extroversion
   b.   agreeableness
   c.   conscientiousness
   d.   sociability
   e.   emotional stability

_____ 10. Which of these refers to the degree to which a person is focused on a few goals, thus behaving in ways that are responsible, dependable, persistent, and achievement oriented?
   a.   Agreeableness
   b.   Conscientiousness
   c.   Emotional stability
   d.   Openness to experience
   e.   Extroversion

_____ 11. Internal locus of control refers to
   a.   having a strong ego.
   b.   having a strong and dominant personality.
   c.   being able to overcome cognitive dissonance.
   d.   the tendency to place the responsibility for one's success or failure on outside forces.
   e.   the tendency to place the responsibility for one's success or failure on oneself.

_____ 12. "The job of the boss is to be tough," is a belief of someone subscribing to
   a.   authoritarianism.
   b.   cognitive dissonance.
   c.   egalitarianism.
   d.   achievement-orientation.
   e.   participative management.

_____ 13. "If you have to choose between being loved and being feared, it is better to be feared," is a statement that agrees with
   a.   socialism.
   b.   communism.
   c.   republicanism.
   d.   machiavellianism.
   e.   all of the above.

_____ 14. According to Carl Jung's typology, a person who is decisive and an applied thinker has the _____ personal style.
   a.   sensation-thinking
   b.   intuitive-thinking
   c.   sensation-feeling
   d.   intuitive-feeling
   e.   sensation-intuitive

_____ 15. A thinking-type person evaluates information by
   a.   using personal values.
   b.   relying on emotional aspects of the situation.
   c.   considering the probability of approval from others.
   d.   using reason and logic.
   e.   considering harmony of the group.

_____ 16. If you put a highly social person into a job having little contact with others you are ignoring
   a.   cognitive dissonance.
   b.   the big five personality theory.
   c.   Jung's typology.
   d.   economies of scale.
   e.   person-job fit.

_____ 17. While watching television with a friend you ask the friend what the first commercial was about during the last break in your show. The fact that your friend cannot tell you what the commercial was about illustrates
   a.   his stupidity.
   b.   perceptual contrast.
   c.   perceptual selectivity.
   d.   perceptual familiarity.
   e.   perceptual learning.

_____ 18. When a stimulus is new or different from stimuli previously perceived, it has
   a.   contrast.
   b.   familiarity.
   c.   Intensity.
   d.   novelty.
   e.   motion.

_____ 19. Once people have selected the sensory data to be perceived, they begin grouping the data into
   a.   perceptual sets.
   b.   proximity clusters.
   c.   recognizable patterns.
   d.   learning paradigms.
   e.   knowledge patterns.

_____ 20. Which of these characteristics support the old truism that first impressions are important?
a. Contrast
b. Values and beliefs
c. Primacy
d. Personality
e. Recency

_____ 21. The tendency to assign an individual to a group or broad category and then to attribute widely held generalizations about the group to the individual is called
a. stereotyping.
b. projection.
c. figure-ground.
d. the halo effect.
e. perceptual defense.

_____ 22. If you are in a line at a movie theater and see someone break in line in front of you and then say, "He must be trying to catch a movie that is about to start," because that is the only reason you would break into line, you are using
a. stereotyping.
b. the halo effect.
c. projection.
d. a perceptual defense.
e. learning.

_____ 23. When other people tend to respond to similar situations in the same way attribution theory calls this
a. distinctiveness.
b. consensus.
c. consistency.
d. the fundamental attribution error.
e. maverick behavior.

_____ 24. In the experiential learning cycle, after concrete experience what comes next?
a. abstract conceptualization
b. reflexive experimentation
c. concrete conceptualization
d. reflective observation
e. active experimentation

_____ 25. The _____ is good at generating ideas, seeing a situation from multiple perspectives, and being aware of meaning and value.
a. diverger
b. assimilator
c. converger
d. accommodator
e. maverick

_____ 26. Abstract conceptualization and reflective observation are dominant learning abilities in which learning?
   a.   Converger
   b.   Assimilator
   c.   Accommodator
   d.   Diverger
   e.   Compromiser

_____ 27. In biological terms, the stress response follows a pattern known as the
   a.   stress model.
   b.   physiological stress pattern.
   c.   general adaptation syndrome.
   d.   physical stress syndrome.
   e.   biological stress syndrome.

_____ 28. The behavior pattern characterized by extreme competitiveness, impatience, aggressiveness, and devotion to work is known as
   a.   Workaholism.
   b.   Type A behavior.
   c.   Type B behavior.
   d.   Machiavellianism.
   e.   maverick behavior.

_____ 29. Uncertainty about what behaviors are expected of a person in a particular role is referred to as
   a.   role conflict.
   b.   task overload.
   c.   nonprogrammed decisions.
   d.   role ambiguity.
   e.   task underload.

_____ 30. _____ is/are stressors associated with the setting in which an individual works.
   a.   Role ambiguity
   b.   Interpersonal demands
   c.   Role demands
   d.   Physical demands
   e.   Task demands

True/False: Please indicate whether the following statements are true or false by writing a T or an F in the blank in front of each question.

_____ 1. Attitudes have three components: cognitive, affective, and behavioral.

_____ 2. The tendency of perceivers to protect themselves by disregarding ideas, objects, or people that are threatening to them is called perceptual defense.

_____ 3. According to research, people with an internal locus of control are easier to motivate, are better able to handle complex information and solve problems, and are oriented towards achievement.

_____ 4. People tend to ignore stimuli that coincide with their values and beliefs.

_____ 5. Stereotyping is the tendency to see one's own personal traits in other people and to allow these traits to affect one's judgment of others.

_____ 6. When the level of stress is low relative to a person's coping resources, stress can be a positive force, stimulating desirable change and achievement.

_____ 7. Research shows that the link between satisfaction and performance is very strong.

_____ 8. Extroversion is the degree to which a person is sociable, talkative, assertive, and comfortable with interpersonal relationships.

_____ 9. A person who feels like a pawn of fate has a high internal locus of control.

_____ 10. People's responses to stressors vary according to their personality, resources available to cope, and the context of the stress.

Short Answer: Please indicate your answer in the space provided.

1. Describe the characteristics associated with each of the Big Five personality factors.

2. List Carl Jung's four functions related to gathering and evaluating information for problem solving and decision making.

3. Define perceptual selectivity. Identify the characteristics of the stimuli and the perceiver that affect this process.

4. List four common perceptual errors that managers make.

Manager's Workbook

High Five: How Many of the "Big Five" Personality Traits Are Yours?

Each individual's collection of personality traits is different; it's what makes us unique. But, although each collection of traits varies, we all share many common traits. To find out which are your most prominent traits, mark "yes" or "no" after each of the following statements. Then, for fun, compare your responses with classmates.

	Yes	No
1. I love meeting and talking with new people at parties.		
2. I try not to hold grudges against others.		
3. I am focused on graduating from college and finding a good job in my field.		
4. I enjoy performing under pressure—for example, in a big athletic event.		
5. When I finish school, I want to travel around the world.		
6. Final exams don't really bother me because I prepare well for them.		
7. I like to take part in group projects.		
8. I don't mind giving oral presentations in class.		

9. Just for fun, I would sign up to take a course in a discipline completely outside my field.

10. I work summers in order to fund as much of my own education as I can.

Statements 1 and 8 deal with extroversion; statements 2 and 7 deal with agreeableness; statements 3, 6, and 10 deal with conscientiousness; statements 4 and 6 deal with emotional stability; statements 5 and 9 deal with openness to new experiences.

Personality Inventory *(Also available on page 406 of text.)*

Your personality is what you are. You have similarities and differences from other people. The differences measured here are not better or worse, merely different. Complete and score the inventory below to find out your personality type.

For each item, circle either "a" or "b." If you feel both "a" and "b" are true, decide which one is more like you, even if it is only slightly more true.

1. When making a decision, the most important considerations are
    a. Rational thoughts, ideas, and data.
    b. People's feelings.

2. When discussing a problem with colleagues, it is easy for me
    a. To see "the big picture."
    b. To grasp the specifics of the situation.

3. When I am working on an assignment, I tend to
    a. Work steadily and consistently.
    b. Work in bursts of energy with "down time" in between.

4. When I listen to someone talk on a subject, I usually try to
    a. Relate it to my own experience and see if it fits.
    b. Assess and analyze the message.

5. In work, I prefer spending a great deal of time on issues of
    a. Ideas.
    b. People.

6. In meetings I am most often annoyed with people who
    a. Come up with many sketchy ideas.
    b. Lengthen meetings with many practical details.

7. I would rather work for an organization where
    a. My job was intellectually stimulating.
    b. I was committed to its goals and mission.

8. I would rather work for a boss who is
   a. Full of new ideas.
   b. Practical.

In the following, choose the word in each pair that appeals to you more.

9. a. Social
   b. Theoretical

10. a. Ingenuity
    b. Practicality

Scoring Key

Count one point for each item listed below that you circled in the inventory.

Score for S	Score for N
2b	2a
3a	3b
6a	6b
8b	8a
10b	10a
Total:	

Circle the one with more points: S or N

Score for T	Score for F
1a	1b
4b	4a
5a	5b
7a	7b
9b	9a
Total:	

Circle the one with more points: T or F

Your Score is:

S or N_____   T or F_____

S = Sensation
N = Intuitive
T = Thinking
F = Feeling
(see Exhibit 11.5 in text)

Manager's Workshop

Apply What You Know about Perceptual Biases and Rater Errors *(Also available on page 407 of text.)*

Scully and Mulder have to speak with a number of informants about a UFO sighting that occurred in Flatbush, Kansas. The informants are all poor, middle-aged farmers who have little education and strong rural accents. It appears that they don't bathe very often, and they also happen to have poor dental hygiene (many in fact are missing their teeth). Listed below are a number of perceptual biases and rater errors and examples of how Scully and Mulder may be susceptible to each of them when interacting with these people or evaluating the quality of their stories. Match each of the biases with the example that best reflects that error.

- Implicit personality theory
- Contrast effects
- Central tendency (seeing all things at same level)

- Primacy effect
- Projection
- Leniency (too easy on some things)
- Halo effect

- Recency effect
- Stereotyping
- Harshness (intensity)
- Similar-to-me effect (familiarity)

1. At the beginning of her first interview, Scully discovers that the informant can't read and has very slow, drawn out speech, which leads her to conclude that the person is probably mentally disabled. She conducts the rest of her interview based on that assumption.

2. Scully is a Christian, and her religion is very important to her. As a result, she is very skeptical about the whole UFO phenomenon and thinks that others are as well. Her interview questions are often phrased to reflect her skepticism: Do you think the light you saw might have been an airplane? You don't really believe that what you saw were visitors from another planet, do you?

3. Because Scully thinks that there is no such thing as UFOs, she has a tendency to invalidate the stories of all the farmers by finding flaws and inconsistencies in them.

4. Mulder has interviewed three people, all of whom fit the general description of the residents of this area. The fourth person who arrives is clean, well dressed, and very articulate. The difference is amazing and leads Mulder to put more weight on what this individual has to tell him.

5. On their way into town, Scully and Mulder nearly get into an accident with one of the local farmers. An argument ensues, and Mulder is tempted to arrest the man for obstruction of justice. When they

meet later during one of the interview sessions, Mulder can't shake his negative impression of the guy and finds himself being very harsh.

6. At the conclusion of an interview that was going very well, an informant suddenly bursts into a medley of Broadway show tunes. Mulder is stunned by how nutty this person appears to be and forgets all the apparently rational things the individual has told him.

7. Because Mulder believes that UFOs are very real, he has a tendency to accept all of the farmers' stories as being highly accurate and valid.

8. The sheriff helped Mulder and Scully conduct the interviews. When it came time to evaluate them, however, he had a hard time distinguishing the good stories from the bad, so he classified them all as somewhat believable but flawed.

9. Scully thinks personal hygiene is extremely important; therefore, she concludes that if these people aren't very good at taking care of themselves, they are probably not very reliable as witnesses due to a lack of attention to detail.

10. One person whom Scully interviews is also a devout Christian, and she articulates many of the same concerns and skepticism that Scully has. Because of their obvious similarities, Scully is predisposed to like this woman and to believe her version of events.

11. Mulder thinks of farmers as having a strong work ethic and being very honest and forthright. Therefore, he is predisposed to believe everything that the informants tell him, even though the sheriff has told him that one of the farmers is a known liar and a convicted criminal.

12. Mulder thinks that people who are hard working and make a lot of sacrifices are also generally honest. He therefore tends to believe the stories of the farmers who seem to be very hard working and self-sacrificing.

Source: Courtney Hunt, Northern Illinois University.

World Trade Center Perceptions

We all engaged in perceptual distortions although we may not be aware of it. Reflect on the terrorist attacks of the World Trade Center. Comment on the perceptual distortions of both the Americans and the Moslem world to this event as applied to the following types of distortions. Discuss this in groups of 2 – 4 persons.

Type of Distortion	Americans	Moslem World
Stereotyping		
The Halo Effect		
Projection		
Perceptual Defense		

Study Guide Solutions

Chapter Review

Multiple-Choice Questions

1	2	3	4	5	6	7	8	9	10
A	D	C	B	C	B	A	A	D	B

11	12	13	14	15	16	17	18	19	20
E	A	D	A	D	E	C	D	C	C

21	22	23	24	25	26	27	28	29	30
A	C	B	D	A	B	C	B	D	D

True/False Questions

1	2	3	4	5	6	7	8	9	10
T	T	T	F	F	T	F	T	F	T

Short Answer Questions

1. Extroversion: sociable, talkative, assertive, and comfortable with interpersonal relationships

    Agreeableness: able to get along with others by being good-natured, cooperative, forgiving, understanding, and trusting

    Conscientiousness: focused on a few goals, thus behaving in ways that are responsible, dependable, persistent, and achievement oriented

    Emotional stability: calm, enthusiastic, and secure

    Openness to experience: broad range of interests, imaginative, creative, artistically sensitive, and willing to consider new ideas

2. The four functions are sensation, intuitive, thinking, and feeling.

3. Perceptual selectivity is the process by which individuals screen and select the various objects and stimuli that vie for their attention. Characteristics of the stimuli are contrast, novelty, familiarity, intensity, motion, repetition, and size. Characteristics of the perceiver are needs and motivation, values and beliefs, personality, learning, primacy, and recency.

4. The common perceptual errors are stereotyping, the halo effect, projection, and perceptual defense.

Manager's Workbook

High Five: How Many of the "Big Five" Personality Traits Are Yours?: Scoring and interpretation provided with exercise.

Personality Assessment: Jung's Typology Scoring and interpretation provided with exercise.

Manager's Workshop

Applying What You Know about Perceptual Biases and Rater Errors

1. Stereotyping is the tendency to assign an individual to a group or broad category and then attribute generalizations about the group to the individual. Because the informant can't read and has slow speech, she stereotypes him as mentally disabled.
2. Projection is the tendency of perceivers to see their own personal traits in other people; that is, judgments come from projecting their own needs, feelings, values, and attitudes onto the situation or person. Scully is skeptical about UFOs so she projects her feelings onto others by asking biased questions such as "You don't really believe what you saw were visitors from another planet, do you?"
3. Harshness or intensity. Errors in perceptual judgment, called perceptual distortion, can arise from inaccuracies in any part of the perception process. Because Scully does not believe in UFOs, she invalidates all the stories even though parts of them might be true.
4. Stereotyping is the tendency to assign an individual to a group or broad category and then attribute generalizations about the group to the individual. A clean, well dressed, articulate person is considered more credible.
5. This is an error in intensity or harshness. Since Scully and Mulder almost got into an accident with a farmer, they have a negative impression about everything that he says.
6. This is an error in central tendency, seeing all things at the same level. Since the informant started singing, Mulder concluded that this inappropriate behavior cast a negative light on what he had said previously even though the two are unrelated.
7. Similarity-to-me effect. Mulder believes in UFOs, so he accepts the stories of the farmers as valid.
8. This is the leniency error, being too easy on some things. Since the sheriff couldn't evaluate the interviews adequately, he accepted all of them and classified them as somewhat believable.
9. The halo effect is an overall impression of a person or situation based on one attribute, either favorable or unfavorable. Poor dental hygiene has led to an unfavorable impression about their reliability as witnesses.
10. Similar-to-me or familiarity effect. One informant is similar to Scully, so Scully believes her view of events.
11. Stereotyping. Mulder thinks all farmers have a strong work ethic and are honest, so these farmers must be ethical and honest. Information to the contrary is rejected.
12. Stereotyping. Mulder thinks people who are hard working are honest, so he believes the farmers' stories because the farmers seem hard working and honest.

World Trade Center Perceptions

The answers you come up with will vary. The following are examples of what may be provided.

Type of Distortion	Americans	Moslem World
Stereotyping	Those who attacked the World Trade Center must be terrorists to kill innocent civilians	Those who attacked the World Trade Center are patriots who are giving America what it deserves in light of its policies.
The Halo Effect	Since those who attacked were Moslems, any subsequent act by Moslems will also be bad.	Since American policies toward the Moslem world have had negative impact, any actions they now take are aimed at inflicting more injuries.
Projection	Anyone who would attack a civilian target is wicked.	Americans want to blame Moslems for their own misdeeds.
Perceptual Defense	We are not attacking the Islamic religion, just trying to get the terrorists who did this act.	Those who attacked the WTC did so out of feelings of patriotism and self defense.

Chapter 12

Leadership in Organizations

Chapter Outline

I. The Nature of Leadership

   A. Leadership versus Management

   B. Position Power

   C. Personal Power

   D. Empowerment

II. Leadership Traits

   A. Autocratic versus Democratic Leaders

III. Behavioral Approaches

   A. Ohio State Studies

   B. Michigan Studies

   C. The Leadership Grid

IV. Contingency Approaches

   A. Fiedler's Contingency Theory

   B. Hersey and Blanchard's Situational Theory

   C. Path-Goal Theory

   D. Substitutes for Leadership

V. Change Leadership

   A. Charismatic and Visionary Leadership

   B. Transformational Leaders

   C. Leading in the New Workplace

Key Terms

Leadership: the ability to influence people toward the attainment of organizational goals.

Power: the potential ability to influence others' behavior.

Legitimate power: power that stems from a formal management position in an organization and the authority granted to it.

Reward power: power that results from the authority to reward others.

Coercive power: power that stems from the authority to punish or recommend punishment.

Expert power: power that stems from special knowledge of or skill in the tasks performed by subordinates.

Referent power: power that results from characteristics that command subordinates' identification with, respect and admiration for, and desire to emulate the leader.

Traits: distinguishing personal characteristics, such as intelligence, values, and appearance.

Autocratic leader: a leader who tends to centralize authority and rely on legitimate, reward, and coercive power to manage subordinates.

Democratic leader: a leader who delegates authority to others, encourages participation, and relies on expert and referent power to manage subordinates.

Consideration: a type of leader behavior that describes the extent to which a leader is sensitive to subordinates, respects their ideas and feelings, and establishes mutual trust.

Initiating structure: a type of leader behavior that describes the extent to which a leader is task oriented and directs subordinates' work activities toward goal achievement.

Leadership grid: a two-dimensional leadership theory that measures a leader's concern for people and concern for production.

Contingency approach: a model of leadership that describes the relationship between leadership styles and specific organizational situations.

LPC scale: a questionnaire designed to measure relationship-oriented versus task-oriented leadership style according to the leader's choice of adjectives for describing the "least preferred co-worker."

Situational theory: a contingency approach to leadership that links the leader's behavioral style with the task readiness of subordinates.

Path-goal theory: a contingency approach to leadership specifying that the leader's responsibility is to increase subordinates' motivation by clarifying the behaviors necessary for task accomplishment and rewards.

Substitute: a situational variable that makes a leadership style unnecessary or redundant.

Neutralizer: a situational variable that counteracts a leadership style and prevents the leader from displaying certain behaviors.

Transactional leader: a leader who clarifies subordinates' role and task requirements, initiates structure, provides rewards, and displays consideration for subordinates.

Charismatic leader: a leader who has the ability to motivate subordinates to transcend their expected performance.

Vision: an attractive, ideal future that is credible yet not readily attainable.

Transformational leader: a leader distinguished by a special ability to bring about innovation and change.

Interactive leadership: a leadership style characterized by values such as inclusion, collaboration, relationship building, and caring.

Servant leader: a leader who works to fulfill subordinates' needs and goals as well as to achieve the organization's larger mission.

Learning Objectives

1. Define leadership and explain its importance for organizations.

2. Identify personal characteristics associated with effective leaders.

3. Explain the five sources of power and how each causes different subordinate behavior.

4. Describe the leader behaviors of initiating structure and consideration and when they should be used.

5. Describe Hersey and Blanchard's situational theory and its application to subordinate participation.

6. Explain the path-goal model of leadership.

7. Discuss how leadership fits the organizational situation and how organizational characteristics can substitute for leadership behaviors.

8. Describe transformational leadership and when it should be used.

9. Explain innovative approaches to leadership in the new workplace, such as Level 5 leadership, interactive leadership, virtual leadership, and servant leadership.

Chapter Review

Multiple Choice: Please indicate the correct response to the following questions by writing the letter of the correct answer in the space provided.

_____ 1. _____ power comes from a formal management position in an organization and the authority granted to it.
   a. Referent
   b. Expert
   c. Coercive
   d. Reward
   e. Legitimate

_____ 2. When workers obey orders they may disagree with and lack enthusiasm, they are exhibiting
   a. commitment.
   b. compliance.
   c. resistance.
   d. consideration.
   e. Referent power.

_____ 3. Expert power and referent power are most likely to elicit _____ from workers.
   a. commitment
   b. compliance
   c. resistance
   d. complaints
   e. efficiency

_____ 4. At top management, it may be that leaders lack _____ power because subordinates know more about technical details than they do.
   a. legitimate
   b. reward
   c. coercive
   d. expert
   e. referent

_____ 5. _____ power most often generates resistance.
   a. Coercive
   b. Legitimate
   c. Expert
   d. Referent
   e. Reward

_____ 6. A democratic leader relies on _____ power to influence subordinates.
   a. expert
   b. referent
   c. both a and b
   d. Legitimate
   e. Reward

_____ 7. When executives share power and are more participatory, they are said to _____ employees.
   a. Pamper
   b. Patronize
   c. Baby
   d. Empower
   e. Enrich

_____ 8. According to Tannenbaum and Schmidt, a leader should be boss centered when
   a. there is plenty of time to make the decision.
   b. the subordinates cannot learn decision-making skills.
   c. there is little or no skill difference between subordinates and the leader.
   d. the subordinates are fast learners.
   e. both a and d.

_____ 9. A leader is exhibiting initiating structure when he or she
   a. emphasizes deadlines.
   b. is mindful of subordinates.
   c. establishes mutual trust.
   d. provides open communication.
   e. is friendly.

_____ 10. The Michigan researchers used the term _____ for leaders who established high performance goals and displayed supportive behavior toward subordinates.
a. job-centered leaders
b. employee-centered leaders
c. initiating structure
d. consideration
e. impoverished management

_____ 11. The leadership grid was developed by
a. Ohio State.
b. the University of Michigan.
c. Fred Fiedler.
d. Blake and Mouton.
e. Hersey and Blanchard.

_____ 12. Several models of leadership explain the relationship between leadership styles and specific situations. These are termed _____ approaches and include the leadership model of Fiedler and his associates.
a. role model
b. management
c. supervisor
d. contingency
e. subversive

_____ 13. The recommended management style from the leadership grid is _____.
a. 1,9
b. 9,1
c. 5,5
d. 1,1
e. 9,9

_____ 14. The leader-member relations can be seen in
a. how well defined the task is.
b. how much authority the leader has to reward subordinates.
c. specific procedures.
d. the evaluation of subordinates.
e. the members' attitude and acceptance of the leader.

_____ 15. The LPC scale of Fiedler stands for
a. Leadership Potential Characteristics.
b. Likely Power Core.
c. Least Preferred Co-worker.
d. Leadership Power Curve.
e. Leader Preference Caliber.

_____ 16. Leadership situations can be analyzed in terms of three elements:
- a. the quantity of the membership, the organizational structure, and position of authority.
- b. the quality of leader-member relationships, task structure, and position power.
- c. the style of leadership, the educational level of the membership, and the use of power.
- d. the power of the leadership, the member relationships, and the organizational structure.
- e. position power, power relationships, and the authority of the members.

_____ 17. The point of Hersey and Blanchard's situational theory of leadership is that subordinates vary in their
- a. individual situations.
- b. task readiness.
- c. desire for responsibility.
- d. motivational level.
- e. hair styles.

_____ 18. Hersey and Blanchard's approach as compared to Fiedler's model is
- a. more difficult to understand.
- b. more difficult to apply.
- c. easier to understand.
- d. more complex.
- e. not a contingency approach.

_____ 19. In the Hersey and Blanchard model the _____ style, the leader explains decisions and give subordinates a chance to ask questions and gain clarity and understanding about work tasks.
- a. selling
- b. telling
- c. participating
- d. delegating
- e. maturing

_____ 20. According to Hersey and Blanchard, if one or more of the followers are low in task readiness, the leader must
- a. delegate to them.
- b. tell them exactly what to do.
- c. sell them on his ideas.
- d. use a participative leadership style.
- e. tell them to grow up.

_____ 21. Which of the following is *not* one of the types of leader behavior from the path-goal theory?
- a. Autocratic
- b. Supportive
- c. Directive
- d. achievement-oriented
- e. Participative

_____ 22. The two important situational contingencies in the path-goal theory are
   a. the importance of self and the amount of pay you receive.
   b. the personal characteristics of group members and the work environment.
   c. the use of rewards and the task structure.
   d. job ambiguity and a subordinate's lack of confidence.
   e. an incorrect reward system and a subordinate unchallenged by tasks.

_____ 23. _____ is/are (an) element(s) of the environmental contingencies.
   a. Ability of subordinates
   b. Motivations of followers
   c. Needs of followers
   d. The nature of the formal authority system
   e. All of the above

_____ 24. Participative leadership means that the leader _____ about decisions.
   a. stresses higher quality performance
   b. consults with his or her subordinates about what to do
   c. tells subordinates exactly what they are supposed to do
   d. classifies the subordinate's path to rewards and says nothing
   e. shows concern about the subordinates' well being and personal needs

_____ 25. According to the path-goal theory, leader behavior that shows concern for subordinate's well-being is known as
   a. achievement-oriented leadership.
   b. participative leadership.
   c. supportive leadership.
   d. directive leadership.
   e. none of the above.

_____ 26. Which leader behavior from the path-goal theory is similar to the initiating-structure leadership?
   a. Supportive leadership
   b. Directive leadership
   c. Participative leadership
   d. Achievement-oriented leadership
   e. None of the above

_____ 27. A transactional leader
   a. clarifies subordinates' roles.
   b. does not initiate structure but lets it develop.
   c. avoids showing consideration for subordinates.
   d. receives rewards.
   e. does not clarify task requirements.

_____ 28. Charismatic leaders
   a. can only exist in religious organizations.
   b. are usually lacking in vision.
   c. get subordinates to look out for their own interests.
   d. are more predictable than transactional leaders.
   e. may have visionary ideas.

_____ 29. A leader who works to fulfill subordinates' needs and goals as well as to achieve the organization's larger mission is called a(n) _____ leader.
    a. autocratic
    b. servant
    c. democratic
    d. ineffective
    e. maverick

_____ 30. Servant leaders tend to
    a. have an inappropriate style for today's corporate environment.
    b. be too "soft" to be effective.
    c. give things away—power, ideas, information, recognition.
    d. discourage empowerment.
    e. overcompensate in aggressiveness.

True/False: Please indicate whether the following statements are true or false by writing a T or an F in the blank in front of each question.

_____ 1. Management power comes from personal sources, whereas leadership power comes from organizational structure.

_____ 2. Some of the distinguishing personal characteristics associated with successful leaders includes intelligence, verbal ability, and high values.

_____ 3. According to the Michigan studies, the less effective leaders were called job-centered leaders.

_____ 4. The leader can increase employee motivation, according to the Path-Goal theory, by either (1) clarifying the employee's path to accomplish goals, or (2) maximizing the value of the rewards available to successful employees.

_____ 5. Expert power depends on the leader's personal characteristics rather than formal title or position.

_____ 6. When leaders use legitimate power and reward power, the most likely outcome will be commitment.

_____ 7. Research has found a strong relationship between personal traits and leader success.

_____ 8. Fiedler suggests that if a leader finds that his or her style does not match the situation, the leader should try to change styles.

_____ 9. The traditional management function of leading has been called transactional leadership.

_____ 10. The servant leader will help employees become empowered.

Short Answer: Please indicate your answer in the space provided.

1. List the two dimensions used in Blake and Mouton's Leadership Grid.

2. Do you agree with the original Ohio State studies that concluded that high consideration and high initiating structure are always the best? Why or why not?

3. What is the difference between reward power and coercive power?

4. Why is the Hersey and Blanchard approach to leadership better for practicing managers than the Fiedler model?

Manager's Workbook

T–P Leadership Questionnaire: An Assessment of Style *(Also available on page 438 of text.)*

Some leaders deal with general directions, leaving details to subordinates. Other leaders focus on specific details with the expectation that subordinates will carry out orders. Depending on the situation, both approaches may be effective. The important issue is the ability to identify relevant dimensions of the situation and behave accordingly. Through this questionnaire, you can identify your relative emphasis on two dimensions of leadership: task orientation (T) and people orientation (P). These are not opposite approaches, and an individual can rate high or low on either or both.

Directions: The following items describe aspects of leadership behavior. Respond to each item according to the way you would most likely act if you were the leader of a work group. Circle whether you would most likely behave in the described way: **always (A), frequently (F), occasionally (O), seldom (S), or never (N).**

1.	I would most likely act as the spokesperson of the group.	A	F	O	S	N
2.	I would encourage overtime work.	A	F	O	S	N
3.	I would allow members complete freedom in their work.	A	F	O	S	N
4.	I would encourage the use of uniform procedures.	A	F	O	S	N
5.	I would permit members to use their own judgment in solving problems.	A	F	O	S	N
6.	I would stress being ahead of competing groups.	A	F	O	S	N
7.	I would speak as a representative of the group.	A	F	O	S	N
8.	I would needle members for greater effort.	A	F	O	S	N
9.	I would try out my ideas in the group.	A	F	O	S	N
10.	I would let members do their work the way they think best.	A	F	O	S	N
11.	I would be working hard for a promotion.	A	F	O	S	N
12.	I would tolerate postponement and uncertainty.	A	F	O	S	N
13.	I would speak for the group if there were visitors present.	A	F	O	S	N
14.	I would keep the work moving at a rapid pace.	A	F	O	S	N
15.	I would turn the members loose on a job and let them go to it.	A	F	O	S	N
16.	I would settle conflicts when they occur in the group.	A	F	O	S	N
17.	I would get swamped by details.	A	F	O	S	N
18.	I would represent the group at outside meetings.	A	F	O	S	N
19.	I would be reluctant to allow the members any freedom of action.	A	F	O	S	N
20.	I would decide what should be done and how it should be done.	A	F	O	S	N
21.	I would push for increased production.	A	F	O	S	N
22.	I would let some members have authority that I could keep.	A	F	O	S	N
23.	Things would usually turn out as I had predicted.	A	F	O	S	N
24.	I would allow the group a high degree of initiative.	A	F	O	S	N
25.	I would assign group members to particular tasks.	A	F	O	S	N
26.	I would be willing to make changes.	A	F	O	S	N
27.	I would ask the members to work harder.	A	F	O	S	N
28.	I would trust the group members to exercise good judgment.	A	F	O	S	N
29.	I would schedule the work to be done.	A	F	O	S	N
30.	I would refuse to explain my actions.	A	F	O	S	N
31.	I would persuade others that my ideas are to their advantage.	A	F	O	S	N
32.	I would permit the group to set its own pace.	A	F	O	S	N
33.	I would urge the group to beat its previous record.	A	F	O	S	N
34.	I would act without consulting the group.	A	F	O	S	N
35.	I would ask that group members follow standard rules and regulations.	A	F	O	S	N

T _____   P_____

The T–P Leadership Questionnaire is scored as follows:

a. Circle the item number for items 8, 12, 17, 18, 19, 30, 34, and 35.
b. Write the number 1 in front of a circled item number if you responded S (seldom) or N (never) to that item.
c. Also write a number 1 in front of item numbers not circled if you responded A (always) or F (frequently).
d. Circle the number 1s that you have written in front of the following items: 3, 5, 8, 10, 15, 18, 19, 22, 24, 26, 28, 30, 32, 34, and 35.
e. Count the circled number 1s. This is your score for concern for people. Record the score in the blank following the letter P at the end of the questionnaire.
f. Count uncircled number 1s. This is your score for concern for task. Record this number in the blank following the letter T.

SOURCE: The T–P Leadership Questionnaire was adapted by J. B. Ritchie and P. Thompson in Organization and People (New York: West, 1984). Copyright 1969 by the American Educational Research Association. Adapted by permission of the publisher.

Assumptions About Leaders *(also available on page 439 in text)*

Complete the sentences below.

A leader must always…

Leaders should never…

The best leader I ever had did…

The worst leader I ever had did…

When I am doing a good job as a leader, I…

I am afraid of leaders who…

I would follow a leader whom…

I am repelled by leaders who…

Some people think they are good leaders, but they are not because they…

I want to be the kind of leader who…

What did you learn about your own assumptions about leadership? Trace those assumptions back to theories on leadership in this chapter.

Copyright 2000 by Dorothy Marcic.

Manager's Workshop

The Many Faces of Leadership

1. Think of examples of leaders who used their leadership abilities as a positive force, and those as a negative force. Fill in the table below.

Individual responses:

Leaders with positive force (Name)	Leader 1:	Leader 2:	Leader 3:	Leader 4:
General leadership characteristics				
List characteristics according to Fiedler's contingency and Path-Goal Theory				
Which type of position power did leader use? (i.e., coercive, referent, etc)				
Which style used most, according to Leadership Grid?				
Task or people style? Delegating, participating, selling or telling? (according to Hersey and Blanchard)				

	Leader 1:	Leader 2:	Leader 3:	Leader 4:
Results/outcome of their leadership				
Leaders with negative force (Name)	Leader 1:	Leader 2:	Leader 3:	Leader 4:
General leadership characteristics				
List characteristics according to Fiedler's contingency and Path-Goal Theory				
Which type of position power did leader use? (i.e., coercive, referent, etc)				
Which style used most, according to Leadership Grid?				
Task or people style? Delegating, participating, selling or telling? (according to Hersey and Blanchard)				
Results/outcome of their leadership				

2. Divide into groups of 4-7 members. Develop a "group list" of positive and negative leaders, having about five positive and five negative. Complete the second table as you answer each question.

3. What were the similarities between the positive and negative? What were the characteristics of leadership that were comparable?

4. What was it about the positive and negative leaders that made their outcomes so very different? Can you identify one of two critical elements that distinguish positive leaders from negative ones?

5. Refer to "Are You a Charismatic Leader?" in the Leading Revolution: Leadership box. What similarities can you find with those characteristics and the leaders you identified?

Group responses:

Positive leader names	Positive characteristics identified which have commonality with other leaders on your lists	What makes positive leader outcomes positive?	Level of moral development for each	Similarities to charismatic leaders
1.				
2.				

Positive leader names	Positive characteristics identified which have commonality with other leaders on your lists	What makes positive leader outcomes positive?	Level of moral development for each	Similarities to charismatic leaders
3.				
4.				
5.				

Negative leader names	Positive characteristics identified which have commonality with other leaders on your lists	What makes negative leader outcomes negative?	Level of moral development for each	Similarities to charismatic leaders
1.				
2.				
3.				
4.				
5.				

Developing Meeting Leadership Roles

Divide class into groups of 6-8 students. Each group develops a list of desirable ("Do") and undesirable ("Do Not") behavioral roles for leading a meeting.

To run an effective meeting a leader must:

Do the following	Do not do the following

Each group develops a plan of action for a convenience store that is continually plagued by random cash drawer shortages.

A participant from each group is selected to serve as the group meeting leader for each group during the decision making process to develop the action plans.

Plan of Action:

a.

b.

c.

d.

e.

f.

After 10 minutes, the group leader describes what it was like to serve as group leader. The group then provides feedback to the group leader, using the previously developed list of "Do" and "Do Not" group leadership roles.

South-Western

Next, a new leader is selected to continue the development of the action plan. After five minutes, the steps described in step 3 are repeated for the new leader. This process continues until each group participant has had an opportunity to serve as group leader.

Discussion questions:

1. What is the difference between listing a desirable behavior and exhibiting it?

2. How can leaders learn to be more effective?

SOURCE: Adapted from Gerald Klein, Meeting Leadership. *Journal of Management Education*, Vol. 18 (3), 1994, 375-379.

Study Guide Solutions

Chapter Review

Multiple-Choice Questions

1	2	3	4	5	6	7	8	9	10
E	B	A	D	A	C	D	B	A	B

11	12	13	14	15	16	17	18	19	20
D	D	E	E	C	B	B	C	A	B

21	22	23	24	25	26	27	28	29	30
A	B	D	B	C	B	A	E	B	C

True/False Questions

1	2	3	4	5	6	7	8	9	10
F	T	T	T	F	F	F	F	T	T

Short Answer Questions

1. The two dimensions are concern for people and concern for production.

2. New research has shown the effective leadership style depends on the situation, and the high consideration and initiating structure is not the best in every situation.

3. Reward power is the ability to influence others because of the rewards you have to offer them such as praise, attention, and recognition. Coercive power refers to the ability to influence others because of the leader's authority to punish them by firing, demotions, criticism, or withdrawing a pay increase. Reward power is positive by nature, while coercive power is negative.

4. The Hersey and Blanchard model is easier to understand than the Fiedler model. It is also easier to apply because it describes the best leadership for the manager to take.

Manager's Workbook

T–P Leadership Questionnaire: An Assessment of Style: Scoring and interpretation provided with exercise.

Assumptions About Leaders: Answers to this application will vary according to perceptions and unique experiences of each student.

Manager's Workshop

The Many Faces of Leadership: Answers to this application will vary according to perceptions and unique experiences of each student.

Developing Meeting Leadership Roles: Answers will vary.

Chapter 13

Motivation in Organizations

Chapter Outline

I. The Concept of Motivation

II. Foundations of Motivation

    A. Traditional Approach

    B. Human Relations Approach

    C. Human Resource Approach

    D. Contemporary Approaches

III. Content Perspectives on Motivation

    A. Hierarchy of Needs Theory

    B. ERG Theory

    C. Two-Factor Theory

    D. Acquired Needs Theory

IV. Process Perspectives on Motivation

    A. Equity Theory

    B. Expectancy Theory

V. Reinforcement Perspective on Motivation

    A. Reinforcement Tools

    B. Schedules of Reinforcement

VI. Job Design for Motivation

    A. Job Simplification

    B. Job Rotation

    C. Job Enlargement

    D. Job Enrichment

    E. Job Characteristics Model

VII. Motivating in the New Workplace

VIII. Empowerment

IX. Giving Meaning to Work

Key Terms

Motivation: the arousal, direction, and persistence of behavior.

Intrinsic reward: the satisfaction received in the process of performing an action.

Extrinsic reward: a reward given by another person.

Content theories: a group of theories that emphasize the needs that motivate people.

Hierarchy of needs theory: a content theory that proposes that people are motivated by five categories of needs—physiological, safety, belongingness, esteem, and self-actualization—that exist in a hierarchical order.

ERG theory: a modification of the needs hierarchy theory that proposes three categories of needs: existence, relatedness, and growth.

Frustration-regression principle: the idea that failure to meet a high-order need may cause a regression to an already satisfied lower-order need.

Hygiene factors: factors that involve the presence or absence of job dissatisfiers, including working conditions, pay, company policies, and interpersonal relationships.

Motivators: factors that influence job satisfaction based on fulfillment of high-level needs such as achievement, recognition, responsibility, and opportunity for growth.

Process theories: a group of theories that explain how employees select behaviors with which to meet their needs and determine whether their choices were successful.

Equity theory: a process theory that focuses on individuals' perceptions of how fairly they are treated relative to others.

Equity: a situation that exists when the ratio of one person's outcomes to inputs equals that of another's.

Expectancy theory: a process theory that proposes that motivation depends on individuals' expectations about their ability to perform tasks and receive desired rewards.

$E \rightarrow P$ *expectancy*: expectancy that putting effort into a given task will lead to high performance.

$P \rightarrow O$ *expectancy*: expectancy that successful performance of a task will lead to the desire outcome.

Valence: the value or attraction an individual has for an outcome.

Reinforcement theory: a motivation theory based on the relationship between a given behavior and its consequence.

Behavior modification: the set of techniques by which reinforcement theory is used to modify human behavior.

Law of effect: the assumption that positively reinforced behavior tends to be repeated and unreinforced or negatively reinforced behavior tends to be inhibited.

Reinforcement: anything that causes a given behavior to be repeated or inhibited.

Schedule of reinforcement: the frequency with which and intervals over which reinforcement occurs.

Continuous reinforcement schedule: a schedule in which every occurrence of the desired behavior is reinforced.

Partial reinforcement schedule: a schedule in which only some occurrences of the desired behavior are reinforced.

Job design: the application of motivational theories to the structure of work for improving productivity and satisfaction.

Job simplification: a job design whose purpose is to improve task efficiency by reducing the number of tasks a single person must perform.

Job rotation: a job design that systematically moves employees from one job to another to provide them with variety and stimulation.

Job enlargement: a job design that combines a series of tasks into one new, broader job to give employees variety and challenge.

Job enrichment: a job design that incorporates achievement, recognition, and other high-level motivators into the work.

Work redesign: the altering of jobs to increase both the quality of employees' work experience and their productivity.

Job characteristics model: a model of job design that comprises core job dimensions, critical psychological states, and employee growth-need strength.

Empowerment: the delegation of power or authority to subordinates.

Learning Objectives

1. Define motivation and explain the difference between current approaches and traditional approaches to motivation.

2. Identify and describe content theories of motivation based on employee needs.

3. Identify and explain process theories of motivation based on employee needs.

4. Describe reinforcement theory and how it can be used to motivate employees.

5. Discuss major approaches to job design and how job design influences motivation.

6. Discuss how empowerment heightens employee motivation.

Chapter Review

Multiple Choice: Please indicate the correct response to the following questions by writing the letter of the correct answer in the space provided.

_____ 1. _____ is an example of an extrinsic reward.
   a. A good feeling
   b. A promotion
   c. Enjoying the job
   d. A sense of accomplishment
   e. All of the above

_____ 2. An example of contemporary approaches to employee motivation is
     a.   content theories.
     b.   the economic man theory.
     c.   scientific management.
     d.   the human relations approach.
     e.   all of the above.

_____ 3. Content theories emphasize the _____ that motivate people.
     a.   expectancies
     b.   rewards
     c.   equities
     d.   needs
     e.   valences

_____ 4. The most basic need according to Maslow's hierarchy is _____ needs.
     a.   physiological
     b.   safety
     c.   belongingness
     d.   esteem
     e.   self-actualization

_____ 5. The highest level of needs according to Maslow is developing one's full potential. Maslow named this set of needs
     a.   physiological.
     b.   safety.
     c.   belongingness.
     d.   esteem.
     e.   self-actualization.

_____ 6. According to the frustration-regression principle,
     a.   failure to have an adequate sexual relationship may lead to rape.
     b.   failure to have one's needs met on the job may lead one to be more aggressive on the job.
     c.   failure to meet a higher-order need may trigger a regression to an already fulfilled lower-order need.
     d.   frustration is a good thing because it makes us more assertive.
     e.   when we are frustrated, we begin to act like babies.

_____ 7. According to Herzberg, making the work more safe will
     a.   result in increased motivation of the workers.
     b.   increase the level of satisfaction.
     c.   decrease the level of dissatisfaction.
     d.   make the workers want to work harder.
     e.   make the workers want higher pay.

_____ 8. According to Herzberg's two-factor theory, _____ is a hygiene factor, not a motivator.
   a. achievement
   b. pay
   c. recognition
   d. responsibility
   e. work itself

_____ 9. McClelland describes the need for _____ as the desire to accomplish something difficult.
   a. affiliation
   b. attention
   c. power
   d. achievement
   e. self-actualization

_____ 10. The desire to influence or control others is the _____ need.
   a. esteem
   b. achievement
   c. affiliation
   d. expectancy
   e. power

_____ 11. People with a high need for _____ tend to be top managers.
   a. achievement
   b. affiliation
   c. power
   d. relatedness
   e. existence

_____ 12. If a person chooses to increase his inputs to the organization without an increase in income, it is because he or she has perceived
   a. equity.
   b. inequity.
   c. valence.
   d. a continuous reinforcement schedule.
   e. a pay-for-performance plan.

_____ 13. In a situation where one perceives unfavorable inequity, he is likely to
   a. increase effort.
   b. quit the union.
   c. distort others' perceived rewards.
   d. stay on the job longer to improve equity.
   e. all of the above.

_____ 14. According to equity theory, which of the following is an input?
   a. experience
   b. recognition
   c. Pay
   d. promotions
   e. all of the above

_____ 15. Which of the following is an example of a process perspective of motivation?
   a. Need hierarchy theory
   b. Equity theory
   c. Two-factor theory
   d. ERG theory
   e. Acquired needs theory

_____ 16. For the expectation that effort will lead performance to be high, the individual must have
   a. ability.
   b. previous experience.
   c. necessary tools.
   d. opportunity to perform.
   e. all of the above.

_____ 17. _____ is the value of the outcomes for the individual.
   a. Expectancy
   b. Valence
   c. E → P
   d. P → O
   e. Achievement

_____ 18. Which of the following theories is based on the relationships between effort, performance, and outcomes?
   a. Equity theory
   b. Expectancy theory
   c. Reinforcement theory
   d. Two-factor theory
   e. ERG theory

_____ 19. Reinforcement theory focuses on changing _____ through the appropriate use of immediate rewards and punishments.
   a. attitudes
   b. opinions
   c. expectancies
   d. behavior
   e. organizational structure

_____ 20. The removal of an unpleasant consequence following a desired behavior is called
   a. positive reinforcement.
   b. avoidance learning.
   c. punishment.
   d. extinction.
   e. positive extinction.

_____ 21. A farm worker who is paid $2.00 for picking 20 pounds of peppers is being rein-
       forced according to a _____ schedule.
   a. fixed-interval
   b. fixed-ratio
   c. variable-interval
   d. variable-ratio
   e. continuous

_____ 22. The most powerful reinforcement schedule is the _____ schedule.
   a. fixed-interval
   b. fixed-ratio
   c. variable-interval
   d. variable-ratio
   e. continuous

_____ 23. To motivate employees at Emerald Packaging, top management
   a. offered monthly quality awards
   b. gave them authority to make many of their own decisions.
   c. required them to make a $25,000 investment.
   d. required them to sign a five-year contract.
   e. wiped out all individual incentives.

_____ 24. Job simplification is based on principles drawn from
   a. adolescent psychology.
   b. social psychology.
   c. the human relations movement.
   d. industrial engineering.
   e. Elton Mayo.

_____ 25. Which of these systematically moves employees from one job to another, thereby
       increasing the number of different tasks an employee performs without increasing
       the complexity of any one job?
   a. Job simplification
   b. Job rotation
   c. Job enlargement
   d. Job enrichment
   e. None of the above

_____ 26. Giving an employee control over resources, decision making, the pace of work, and providing growth is called
   a. job enlargement.
   b. task significance.
   c. task identity.
   d. job enrichment.
   e. psychological fulfillment.

_____ 27. Autonomy refers to
   a. the degree to which a job is considered important and having impact.
   b. the degree to which an employee performs a total job with a recognizable beginning and end.
   c. the degree to which an employee has freedom and discretion in planning and carrying out tasks.
   d. the degree to which a job provides information to the employee regarding performance.
   e. none of the above.

_____ 28. Which core job dimension refers to the degree to which a job is considered important and having an impact?
   a. Task significance
   b. Task identity
   c. Skill variety
   d. Autonomy
   e. Feedback

_____ 29. The core job dimension from the job characteristics model which is the degree to which an employee performs a total job with a recognizable beginning and ending is
   a. skill variety.
   b. task identity.
   c. task significance.
   d. autonomy.
   e. feedback.

_____ 30. Which of the following is true of empowered employees?
   a. they receive little information about company performance to reduce anxiety
   b. they make only minor decisions
   c. they do not really have the skills and abilities to contribute to company goals, but are made to feel that they do
   d. they are rewarded based on company performance
   e. all of the above are true

True/False: Please indicate whether the following statements are true or false by writing a T or an F in the blank in front of each question.

_____ 1. E→P expectancy involves whether putting effort into a task will lead to high performance.

_____ 2. The law of effect states that behavior that is positively reinforced tends to be repeated, and behavior that is not reinforced tends not to be repeated.

_____ 3. Extinction is the withdrawal of a positive reward.

_____ 4. An extrinsic reward is one received as a direct consequence of a person's actions.

_____ 5. According to Maslow's theory, higher-level needs take priority over the lower-level needs.

_____ 6. The ERG model is more rigid than Maslow's need hierarchy.

_____ 7. Good hygiene factors can cause people to become highly satisfied and motivated in their work.

_____ 8. Equity theory focuses on individuals' perceptions of how fairly they are treated compared to others.

_____ 9. Expectancy theory is concerned with identifying types of needs, not with the thinking process that individuals use to achieve rewards.

_____ 10. Valence is the value of outcomes for the individual.

_____

Short Answer: Please indicate your answer in the space provided.

1. List the five core job dimensions found in the job characteristics model.

2. Describe the evolution of motivation approaches to work.

3. In equity theory, what are the ways in which an individual might reduce a perceived inequity?

4. If you were manager and you wanted to increase the meaningfulness of the activities performed in a job, which core dimensions of the job characteristics model would you use? Apply it to a job with which you are familiar.

Manager's Workbook

What Motivates You? *(Also available on page 473 of text.)*

You are to indicate how important each characteristic is to you. Answer according to your feelings about the most recent job you had or about the job you currently hold. Circle the number on the scale that represents your feeling: 1 (very unimportant) to 7 (very important).

When you have completed the questionnaire, score it as follows:

    Rating for question 5: Divide by 1:   security.
    Rating for questions 9 and 13: Divide by 2:   social.
    Rating for questions 1, 3, and 7: Divide by 3:   esteem.
    Rating for questions 4, 10, 11, and 12: Divide by 4:   autonomy.
    Rating for questions 2, 6, and 8: Divide by 3:   self-actualization.

The instructor has national norm scores for presidents, vice-presidents, and upper middle-level, lower middle-level, and lower-level managers with which you can compare your mean importance scores. How do your scores compare with the scores of managers working in organizations?

1. The feeling of self-esteem a person gets from being in that job   1   2   3   4   5   6   7

2. The opportunity for personal growth and development in that job   1   2   3   4   5   6   7

3.	The prestige of the job inside the company (that is, regard received from others in the company)	1	2	3	4	5	6	7
4.	The opportunity for independent thought and action in that job	1	2	3	4	5	6	7
5.	The feeling of security in that job	1	2	3	4	5	6	7
6.	The feeling of self-fulfillment a person gets from being in that position (that is, the feeling of being able to use one's own unique capabilities, realizing one's potential)	1	2	3	4	5	6	7
7.	The prestige of the job outside the company (that is, the regard received from others not in the company)	1	2	3	4	5	6	7
8.	The feeling of worthwhile accomplishment in that job	1	2	3	4	5	6	7
9.	The opportunity in that job to give help to other people	1	2	3	4	5	6	7
10.	The opportunity in that job for participation in the setting of goals	1	2	3	4	5	6	7
11.	The opportunity in that job for participation in the determination of methods and procedures	1	2	3	4	5	6	7
12.	The authority connected with the job	1	2	3	4	5	6	7
13.	The opportunity to develop close friendships in the job	1	2	3	4	5	6	7

SOURCE: Lyman W. Porter, Organizational Patterns of Managerial Job Attitudes (New York: American Foundation for Management Research, 1964), 17, 19.

Equity Theory in Action

The President of Binford Tools wanted to create a permanent vehicle for advertising the company's products, so he decided to start a cable show called Tool Time. He chose Tim Taylor to be the host of the show because of his love and knowledge of tools and because he had been Binford's best sales rep for the last ten years. He decided to give Tim a starting salary of $80,000. Tim decided that he needed an assistant for the show, so he hired Al Borland. Al had been a master craftsman for 15 years and had worked on building or renovating almost a dozen houses. Al's starting salary was $50,000. Tim's perception is that his role in the show is to promote Binford's products and to make people enthusiastic about initiating home improvement projects. Al's perception is that his role in the show is to do all the "real" work so that the viewers can see how the tools work and know how to use them safely.

- Assuming that each man knows the other's starting salary, use equity theory to demonstrate how Tim and Al are each likely to perceive this situation. Use the ratios to show your analysis.

Tim:

Al:

- Assuming that Al perceives an underpayment inequity, what are some of the ways he might try to restore equity?

SOURCE: Courtney Hunt, Northern Illinois University, "Must see TV: The timelessness of television as a teaching tool," presented at Academy of Management, August 2000. Used with permission.

Expectancy Theory in Action

Your assignment, your job, is to use expectancy theory to determine how much you are going to study for this course. The outcomes and performance alternatives that are relevant to this determination are listed below. You should draw the expectancy theory diagram and do the necessary calculations to identify the most motivating option. In particular, you will need to:

1. Assign valences to the outcomes;
2. Identify the instrumentalities for each performance-outcome relationship;
3. Calculate the values for each performance alternative;
4. Assign expectancies to each performance alternative; and
5. Calculate the force for each performance alternative.

Outcomes	Assign valences to outcomes
• Getting a good grade in the course	
• Socializing with friends	
• Money from part-time job	

	Identify instrumentalities for each performance-outcome relationship
Performance-outcome relationships	
• Study a lot —good grade	
—socializing	
—money	
• Study moderate— good grade	
—socializing	
—money	
• Don't study— good grade	
—socializing	
—money	

Performance alternatives	Calculate values, assign expectancies, calculate forces
• Study a lot	
Value of performance alternative	
Expectancy	
Force	
• Study a moderate amount	
Value of performance alternative	
Expectancy	
Force	
• Don't study at all	
Value of performance alternative	
Expectancy	
Force	

SOURCE: Adapted from Courtney Hunt, Northern Illinois University, "Must see TV: The timelessness of television as a teaching tool," presented at Academy of Management, August 2000. Used with permission.

Manager's Workshop

Hey, That's Not Fair! *(Also available on page 474 of text.)*

Listed below are six vignettes depicting situations in which the Brady kids have perceived an unfair situation. For each vignette, identify the equity theory method (change inputs, change outcomes, distort perceptions or leave the situation) that you feel the Brady kid should employ. Then, in groups of 4-6 discuss which method is most relevant for each situation.

• Greg just found out that Tommy has been picked by the coach to be the new quarterback for the football team because his dad and the coach are old high school buddies. He is really bummed because that is the position he has been hoping to play ever since junior high.

- Marcia was upset about being turned down for the job of emcee for the school talent show, but she was even more bothered by the fact that the director of the show made her wait for half an hour and was rude and inconsiderate when giving her feedback about her tryout performance. To top it off, she found out later the person chosen as emcee was the homecoming queen.

  _____

- Jan studied about 5 hours for her geometry final, but her friend Sue only spent about 30 minutes cramming at the last minute. They just got back their test results today -- much to Jan's surprise, she only got a B-, but Sue got an A!

  _____

- Peter has been working really hard at the malt shop for the last six months, doing extra chores and helping out other employees when they needed it. The manager of the store just told him that he was going to give him a raise, but Peter is frustrated by the fact that it's only an extra 15¢ an hour. He thought he deserved more. Then yesterday he found out that the new guy, hired just two months ago got the same raise.

  _____

- Bobby and his friend Dennis just finished doing a bunch of yard work for Mr. Wilson. Bobby worked non-stop, rarely taking a break, but Dennis kept goofing off and playing around. In the end Mr. Wilson gave them both the same amount of money, which Bobby didn't think was right.

  _____

- Cindy is upset because her science teacher selected three other people to compete in the upcoming science fair without first asking if anybody wanted to volunteer to participate in it.

  _____

SOURCE: Courtney Hunt, Northern Illinois University, "Must see TV: The timelessness of television as a teaching tool," presented at Academy of Management, August 2000. Used with permission.

My Absolute Worst Job

1. By yourself, complete the table below, except for the "group" row answers.

2. Divide into groups of 4-7 members. Groups discuss individual answers and complete the group rows.

Reasons for job being so awful

	Title & Duties?	Working Conditions?	Supervision? Boss?	Work itself, lack of rewards, coworkers?	Other?	Compare to best job
Your worst job						
Groups-- Member #1						
Member #2						
#3						
#4						
#5						
#6						

3. The instructor asks for a show of hands on the number of people whose worst jobs fit into the following categories:

    a. Factory
    b. Restaurant
    c. Manual labor
    d. Driving or delivery

    e. Professional
    f. Health care
    g. Phone sales or communications
    h. Other

4. Instructor gathers data from each group on worst jobs and asks groups to answer:

    a. What are any common characteristics of the worst jobs in your group?

b. How did your co-workers feel about their jobs?

c. What happens to morale and productivity when a worker hates the job?

d. What was the difference in your own morale/productivity in your worst job versus a job you really enjoyed?

e. Why do organizations continue to allow unpleasant working conditions to exist?

f. What motivation theories are relevant for understanding how to prevent these "worst" jobs?

Study Guide Solutions

Chapter Review

Multiple-Choice Questions

1	2	3	4	5	6	7	8	9	10
B	A	D	A	E	C	C	B	D	E

11	12	13	14	15	16	17	18	19	20
C	B	C	A	B	E	B	B	D	B

21	22	23	24	25	26	27	28	29	30
B	D	A	D	B	D	C	A	B	D

True/False Questions

1	2	3	4	5	6	7	8	9	10
T	T	T	F	F	F	F	T	F	T

Short Answer Questions

1. The five dimensions are (a) skill variety, (b) task identity, (c) task significance, (d) autonomy, and (e) feedback.

2. The early emphasis was on pay and incentive pay systems. Later the human relations approach evolved, which studied workers as people with basic needs. The concept of the "whole person" developed to explain that employees are complex, motivated by many factors, competent, and able to make major contributions. Contemporary approaches take three forms. Content theories stress understanding human behavior by analyzing underlying human needs. Process theories concern thought processes that influence behavior. Reinforcement theories focus on employee learning of desired work behaviors.

3. An individual could change inputs -- increase or decrease amount of effort; change outcomes -- request a salary increase or bigger office; distort perceptions -- artificially increase status of job or distort others' perceived rewards; or leave the job.

4. The three core dimensions that should be used to increase a job's motivational potential are skill variety, task identity, and task significance.

Manager's Workbook

What Motivates You?: Scoring and interpretation provided with exercise.

Below are shown the scores of executives and three levels of managers that Porter obtained in a study using this questionnaire.

Sample	Security	Social	Esteem	Autonomy	Self-Actualization
President (n=114)	5.69	5.38	5.27	6.11	6.50
Vice President (n=611)	5.44	5.46	5.33	6.10	6.40
Upper-Middle (n=569)	5.20	5.31	5.27	5.89	6.34
Lower-Middle (n=431)	5.29	5.33	5.26	5.74	6.25
Lower (n=101)	5.30	5.27	5.18	5.58	6.32

Note: 1 = lowest degree of importance; 7 = highest degree of importance.

Source: K. Stewart, Instructor's Manual to accompany Gibson, Ivancevich, and Donnelly, *Organizations*, Plano, TX: BPI, 1988, 36.

It is interesting to note that self-actualization needs were rated by managers at all levels as most important. For all but upper-middle level managers, esteem needs were rated as least important of the five categories. The only category of needs which shows a clear progression (increase in importance) from lower-level management to top management is autonomy. It is also probably accurate to say that managers at higher levels in the organization actually have more autonomy than managers at lower levels.

Equity Theory in Action: Answers will vary.

Expectancy Theory in Action: Answers will vary.

Manager's Workshop

Hey, That's Not Fair: Answers will vary.

My Absolute Worst Job: Answers to this application will vary.

Chapter 14

Communicating in Organizations

Chapter Outline

I. Communication and the Manager's Job

    A. What Is Communication?

    B. The Communication Process

II. Communicating among People

    A. Communication Channels

    B. Persuasion and Influence

    C. Nonverbal Communication

    D. Listening

III. Organizational Communication

    A. Formal Communication Channels

    B. Team Communication Channels

    C. Informal Communication Channels

IV. Communicating in the New Workplace

    A. Open Communication

    B. Dialogue

    C. Feedback and Learning

V. Managing Organizational Communication

    A. Barriers to Communication

    B. Overcoming Communication Barriers

Key Terms

Communication: the process by which information is exchanged and understood by two or more people, usually with the intent to motivate or influence behavior.

Encode: to select symbols with which to compose a message.

Message: the tangible formulation of an idea to be sent to a receiver.

Channel: the carrier of a communication.

Decode: to translate the symbols used in a message for the purpose of interpreting its meaning.

Feedback: a response by the receiver to the sender's communication.

Channel richness: the amount of information that can be transmitted during a communication episode.

Nonverbal communication: a communication transmitted through actions and behaviors rather than through words.

Listening: the skill of receiving messages to accurately grasp facts and feelings to interpret the genuine meaning.

Formal communication channel: a communication channel that flows within the chain of command or task responsibility defined by the organization.

Downward communication: messages sent from top management down to subordinates.

Upward communication: messages transmitted from the lower to the higher levels in the organization's hierarchy.

Horizontal communication: the lateral or diagonal exchange of messages among peers or coworkers.

Centralized network: a team communication structure in which team members communicate through a single individual to solve problems or make decisions.

Decentralized network: a team communication structure in which team members freely communicate with one another and arrive at decisions together.

Informal communication channels: a communication channel that exists outside formally authorized channels without regard for the organization's hierarchy of authority.

Management by wandering around (MBWA): a communication technique in which managers interact directly with workers to exchange information.

Grapevine: an informal person-to-person communication network of employees that is not officially sanctioned by the organization.

Open communication: sharing all types of information throughout the company, across functional and hierarchical levels.

Dialogue: a group communication process aimed at creating a culture based on collaboration, fluidity, trust, and commitment to shared goals.

Feedback: using communication and evaluation to help the organization learn and improve.

Defense mechanism: emotional blocks that serve to minimize anxiety, protect the ego, and maintain repression of true feelings.

Semantics: the meaning of words and the way they are used.

Learning Objectives

1. Explain why communication is essential for effective management and describe how nonverbal behavior and listening affect communication among people.

2. Explain how managers use communication to persuade and influence others.

3. Describe the concept of channel richness, and explain how communication channels influence the quality of communication in organizations.

4. Explain the difference between formal and informal organizational communications and the importance of each for organization management.

5. Identify how structure influences team communication outcomes.

6. Explain why open communication, dialogue, and feedback are essential to communication in the new workplace.

7. Describe barriers to organizational communication, and suggest ways to avoid or overcome them.

Chapter Review

Multiple Choice: Please indicate the correct response to the following questions by writing the letter of the correct answer in the space provided.

_____ 1. About _____ minutes of every working hour is spent communicating by managers.
    a.   10
    b.   22
    c.   36
    d.   48
    e.   54

_____ 2. The tangible formulation of an idea to be sent to a receiver is called
    a.   encoding.
    b.   the message.
    c.   the channel.
    d.   decoding.
    e.   feedback.

_____ 3. Which of the following is an example of "noise" which impedes communication?
    a.   lack of knowledge
    b.   negative attitude
    c.   different backgrounds of sender and receiver
    d.   all of the above
    e.   a and b only

_____ 4. Which of the following is *not* a communication channel?
    a.   telephone
    b.   Memo
    c.   newsletter
    d.   Letter
    e.   perceptual background

_____ 5. Without feedback communication is
    a.   two-way.
    b.   one-way.
    c.   informal.
    d.   Bottom up.
    e.   most effective.

_____ 6. The richest communication channel is a
    a.   telephone.
    b.   Memo.
    c.   face-to-face talk.
    d.   flyer.
    e.   letter.

_____ 7. _____ is a characteristic of a non-routine message.
    a.   Simplicity
    b.   Prior agreement
    c.   Pertaining to statistics
    d.   Dealing with a novel event
    e.   Straightforwardness

_____ 8. To persuade and influence, managers connect with others by using
    a.   a policy manual.
    b.   symbols, metaphors, and stories.
    c.   statistical facts and figures.
    d.   rules and regulations.
    e.   external consultants.

_____ 9. The three sources of communication cues during face-to-face communications are
    a.   verbal, vocal, and facial expressions.
    b.   vocabulary, loudness, and eye contact.
    c.   tone, volume, and clarity.
    d.   drift, static, and tone.
    e.   eye contact, eye movement, and voice inflection.

_____ 10. An effective listener
    a.   does not show interest until the other stops talking.
    b.   listens for facts.
    c.   listens for ideas.
    d.   judges by the quality of the delivery.
    e.   never asks questions.

_____ 11. Which of the following is evidence of a good listener?
    a. laid back
    b. listens for facts
    c. prefers recreational material rather than difficult material
    d. judges content and skips over delivery errors
    e. does not ask questions

_____ 12. Our listening efficiency as measured by the amount of material understood and remembered by subjects 48 hours after listening to a 10-minute message is on the average no better than _____ percent.
    a. 50
    b. 45
    c. 30
    d. 25
    e. 15

_____ 13. Keys to effective listening include all of the following EXCEPT
    a. find areas of interest.
    b. listen for ideas.
    c. be responsive.
    d. have preconceptions.
    e. All of the above are keys to effective listening.

_____ 14. The learning organizations emphasize which of these?
    a. Downward communication
    b. Grapevine communication
    c. Horizontal communication
    d. Upward communication
    e. Vertical communication

_____ 15. Which type of downward communication is illustrated by the following words: "Sally, you need to improve your typing skills"?
    a. indoctrination
    b. performance feedback
    c. procedures and practices
    d. job instructions
    e. implementation of goals

_____ 16. The major problem with downward communication is drop-off, which means
    a. the tendency of employees to drop off to sleep while listening.
    b. the distortion or loss of message content.
    c. using poor grammar or slang.
    d. the incongruity with the informal communication channel of the message content.
    e. the conflict between verbal and nonverbal messages.

_____ 17. Recently, a manager received the following note on his desk: "The main computer just went down. We expect to have it fixed in about two hours." What type of communication is this?
    a.   downward
    b.   upward
    c.   horizontal
    d.   rumor
    e.   grapevine

_____ 18. Which of the following would *not* facilitate upward communication?
    a.   suggestion box
    b.   employee survey
    c.   open-door policy
    d.   management by wandering around
    e.   All of the above would facilitate upward communication.

_____ 19. Through _____ and _____ meetings, managers can develop an understanding of the organization and are able to communicate important ideas and values directly to others.
    a.   direct observation; face-to-face
    b.   indirect observation; clandestine
    c.   one-way mirrored observation; backroom
    d.   video-camera observations; face-to-face
    e.   surveillance-type observation; clandestine

_____ 20. The message, "We are streamlining the company travel procedures and would like to discuss them with your department," is an example of _____ communication.
    a.   downward
    b.   upward
    c.   horizontal
    d.   vertical
    e.   informal

_____ 21. Management by wandering around (MBWA) is a communications technique that was made famous by the book written by Tom Peters called
    a.   *Business Can Be Fun.*
    b.   *Quality Communications.*
    c.   *Lazy Communications.*
    d.   *In Search of Excellence.*
    e.   *The 7 Habits of Highly Effective Communicators.*

_____ 22. The grapevine
    a.   will not exist in a well-run company.
    b.   usually carries inaccurate information.
    c.   usually circulates non-business related matters.
    d.   fills in information gaps in the organization.
    e.   usually is inactive during a period of change.

_____ 23. The informal communication channel is called the grapevine because it
    a. links employees in all directions together.
    b. is too strong to be cut.
    c. can be tapped into for the "wine of the message."
    d. contains "grapes" of information.
    e. only exists when employees have drunk a little wine.

_____ 24. When the complexity of a department task is high, a(n) _____ communication process works best.
    a. Decentralized
    b. Centralized
    c. Wheel
    d. "Y"
    e. Informal

_____ 25. The grapevine tends to be more active during periods of
    a. boredom.
    b. change or anxiety.
    c. competition.
    d. stability.
    e. holidays.

_____ 26. A group communication process aimed at creating a culture based on collaboration, fluidity, trust, and commitment to shared goals is referred to as a(n)
    a. MBWA.
    b. dialogue.
    c. open communication.
    d. centralized system.
    e. gossip.

_____ 27. When managing organizational communications, at what two levels do communication barriers occur?
    a. Supervisory, executive
    b. Individual, organizational
    c. Shop floor, executive suite
    d. Street, penthouse
    e. Middle management, customer

_____ 28. Writing works best for _____ messages but _____ the capacity for rapid feedback.
    a. routine; lacks
    b. routine; provides
    c. nonroutine; lacks
    d. nonroutine; provides
    e. None of the above

_____ 29. Attaching different meanings to words is a communication problem pertaining to
    a.   interpersonal dynamics.
    b.   channels and media.
    c.   semantics.
    d.   inconsistent cues.
    e.   nonverbal communication.

_____ 30. To improve organization communication the organization should
    a.   allow subordinates to transmit only positive messages to managers.
    b.   use formal information channels in one direction only.
    c.   use only the formal communication channel.
    d.   create a climate of trust and openness.
    e.   never change the organizational structure.

True/False: Please indicate whether the following statements are true or false by writing a T or an F in the blank in front of each question.

_____ 1. The more similar the frames of reference between people, the more easily they can communicate.

_____ 2. After developing the message, the sender must decode the message and select a communication channel.

_____ 3. Managers can communicate nonroutine messages effectively only by selecting rich channels.

_____ 4. Blushing, perspiring, glancing, crying and laughing are all forms of nonverbal communication.

_____ 5. An example of downward communication is performance feedback.

_____ 6. Horizontal communication is the lateral or diagonal exchange of messages among peers or coworkers.

_____ 7. Informal communication channels exist within the formally authorized channels and adhere to the organization's hierarchy of authority.

_____ 8. MBWA and grapevine are two types of informal channels used in many organizations.

_____ 9. Interpersonal barriers may include problems with emotions and perceptions held by employees.

_____ 10. Perhaps the most important individual skill that managers can develop is active listening.

Short Answer: Please indicate your answer in the space provided.

1. Explain why feedback is an essential part of the communication process.

2. How does nonverbal behavior affect the communication process?

3. Since informal communication is so powerful, fast, and accurate, why do organizations need formal channels of communication?

4. Which type of network would be most appropriate for a team assigned to come up with new ideas?

Manager's Workbook

Listening Self-Assessment *(Also available on page 508 of text.)*

Instructions: Choose one response for each of the items below. Base your choice on what you usually do, not on what you think a person should do.

1. When you are going to lunch with a friend, you:
   a. Focus your attention on the menu and then on the service provided
   b. Ask about events in your friend's life and pay attention to what's said
   c. Exchange summaries of what is happening to each of you while focusing attention on the meal

2. When someone talks nonstop, you:
   a. Ask questions at an appropriate time in an attempt to help the person focus on the issue
   b. Make an excuse to end the conversation
   c. Try to be patient and understand what you are being told

3. If a group member complains about a fellow employee who, you believe, is disrupting the group, you:
   a. Pay attention and withhold your opinions
   b. Share your own experiences and feelings about that employee
   c. Acknowledge the group member's feelings and ask the group member what options he or she has

4. If someone is critical of you, you:
   a. Try not to react or get upset
   b. Automatically become curious and attempt to learn more
   c. Listen attentively and then back up your position

5. You are having a very busy day and someone tells you to change the way you are completing a task. You believe the person is wrong, so you:
   a. Thank her or him for the input and keep doing what you were doing
   b. Try to find out why she or he thinks you should change
   c. Acknowledge that the other may be right, tell her or him you are very busy, and agree to follow up later

6. When you are ready to respond to someone else, you:
   a. Sometimes will interrupt the person if you believe it is necessary
   b. Almost always speak before the other is completely finished talking
   c. Rarely offer your response until you believe the other has finished

7. After a big argument with someone you have to work with every day, you:
   a. Settle yourself and then try to understand the other's point of view before stating your side again
   b. Just try to go forward and let bygones be bygones
   c. Continue to press your position

8. A colleague calls to tell you that he is upset about getting assigned to a new job. You decide to:
   a. Ask him if he can think of options to help him deal with the situation
   b. Assure him that he is good at what he does and that these things have a way of working out for the best
   c. Let him know you have heard how badly he feels

9. If a friend always complains about her problems but never asks about yours, you:
   a. Try to identify areas of common interest
   b. Remain understanding and attentive, even if it becomes tedious
   c. Support her complaints and mention your own complaints

10. The best way to remain calm in an argument is to:
    a. Continue to repeat your position in a firm but even manner
    b. Repeat what you believe is the other person's position
    c. Tell the other person that you are willing to discuss the matter again when you are both calmer

Score each item of your Listening Self-Assessment

1. (a) 0   (b) 10   (c) 5
2. (a) 10   (b) 0   (c) 5
3. (a) 5   (b) 0   (c) 5
4. (a) 5   (b) 10   (c) 0
5. (a) 0   (b) 10   (c) 5
6. (a) 5   (b) 0   (c) 10
7. (a) 10   (b) 5   (c) 0
8. (a) 5   (b) 5   (c) 10
9. (a) 0   (b) 10   (c) 5
10. (a) 0   (b) 10   (c) 5

Add up your total score_____

80–100 You are an active, excellent listener. You achieve a good balance between listening and asking questions, and you strive to understand others.

50–75 You are an adequate-to-good listener. You listen well, although you may sometimes react too quickly to others before they are finished speaking.

25–45 You have some listening skills but need to improve them. You may often become impatient when trying to listen to others, hoping they will finish talking so you can talk.

0–20 You listen to others very infrequently. You may prefer to do all of the talking and experience extreme frustration while waiting for others to make their point.

SOURCE: Richard G. Weaver and John D. Farrell, *Managers As Facilitators: A Practical Guide to Getting Work Done in a Changing Workplace* (San Francisco: Berrett-Koehler Publishers, 1997), 134–136. Used with permission.

Do You Love Your Company? *(Also available on page 509 of text.)*

Open, honest and authentic communication can help create the kind of organization that employees love. Here's an instrument to determine which of five key principles your company does best.

	Strongly Agree	Somewhat Agree	Neutral	Somewhat Disagree	Strongly Disagree
Capture the Heart					
1. We have a written vision that is known to all and lived every day.	1	2	3	4	5
2. We seek creative, low-cost ways to balance work and family.	1	2	3	4	5
3. We love to celebrate and find innovative ways to inject fun into the workplace.	1	2	3	4	5
Open Communication					
1. It is obvious that management considers internal listening a priority.	1	2	3	4	5
2. Attention is given to using multiple communication channels--more than just using memos and e-mail.	1	2	3	4	5
3. Employees receive feedback in real time (immediate, direct, positive) rather than merely occasional performance appraisals.	1	2	3	4	5
Create Partnerships					
1. There are few, if any, status barriers between employees (i.e., reserved parking, bonuses only for top management, special benefits).	1	2	3	4	5
2. We actively share financial numbers, ratios and company performance measures with all employees.	1	2	3	4	5
3. Management visibly serves the front-line, customer-contact employee first (providing tools, resources and training) before asking the front-line employee to serve us with reports, paperwork, etc.	1	2	3	4	5

Drive Learning					
1. We guarantee lifelong employability (rather than lifetime employment) through offering extensive training, cross-training and work variety.	1	2	3	4	5
2. Special attention is given to creating visible, activity-filled programs that help drive learning through all levels of the organization--up, down and laterally.	1	2	3	4	5
3. We actively support a philosophy of lifelong learning for our employees that goes beyond focusing only on today's job needs.	1	2	3	4	5
Emancipate Action					
1. We allow employees the freedom to fail and try again.	1	2	3	4	5
2. Constant attention is given to creating freedom from bureaucracy, unnecessary sign-offs, outdated procedures and office politics.	1	2	3	4	5
3. All employees are encouraged to openly challenge the status quo to help find better, faster, more profitable ways to serve our customers.	1	2	3	4	5

Summary score: The higher the score (on any of the five principles), the more you believe this principle is alive and well in your organization. The lower the score, the more your organization needs to address this principle.

SOURCE: Jim Harris, "The partnership facade: What's your love quotient?" *Management Review*, April 1996, pp.45-48.

Manager's Workshop

Defense Mechanism Exercise *(Also available on page 510 of text.)*

    1. Preparation: Students form up to nine groups of 3 – 6 members. Instructor hands out a slip of paper with one of the defense mechanisms listed below to each group, which should not reveal its role to the other groups. Each group designs a role-play based on their assigned defense mechanism. If there are more than nine groups, more than one group can receive the same mechanism.

2. **Role Play:** The role-plays are then presented to the entire class. Other groups guess which defense mechanism is represented.

3. **Class Discussion:** Instructor will ask the class to address the following:
   a. Did you recognize any behaviors that you have used? Provide examples.
   b. Give examples of situations when these behaviors may have been used with you.

Behavioral Defense Mechanisms

Devaluation: Exaggerating negative attributes in self or others.

Distortion: Reshaping external reality to suit inner needs.

Idealization: Exaggerating positive qualities in self or others.

Intellectualization: Engaging in excessive abstract thought to avoid disturbing feelings.

Passive Aggressive: Expressing indirect and unassertive aggression toward others.

Projection: Attributing one's own feelings, impulses, or thoughts to others.

Rationalization: Devising reassuring or self-serving, but incorrect, explanations for one's behavior.

Reaction Formation: Substituting behaviors, thoughts, or feelings which are opposed to one's true behaviors, thoughts or feelings.

Repression: Inhibiting the ability to remember or be aware of disturbing thoughts, feelings, or experiences.

SOURCE: Adapted from an exercise by Dorothy A. Marcic (Vanderbilt University) and Susanne Fest (Vanderbilt University). Used with permission.

Evaluate This!

1 Form groups of 5-8 members. Instructor will assign role of either Pat OR Chris to each group. In other words, some groups will be "Pat" groups and some will be "Chris" groups. Only read the role you are assigned. DO NOT read the other role.

2 Fill in the box after each role, answering the questions. Role play the next meeting between Pat and Chris. Be prepared to do your role play in front of the class.

3 The instructor will call certain people to the front for the role play.

4 Class discussion on communication in organizations.

Role for Pat to read:

It's time for annual performance evaluations at the Topflight Music Publishing Company. Pat, the new manager of the marketing department has one employee, Bob, who is not cutting it. Pat has convinced his/her boss, Chris, the VP of Marketing, to reassign Bob to a less client-oriented position. It was difficult for Chris to accept the fact that Bob was a nuisance in the department. After all Bob's wife, Veronica, Executive Vice President at Oldies Records, is an old friend and mentor of Chris' and helped Chris get the job with Topflight.

Bob has been very erratic in his behaviors for the past two months. He comes in late to work 3 out of 5 days a week. He has become disruptive in the workplace and has thrown papers and files at co-workers. No one can explain his unpredictable behavior.

Pat meets with Bob on Thursday afternoon. Pat reviews Bob's past performance for the entire year with him. Near the end of the evaluation Pat explains to Bob that there is going to be a bit of a change in his workday. Pat demotes Bob. Bob is devastated. Suddenly he jumps up and begins yelling obscenities. He says to Pat, "With everything else going wrong in my life, I thought I could count on you for friendship and understanding. I'm going to talk to your boss Chris and I'll take you on later." He leaves Pat's office.

Thirty minutes later, Pat's phone rings. It's Chris saying, "I think we ought to give Bob another chance. I've told Bob that we want to meet with him tomorrow to discuss your meeting with him today."

	What concepts or principles are important in this interaction relevant to each player? What communication principles are important here?	What should have been done differently?	What should happen at the next meeting between Pat and Chris? What will you say?
Chris			
Pat			
Bob			

Role for Chris to read:

It's time for annual performance evaluations at the Topflight Music Publishing Company. Pat, the new manager of the marketing department has one employee, Bob, who is not cutting it. Pat has convinced his/her boss, Chris, the VP of Marketing, to reassign Bob to a less client-oriented position. It was difficult for Chris to accept the fact that Bob was a nuisance in the department. After all Bob's wife, Veronica, Executive Vice President at Oldies Records, is an old friend and mentor of Chris' and helped Chris get the job with Topflight.

Bob has been very erratic in his behaviors for the past two months. He comes in late to work 3 out of 5 days a week. He has become disruptive in the workplace and has thrown papers and files at co-workers. No one can explain his unpredictable behavior.

Pat has just met with Bob to tell him that he is fired, after reviewing his performance for the year. Right after the meeting, Bob storms into Chris's office and sputters at Chris, as Bob leans menacingly over Chris's desk, "You better watch out. If you two fire me, I'll, why, well, my wife has friends in high places, at record companies and in the media, some who know where the bones are buried—if you get my drift." His eyes were wide and bulging as he came around the desk and poked his finger into Chris's face. "You better not mess with me, not if you want to…." And then Bob stood staring hatefully at Chris, turned and stalked out of the office.

After a few minutes, Chris realized there could be a big mess if Bob was not appeased, so Chris telephoned Bob. Then Chris call Pat and said, "I think we ought to give Bob another chance. I've told Bob that we want to meet with him tomorrow to discuss your meeting with him today."

	What concepts or principles are important in this interaction relevant to each player? What communication principles are important here?	What should have been done differently?	What should happen at the next meeting between Pat and Chris? What will you say?
Chris			
Pat			
Bob			

Adapted by Dorothy Marcic from Lee Bolman's case. Used with permission.

Study Guide Solutions

Chapter Review

Multiple-Choice Questions

1	2	3	4	5	6	7	8	9	10
D	B	D	E	B	C	D	B	A	C

11	12	13	14	15	16	17	18	19	20
D	D	D	C	B	B	B	E	A	C

21	22	23	24	25	26	27	28	29	30
D	D	A	A	C	B	B	A	C	D

True/False Questions

1	2	3	4	5	6	7	8	9	10
T	F	T	T	T	T	F	T	T	T

Short Answer Questions

1. Feedback is necessary for the sender to know that the receiver grasped the intended message. It can tell the sender if improper encoding took place, if the channel was improper, or if noise impeded the communication process.

2. Nonverbal behavior is the most important part of the communication media. It is more powerful than the words or the voice. It can override or completely change the meaning of words.

3. Formal communication channels are needed to implement goals; to give job instructions and rationale; to communicate procedures, practices, performance feedback, and indoctrination; to deal with problems; to provide suggestions and performance reports; and as a means of airing grievances and officially providing financial information.

4. The decentralized network would be the best structure for a team assigned to come up with new ideas. It allows members to communicate freely with each other and would therefore facilitate brainstorming and piggybacking on the ideas of others, thus fostering creativity.

Manager's Workbook

Listening Self-Assessment: Scoring and interpretation provided with exercise.

Do You Love Your Company?: Scoring and interpretation provided with exercise.

Manager's Workshop

Defense Mechanism Exercise: Answers will vary.

Evaluate This! Answers will vary. However, several communication principles apply.

1. Bob is demoted or fired without ever being given a chance to communicate. Communication is one-sided, not two sided.

2. In both roles, the manager does not listen to the employee. The keys to effective listening should be reviewed and applied to Bob. Why has his behavior been erratic for the past two months? Why is he late? Why is he disruptive? Why is his behavior unpredictable?

3. Using Exhibit 14.5, the principles of downward and upward communication should be applied here. Downward communication refers to the flow of communication from top management to subordinates. (Pat to Bob, and Chris to Pat) Downward communication should encompass company goals and strategies, job instructions and rationale, procedures and practices, performance feedback, and indoctrination. These were omitted in the role for Pat and for Chris. Chris overrides Pat's decision and gives Bob another chance.

   Upward communication is the flow of messages from the lower to the higher levels in the organization's hierarchy. (Bob to Pat) (Bob to Chris) Upward communication should encompass problems and exceptions, suggestions for improvement, and grievances and disputes. Bob presented none of these.

4. There are communication barriers to overcome based on status and power differences that exist between Chris, Pat, and Bob. Also, the absence of formal channels reduces communication effectiveness. This organization should provide employee surveys, open-door policies, liaison personnel to improve communication.

5. The use of dialogue is recommended for the follow-up meeting. Dialogue, or "stream of meaning," is a communication process in which groups create a stream of shared meaning that would enable Bob, Chris, and Pat to understand each other a share a view of the world. Bob, Pat, and Chris may start out at polar opposites, but by talking openly to one another, they can discover common ground, common issues and shared goals on which they can build cooperation.

Chapter 15

Teamwork in Organizations

Chapter Outline

I. Teams at Work

   A. What Is a Team?

   B. Model of Work Team Effectiveness

II. Types of Teams

   A. Formal Teams

   B. Self-Directed Teams

   C. Teams in the New Workplace

III. Work Team Characteristics

   A. Size

   B. Member Roles

IV. Team Processes

   A. Stages of Team Development

   B. Team Cohesiveness

   C. Team Norms

V. Managing Team Conflict

   A. Causes of Conflict

   B. Styles to Handle Conflict

VI. Benefits and Costs of Teams

   A. Potential Benefits of Teams

   B. Potential Costs of Teams

Key Terms

Team: a unit of two or more people who interact and coordinate their work to accomplish a specific goal.

Formal team: a team created by the organization as part of the formal organization structure.

Vertical team: a formal team composed of a manager and his or her subordinates in the organization's formal chain of command.

Horizontal team: a formal team composed of employees from about the same hierarchical level but from different areas of expertise.

Committee: a long-lasting, sometimes permanent team in the organization structure created to deal with tasks that recur regularly.

Special-purpose team: a team created outside the formal organization to undertake a project of special importance or creativity.

Problem-solving team: typically 5 to 12 employees from the same department who meet to discuss ways of improving quality, efficiency, and the work enviornmnt.

Self-directed team: a team consisting of 5 to 20 multiskilled workers who rotate jobs to produce an entire product or service, often supervised by an elected member.

Virtual team: a team that uses advanced information and telecommunications technologies so that geographically distant members can collaborate on projects and reach common goals.

Global team: a work team made up of members of different nationalities whose activities span multiple countries; may operate as a virtual team or meet face to face.

Task specialist role: a role in which the individual devotes personal time and energy to helping the team accomplish its task.

Socioemotional role: a role in which the individual provides support for team members' emotional needs and social unity.

Dual role: a role in which the individual both contributes to the team's task and supports members' emotional needs.

Nonparticipator role: a role in which the individual contributes little to either the task or members' socioemotional needs.

Forming: the stage of team development characterized by orientation and acquaintance.

Storming: the stage of team development in which individual personalities and roles, and resulting conflicts emerge.

Norming: the stage of team development in which conflicts developed during the storming stage are resolved and team harmony and unity emerge.

Performing: the stage of team development in which members focus on problem solving and accomplishing the team's assigned task.

Adjourning: the stage of team development in which members prepare for the team's disbandment.

Team cohesiveness: the extent to which team members are attracted to the team and motivated to remain in it.

Norm: a standard of conduct that is shared by team members and guides their behavior.

Conflict: antagonistic interaction in which one party attempts to thwart the intentions or goals of another.

Superordinate goal: a goal that cannot be reached by a single party.

Mediation: the process of using a third party to settle a dispute.

Social facilitation: the tendency for the presence of others to influence an individual's motivation and performance.

Free rider: a person who benefits form team membership but does not make a proportionate contribution to the team's work.

Coordination costs: the time and energy needed to coordinate the activities of a team to enable it to perform its task.

Learning Objectives

1. Identify the types of teams in organizations.

2. Discuss new applications of teams to facilitate employee involvement.

3. Identify roles within teams and the type of role you could play to help a team be effective.

4. Explain the general stages of team development.

5. Explain the concepts of team cohesiveness and team norms and their relationship to team performance.

6. Understand the causes of conflict within and among teams and how to reduce conflict.

7. Discuss the assets and liabilities of organizational teams.

Chapter Review

Multiple Choice: Please indicate the correct response to the following questions by writing the letter of the correct answer in the space provided.

_____ 1. To have a team, you must have _____ people.
   a. hundreds of
   b. at least 7
   c. a diverse collection of
   d. two or more
   e. a homogeneous group of

_____ 2. Which of the following factors affect(s) team effectiveness?
   a. organizational context
   b. team type
   c. team characteristics
   d. team composition
   e. all of the above

_____ 3.   A _____ team is sometimes called a functional team or a command team.
a.   Horizontal
b.   Vertical
c.   Matrix
d.   task force
e.   cross-functional

_____ 4.   Horizontal teams
a.   reflect the organization's command structure.
b.   have an indefinite life span.
c.   may be drawn from several departments.
d.   are run by autocrats.
e.   may have no real purpose at all.

_____ 5.   Companies are gradually moving toward greater _____ for employees, which led first to problem-solving teams and then to self-directed teams.
a.   autonomy
b.   containment
c.   circumscription
d.   salaries
e.   restrictions

_____ 6.   A cross-functional team is a type of _____ team.
a.   horizontal
b.   vertical
c.   matrix
d.   functional
e.   command

_____ 7.   Membership on a committee is usually decided by a person's
a.   area of expertise.
b.   functional specialty.
c.   individual qualifications.
d.   title or position.
e.   supervisor.

_____ 8.   Which of the following is/are true of problem-solving teams?
a.   They consist of 5 to 12 volunteer hourly employees.
b.   They meet two hours a week.
c.   They discuss ways of improving quality.
d.   Their recommendations are proposed to management for approval.
e.   All of the above are true.

_____ 9.   Which of the following is/are true of self-directed teams?
a.   They consist of 5 to 20 multiskilled employees.
b.   They meet two hours a week.
c.   They discuss ways of improving quality.
d.   Their recommendations are proposed to management for approval.
e.   All of the above are true.

_____ 10. A virtual team is a group which
    a. almost acts like a team.
    b. is geographically dispersed, but linked by technology.
    c. exists only in the mind of the creator.
    d. only imaginary characters exist.
    e. none of the above.

_____ 11. A characteristic of a small team is
    a. that it has more disagreement than larger teams.
    b. that fewer questions are asked.
    c. that fewer opinions are offered.
    d. that more satisfaction is enjoyed by members.
    e. that sub-teams form rather easily.

_____ 12. The role of the task specialist may involve
    a. proposing new solutions to team problems.
    b. being warm and receptive to the ideas of others.
    c. reconciling team conflicts.
    d. telling jokes.
    e. shifting one's own opinion to maintain team harmony.

_____ 13. A team member who plays the task specialist role would display which of the following behaviors?
    a. energize
    b. encourage
    c. harmonize
    d. compromise
    e. reduce tension

_____ 14. A team member who plays the socioemotional role would display which of the following behaviors?
    a. initiation
    b. give opinions
    c. seek information
    d. energize
    e. follow

_____ 15. Some team members are asked to play a dual role. These members
    a. engage in two sets of behaviors: initiation and energize.
    b. perform both role: task specialist and socioemotional.
    c. perform both roles: liaison and negotiator.
    d. engage in two sets of behavior: follow and compromise.
    e. do not do anything.

_____ 16. Which stage of team development is characterized by cooperation and problem solving?
   a.   forming
   b.   storming
   c.   norming
   d.   performing
   e.   adjourning

_____ 17. In the _____ stage of team development many people disagree over their perceptions of the team's mission.
   a.   Forming
   b.   Storming
   c.   Norming
   d.   Performing
   e.   Adjourning

_____ 18. Why is morale higher in cohesive teams?
   a.   because of less communication to waste time
   b.   because one doesn't have to feel so loyal to the team
   c.   because less participation is needed in decision making
   d.   because of a friendly climate
   e.   all of the above

_____ 19. The highest productivity in a team occurs when the team is _____ in cohesiveness and has a(n) _____ performance norm.
   a.   high, high
   b.   low, low
   c.   high, low
   d.   low, high
   e.   high, average

_____ 20. The highest productivity results when
   a.   the team is not cohesive but has a high performance norm.
   b.   the team is not cohesive and has no performance norm.
   c.   the team is cohesive but has a low performance norm.
   d.   the team is cohesive and also has a high performance norm.
   e.   the team is cohesive but has no performance norm.

_____ 21. Team norms
   a.   are formal.
   b.   are usually written down by a team member called the "secretary" by sociologists.
   c.   make life harder for team members because they must now conform.
   d.   provide a frame of reference for members.
   e.   do not tell members what is acceptable behavior, only what is unacceptable.

_____ 22. A critical event in a team's history will
   a.   help determine group norms.
   b.   usually lead to the group's demise.
   c.   destroy the group's norms.
   d.   occur during the storming stage.
   e.   require a critical mass manager.

_____ 23. Norms are usually
   a.   formal.
   b.   written.
   c.   informal.
   d.   not very valuable.
   e.   not developed until the organization has been in existence for years.

_____ 24. Which of the following is *not* a cause of conflict among people as described in the text?
   a.   communication overload
   b.   scarce resources
   c.   jurisdictional ambiguities
   d.   power and status differences
   e.   goal differences

_____ 25. The _____, which reflects assertiveness to get one's own way, should be used for quick, decisive action.
   a.   collaborating style
   b.   accommodating style
   c.   compromising style
   d.   avoiding style
   e.   competing style

_____ 26. The collaborating style of conflict resolution is based on a _____ degree of assertiveness and a _____ degree of cooperativeness.
   a.   high; high
   b.   high; low
   c.   low; high
   d.   low; low
   e.   low; medium

_____ 27. If individuals can set aside personal animosities and deal with the conflict in a businesslike way, the _____ approach to conflict resolution will work well.
   a.   superordinate goal appeal
   b.   bargaining or negotiation
   c.   providing of well-defined tasks
   d.   facilitating communication
   e.   Mediation

_____ 28. Social facilitation refers to the
  a. orientation of new members into the team.
  b. teaching of social norms to new team members.
  c. tendency for the presence of others to influence individual motivation and performance.
  d. ease with which a new member learns social norms.
  e. person who enforces team norms by social sanctioning within the team.

_____ 29. One advantage of employee involvement teams is an increase in organizational
  a. communication.
  b. flexibility.
  c. identity.
  d. morale.
  e. pride.

_____ 30. A cost of teams that occurs when a person who benefits from team membership but does not make a proportionate contribution to the team's work is called
  a. free riding
  b. power realignment
  c. coordination costs
  d. unequal burden
  e. scab

True/False: Please indicate whether the following statements are true or false by writing a T or an F in the blank in front of each question.

_____ 1. Work team effectiveness is based on two outcomes--productive output and marketplace acceptance.

_____ 2. The two most common types of horizontal teams are a functional team and a command team.

_____ 3. A committee is generally long-lived and may be a permanent part of the organization's structure.

_____ 4. In a self-directed team, team members take over managerial duties such as scheduling work or ordering materials.

_____ 5. The ideal size of work teams often is thought to be nine.

_____ 6. Individual personalities emerge causing conflict and disagreements during the norming stage.

_____ 7. Team cohesiveness does not necessarily lead to higher team productivity.

_____ 8. The collaborating style reflects assertiveness to get one's own way.

_____ 9. Keeping the teams focused on issues and not personalities helps facilitate communication.

_____ 10. When teams do not work well, the major reasons usually are power realignment, free riding, and coordination costs.

Short Answer: Please indicate your answer in the space provided.

1. List the five stages of team development.

2. List the six factors that can cause people to engage in conflict.

3. What factors influence work team effectiveness?

4. Identify three benefits of using teams.

Manager's Workbook

Is Your Group a Cohesive Team? *(Also available on page 542 of text.)*

Think about a student group with which you have worked. Answer the questions below as they pertain to the functioning of that group.

		Disagree Strongly				Agree Strongly
1	Group meetings were held regularly and everyone attended.	1	2	3	4	5
2	We talked about and shared the same goals for group work and grade.	1	2	3	4	5
3	We spent most of our meeting time talking business, but discussions were open-ended and active.	1	2	3	4	5
4	We talked through any conflicts and disagreements until they were resolved.	1	2	3	4	5
5	Group members listened carefully to one another.	1	2	3	4	5
6	We really trusted each other, speaking personally about what we really felt.	1	2	3	4	5
7	Leadership roles were rotated and shared, with people taking initiative at appropriate times for the good of the group.	1	2	3	4	5
8	Each member found a way to contribute to the final work product.	1	2	3	4	5
9	I was really satisfied being a member of the group.	1	2	3	4	5
10	We freely gave each other credit for jobs well done.	1	2	3	4	5
11	Group members gave and received feedback to help the group do even better.	1	2	3	4	5
12	We held each other accountable; each member was accountable to the group	1	2	3	4	5
13	Group members really liked and respected each other.	1	2	3	4	5
	Total Score					

The questions here are about team cohesion. If you scored **52 or greater**, your group experienced authentic teamwork. Congratulations. If you scored between **39 and 51**, there was a positive group identity that might have been developed even further. If you scored between **26 and 38**, group identity was weak and probably not very satisfying. If you scored **below 26**, it was hardly a group at all, resembling a loose collection of individuals.

Remember, teamwork doesn't happen by itself. Individuals like you have to understand what a team is and then work to make it happen. What can you do to make a student group more like a team? Do you have the courage to take the initiative?

Best and Worst Teams

1. Think of some times you have worked with teams, either on class projects, campus organizations, or in the workplace. Consider the best team you ever had and the worst. Then fill out the boxes below.
2. What were the critical factors in the success of failure of the two teams?
3. What have you learned about teams from this exercise?

	Best team	Worst team
What was the situation?		
How did members of the team behave?		
Was there a leader? What did the leader do?		
What were the norms of this particular team (see chapter concepts)?		
Of the six sources of conflict discussed in the chapter, what were the most important causes of conflict in this team?		
Refer to Exhibit 15.6 and determine the dominant models of conflict resolution used in that team.		

Manager's Workshop

Auntie Kate's Bakery Case Study *(Also available on page 543 of text.)*

A group of management students is assigned to observe the operations at Auntie Kate's Bakery. Initial interviews show that employees identify with company values and practices; things always seem to work well. About 85 percent of the staff have been with the company for other 12 years. Supportive of her employees, the owner has an egalitarian attitude, respects workers, and continually refers to staff as "My family." Seen from the employee's perspective, Auntie Kate's Bakery is the perfect small business.

Class Assignment*:* Observe the bakery's operations and suggest recommendations for improvement.

Results from class members: The task of bagging assorted cookies is inefficient. Eight staff members each stand in front of cartons filled with assorted cookies. The left hand holds a bag, while the right hand makes an extended reach to pick up cookies to place them in the bag. The staff works at a relaxed, informal pace. The tasks do not align with principles of motion economy, because the staff members do not use both hands simultaneously and each hand works in opposite directions. Nor are any materials pre-positioned for ease of reach.

After the students suggest highly structured changes to increase efficiency, the owner graciously rejects their recommendations. The students are confused.

1. In groups of 4-6 members answer the following questions:
   a. Why do you think the owner rejects the recommendations?
   b. What elements regarding team motivation were overlooked by the students in the study?
   c. If you were the student group, what steps would you take if you were studying Auntie Kate's Bakery?
2. The class will discuss the answers of each group. What did you learn about team effectiveness?

Team-based Decision Processes

As organizations shift from traditional hierarchical designs to learning organizations, the reliance on team-based decision processes increases. During this transition, a shift occurs in problem solving. It is from

a) adaptive thinking, where individuals follow established norms, "My way is the only way," to

b) generative thinking, where teams examine the underlying structure of problems to determine cause and effect. Teams can increase their ability to use generative thinking by practice with looking at events or decisions and discussing what would be the impact of those events or decisions.

The purpose of exercise is to help you to better understand this concept of generative thinking in teams.

1. Each student independently completes the immediate and long-term impact/effect for the events or situations described below in the box. Optionally, think of two other events or situations with their impacts. Or you may think of a situation where you made an important decision and look at the possible impacts of that decision.

2. Divide into groups of 4 – 6. The group discusses the three events/situations, coming to a consensus on the immediate and long-term impacts for each situation. If you have time, think of one or two other situations, events or decisions and discuss impacts of those.

3. The entire class shares impacts discussed in small groups and answers the following questions:

   a) How is adaptive thinking different from generative?

b) What are some examples of adaptive and generative thinking you have seen or experienced?

c) Why does understanding impacts help develop more generative thinking?

Situation	Immediate Impact/Effect	Long-Term Impact/Effect
(*Example*) Passed Driving Test	Could drive independently.	Increased self-esteem, greater self-reliance, responsible for safety of other drivers, began part time employment to pay for auto, job expanded social circle outside of homogeneous surroundings.
Admission to Graduate School		
Employed as Research Analyst with Newly Created E-commerce business		
8% of the workforce in your company is retiring in 3 years		

4. With a variety of answers expected, can one answer be ultimately correct? Why or why not? What does the group think?

SOURCE: Adapted from Marcia Salner (1999). The Learning Organization. *Journal of Management Education*, Vol. 23 (5), 489-508.

Study Guide Solutions

Chapter Review

Multiple-Choice Questions

1	2	3	4	5	6	7	8	9	10
D	E	B	C	A	A	D	E	A	B

11	12	13	14	15	16	17	18	19	20
D	A	A	E	B	D	B	D	A	D

21	22	23	24	25	26	27	28	29	30
D	A	C	A	E	A	B	C	B	A

True/False Questions

1	2	3	4	5	6	7	8	9	10
F	F	T	T	F	F	T	F	T	T

Short Answer Questions

1. The five stages are (a) forming, (b) storming, (c) norming, (d) performing, and (e) adjourning.

2. The six factors are (a) scarce resources, (b) jurisdictional ambiguities, (c) communication breakdown, (d) personality clashes, (e) power and status differences, and (f) goal differences.

3. The factors are (a) organizational context, (b) team type, (c) team characteristics, (d) team composition, and (e) team process.

4. Benefits of teams include (a) individual productivity enhancement, (b) increased members' satisfaction, (c) integration of diverse abilities and skills, and (d) greater organizational flexibility.

Manager's Workbook

Is Your Group a Cohesive Team? Scoring and interpretation provided with exercise.

Best and Worst Teams: Results will vary.

Manager's Workshop

Auntie Kate's Bakery Case Study: Answers will vary, but this exercise should generate some interesting discussion.

Team-based Decision Processes: Answers to this application will vary according to perceptions and unique experiences of each student.

Chapter 16

The Importance of Control

Chapter Outline

Key Terms

Organizational control: the systematic process through which managers regulate organizational activities to make the consistent with expectations established in plans, targets, and standards of performance.

Feedforward control: control that focuses on human, material, and financial resources flowing into the organization; also called *preliminary* or *preventive control*.

Concurrent control: control that consists of monitoring ongoing activities to ensure they are consistent with standards.

Feedback control: control that focuses on the organization's output; also called *procrastination* or *output control*.

Responsibility center: an organizational unit under the supervision of a single person who is responsible for its activity.

Expense budget: a budget that outlines the anticipated and actual expenses for a responsibility center.

Revenue budget: a budget that identifies the forecasted and actual revenues of the organization.

Cash budget: a budget that estimates and reports cash flows on a daily or weekly basis to ensure that the company has sufficient cash to meet its obligations.

Capital budget: a budget that plans and reports investments in major assets to be depreciated over several years.

Top-down budgeting: a budgeting process in which middle- and lower-level managers set departmental budget targets in accordance with overall company revenues and expenditures specified by top management.

Bottom-up budgeting: a budgeting process in which lower-level managers budget their departments' resource needs and pass them up to top management for approval.

Bureaucratic control: the use of rules, policies, hierarchy of authority, reward systems, and other formal devices to influence employee behavior and assess performance.

Decentralized control: the use of organizational culture, group norms, and a focus on goals, rather than rules and procedures to foster compliance with organizational goals.

Productivity: the organization's output of products and services divided by inputs.

Total factor productivity: the ratio of total outputs to the inputs from labor, capital, materials, and energy.

Partial productivity: the ratio of total outputs to the inputs from a single major input category.

Total quality management (TQM): an organization-wide commitment to infusing quality into every activity through continuous improvement.

Quality circle: a group of 6 to 12 employees who meet regularly to discuss and solve problems affecting the quality of their work.

Benchmarking: the continuous process of measuring products, services, and practices against major competitors or industry leaders.

Six sigma: a quality control approach that emphasizes a relentless pursuit of higher quality and lower costs.

Cycle time: the steps taken to complete a company process.

Continuous improvement: the implementation of a large number of small, incremental improvements in all areas of the organization on an ongoing basis.

ISO 9000: a set of international standards for quality management, setting uniform guidelines for processes to ensure that products conform to customer requirements.

Economic value added (EVA) system: a control system that measures performance in terms of after-tax profits minus the cost of capital invested in tangible assets.

Market valued added (MVA) system: a control system that measures the stock market's estimate of the value of a company's past and expected capital investment projects.

Activity-based costing (ABC): a control system that identifies the various activities needed to provide a product and allocates costs accordingly.

Open-book management: sharing financial information and results with all employees in the organization.

Balanced scorecard: a comprehensive management control system that balances traditional financial measures with measures of customer service, internal business processes, and the organization's capacity for learning and growth.

Learning Objectives

1. Define organizational control and explain why it is a key management function.

2. Describe differences in control focus, including feedforward, concurrent, and feedback control.

3. Explain the four steps in the control process.

4. Discuss the use of financial statements, financial analysis, and budgeting as management controls.

5. Contrast the bureaucratic and decentralized control approaches.

6. Define productivity and explain why and how managers seek to improve it.

7. Describe the concept of total quality management and major TQM techniques.

8. Identify current trends in financial control and discuss their impact on organizations.

9. Explain the value of open-book management and the balanced scorecard as new workplace approaches to control.

Chapter Review

Multiple Choice: Please indicate the correct response to the following questions by writing the letter of the correct answer in the space provided.

_____ 1. Feedforward control focuses on
      a. human resources.
      b. material resources.
      c. financial resources.
      d. inputs into the organization.
      e. all of the above.

_____ 2. Conducting a survey to determine customer satisfaction is an example of _____ control.
   a. feedforward
   b. total quality
   c. statistical
   d. concurrent
   e. feedback

_____ 3. Feedforward control is
   a. a focus on the transformation process.
   b. a focus on organizational inputs.
   c. a focus on organizational outputs.
   d. sometimes called preliminary control.
   e. sometimes called preventative control.

_____ 4. The selection and hiring of new employees involves _____ control.
   a. total quality
   b. statistical process
   c. feedforward
   d. concurrent
   e. feedback

_____ 5. Direct supervision is most effective for which type of control?
   a. Feedforward
   b. Concurrent
   c. Feedback
   d. Preliminary
   e. Post-action

_____ 6. The first step in the control process is
   a. establish standards.
   b. measure actual performance.
   c. compare performance to standards.
   d. take corrective action.
   e. use feedback.

_____ 7. Frito-Lay's use of handheld computers to monitor daily sales activities is an example of _____ control.
   a. total quality
   b. statistical process
   c. feedforward
   d. concurrent
   e. feedback

_____ 8. What are the key steps in designing a well-designed control system?
   a. Find out what data you need, collect the data, write the report.
   b. Establish standards of performance, measure actual performance, compare performance to standards, take corrective action.
   c. Plan, organize, control, staff/direct.
   d. Appoint a good leader, develop a mission, communicate the mission, step aside, wait for the rank-and-file to achieve the mission.
   e. Establish the standards, communicate the standards, compare the actual with the standard.

_____ 9. According to the control model, after establishing standards of performance, the manager should
   a. compare performance to standards.
   b. get the standards approved by the supervisors and subordinates.
   c. measure actual performance.
   d. take corrective action.
   e. provide feedback.

_____ 10. Which type of control relies on the use of social values and trust to control?
   a. decentralized control
   b. bureaucratic control
   c. feedback control
   d. concurrent control
   e. feedforward control

_____ 11. _____ is/are *not* (an) element(s) of bureaucratic control.
   a. Rules
   b. Written documentation
   c. Reward systems
   d. Social values
   e. Hierarchy of authority

_____ 12. Rewards in a bureaucratic control system are based on
   a. an employee's achievement in his or her own job.
   b. group achievements.
   c. equity across employees.
   d. informal evaluations of performance.
   e. none of the above.

_____ 13. Decentralized control is preferred when
   a. management style is directive.
   b. tasks are quantifiable.
   c. corporate culture supports participation.
   d. subordinates desire not to participate.
   e. the company is owned by a family.

_____ 14. Bureaucratic control relies on the cultural value of
   a.   employee participation.
   b.   top-down control.
   c.   flexibility.
   d.   informal communications.
   e.   self-control.

_____ 15. _____ is/are (a) characteristic of bureaucratic control, while _____ is/are (a) characteristic of decentralized control.
   a.   Employee compliance, tall structure
   b.   Formal authority, flexible authority
   c.   Self-control, mutual influence
   d.   Formalization, rules
   e.   Grievance procedures, measurable standards

_____ 16. The total quality management approach was conceived by
   a.   the Japanese.
   b.   the Germans.
   c.   American researchers and consultants.
   d.   Frederick W. Taylor.
   e.   Donald Trump.

_____ 17. Under total quality management the responsibility for quality rests with
   a.   managers, where it belongs.
   b.   the entire company.
   c.   the control system.
   d.   the control department.
   e.   the computer system.

_____ 18. _____ refers to the continuous process of measuring products, services, and practices against major competitors or industry leaders.
   a.   Resourcing.
   b.   Divestiture.
   c.   Outsourcing.
   d.   Benchmarking.
   e.   Empowerment.

_____ 19. The simplification of work cycles, including the dropping of barriers between work steps and between departments, and the removal of worthless steps in the process is called
   a.   reduced cycle time.
   b.   benchmarking.
   c.   decision support group.
   d.   quality circle.
   e.   continuous improvement.

_____ 20. The process of _____ is the implementation of a large number of small incremental improvements in all areas of the organization on an ongoing basis.
a. reduced cycled time
b. benchmarking
c. continuous improvement
d. quality circle
e. social committee

_____ 21. What is the quality approach that emphasizes a relentless pursuit of higher quality and lower costs?
a. Six sigma.
b. Benchmarking.
c. Quality circle.
d. ISO 9000
e. None of the above.

_____ 22. In attempting to increase organizational productivity, managers can look in which of the following places?
a. Worker productivity
b. Technological productivity
c. Managerial productivity
d. All of the above
e. a and c only

_____ 23. The _____ budget estimates the cash flows on a daily or weekly basis.
a. capital
b. balance sheet
c. bottom-up
d. cash
e. expense

_____ 24. The _____ plans future investments in major assets to be depreciated over several years.
a. capital budget
b. balance sheet budget
c. cash budget
d. revenue budget
e. profit budget

_____ 25. In top-down budgeting
a. lower-level managers are more likely to be committed to achieving budget targets.
b. lower-level managers are included in the process.
c. the budget developers lack reliable information.
d. lower-level managers pass to higher levels their anticipated resource needs.
e. the budget is imposed on lower-level managers.

_____ 26. Many countries have endorsed a universal framework for quality assurance called
   a. the international quality standard.
   b. global standards.
   c. ISO 5000.
   d. ISO 9000.
   e. TQM-Japan/United States Standards.

_____ 27. The term EVA refers to
   a. economic variance analysis.
   b. economic value-added systems.
   c. expected value analysis.
   d. expected variance adjustment.
   e. economic variation adjustment.

_____ 28. In open-book management
   a. any employee is allowed to initiate a complaint.
   b. the public has full access to financial records.
   c. the salaries of top managers are posted on bulletin boards.
   d. financial information and results are shared with all employees in the organization.
   e. none of the above.

_____ 29. Activity-based costing allocates financial resources according to
   a. the true cost of the various activities needed to provide a product.
   b. a zero base.
   c. strategic considerations.
   d. the number of activities associated with production of a product or service.
   e. none of the above.

_____ 30. Which of the following is an element of effective quality control?
   a. independent of strategy
   b. relies totally on objective data
   c. must remain inflexible and stick to standards set
   d. relies solely on subjective data
   e. accepted by members

True/False: Please indicate whether the following statements are true or false by writing a T or an F in the blank in front of each question.

_____ 1. Feedforward control focuses on the organization's inputs.

_____ 2. Effective management control involves subjective judgment and employee discussions as well as objective analysis of data.

_____ 3. Corrective action when performance is inadequate does not include adjusting the standards.

_____ 4. Decentralized control represents the absence of control because visible rules, supervision, and procedures are absent.

_____ 5. The continuous process of measuring products, services, and practices against the toughest competitors or the industry leaders is called benchmarking.

_____ 6. Outsourcing is the implementation of a large number of small, incremental improvements in all areas of the organization and an ongoing basis.

_____ 7. The use of more efficient machines, robots, and computers to increase output refers to the increased managerial productivity.

_____ 8. The fundamental unit of analysis for a budget control system is called a responsibility center.

_____ 9. Open-book management ties employee rewards to the company's overall success.

_____ 10. The balanced scorecard is a comprehensive management control system that balances traditional financial measures with measures of customer service, internal business processes, and the organization's capacity for learning and growth.

Short Answer: Please indicate your answer in the space provided.

1. List the four steps in the feedback control model.

2. List and discuss the elements of effective control systems.

3. Explain the advantages of top-down and bottom-up budgeting.

4. Describe the TQM technique of benchmarking.

Manager's Workbook

Is Your Budget in Control? *(Also available on page 570 of text.)*

By the time you are in college, you are in charge of at least some of your own finances. How well you manage your personal budget may indicate how well you will manage your company's budget on the job. Respond to the following statements to evaluate your own budgeting habits. If the statement doesn't apply directly to you, respond the way you think you would behave in a similar situation.

		Yes	No
1	I spend all my money as soon as I get it.	Y	N
2	At the beginning of each week (or month, or term), I write down all my fixed expenses.	Y	N
3	I never seem to have any money left over at the end of the week (or month).	Y	N
4	I pay all my expenses, but I never seem to have any money left over for fun.	Y	N
5	I am not putting any money away in savings right now; I'll wait until after I graduate from college.	Y	N
6	I can't pay all my bills.	Y	N
7	I have a credit card, but I pay the balance in full each month.	Y	N
8	I take cash advances on my credit card.	Y	N
9	I know how much I can spend on eating out, movies, and other entertainment each week.	Y	N
10	I pay cash for everything.	Y	N
11	When I buy something, I look for value and determine the best buy.	Y	N
12	I lend money to friends whenever they ask, even if it leaves me short of cash.	Y	N
13	I never borrow money from friends.	Y	N
14	I am putting aside money each month to save for something that I really need.	Y	N

Yes responses to statements 2, 9, 10, 13, and 14 point to the most disciplined budgeting habits; yes responses to 4, 5, 7, and 11 reveal adequate budgeting habits; yes responses to 1, 3, 6, 8, and 12 indicate the poorest budgeting habits. If you have answered honestly, chances are you'll have a combination of all three. Look to see where you can improve your budgeting.

Anna's Turn to Do the Dishes

Delores checked her chores chart and discovered that it was Anna's turn to do the dishes. "It's time to do the dishes now, Anna. Make sure you do a good job!"

"Yes, Mother," replied Anna as she headed for the stack of dirty dishes next to the kitchen sink.

Thirty minutes later Anna reported the dishes done and went into the family room to watch her favorite television show. Delores went into the kitchen just before going to bed for a drink of water. She picked up a glass from the drain rack and was repulsed. It still was filthy. She checked a few other dishes and found many of them to be dirty also. Then she looked at the kitchen counter and the dining room table and noticed that they had not been properly cleaned off either. She was mad!!

Delores stormed into Anna's room, threw on the light switch, and yelled, "I thought I told you to do the dishes, young lady! Now get out of that bed and get in there and do the job right!"

What followed was not a pretty sight. The entire family became involved in a major dispute, and it was two hours before Dad—as a gesture of peace—finished the dishes and everyone went to bed. Everyone was now in a bad mood, and Delores was wondering where she had gone wrong.

1. Where did Delores go wrong?

2. Would feedforward, concurrent, or feedback control have solved this problem?

Manager's Workshop

Organizational Control Mechanisms *(Also available on page 570 of text.)*

1. Divide into groups of 5-6 members.
2. Each group examines the following university request form for a complimentary parking pass and identifies flaws with the design of the form.
3. After identifying basic design flaws, groups then answer the following questions:

    a.   *Is the control cost effective?* Are the costs associated with the control mechanism offset by the benefits derived?

    b.   *Is the control acceptable?* Do the people affected believe it is necessary?

c.   *Is the control appropriate?* Are the steps involved commensurate with the activity?

d.   *Is the process strategic?* Is it a critical activity in the operation of the university?

e.   *Is the control reliable and effective?* Is it clear what criteria are necessary for the approval of the request and what will be construed as sufficient justification?

REQUEST FOR COMPLIMENTARY CAMPUS PARKING PERMITS

Requesting Department: _____   Person Requesting: _____

Phone: _____   Event: _____

Date(s): _____   Time(s): _____

Number of Persons for Event: _____   Number of Permits Requested: _____

Permits Mailed: _____   Justification for Waived Fee: _____

Dean Signature   Vice-President Signature

_____   _____

Approve: _____   Approve: _____
Disapprove: _____   Disapprove: _____

SOURCE: Baker III, H. Eugene, Jennings, Kenneth M. (1994). "An Out of Control Organizational Control Mechanism," *Journal of Management Education*, Vol. 18 (3), 380-384.

Management Control and Organizational Effectiveness

1. Divide into groups of 4-6 members.
2. Consider the four organizational settings below along the top of the table/chart. As a group, discuss how you would measure the effectiveness of your efforts in each control/outcome. List two measurements under each control/outcome for each of the four settings. Therefore, you will have eight measurement techniques for each setting.
3. How will applying these measurements help the organization to become more effective? Which measures could be given more weight than others? Why?
4. Present your chart to the rest of the class. Each group should explain why it chose those particular measures and which are more important. Be prepared to defend your position to the other groups, which are encouraged to question your choices.

Type of control or outcome	Small Manufacturing Plant	Counseling Center (univ. or other)	Local courier service	College Basketball Team
Quality	1.			
	2.			
Feedback	1.			
	2.			
Feedforward	1.			
	2.			
Productivity	1.			
	2.			

Source: Adapted by Dorothy Marcic from general ideas in Jennifer Howard and Larry Miller, *Team Management*, The Miller Consulting Group, 1994, pp. 92.

Study Guide Solutions

Chapter Review

Multiple-Choice Questions

1	2	3	4	5	6	7	8	9	10
E	E	B	C	B	A	D	B	C	A

11	12	13	14	15	16	17	18	19	20
D	A	C	B	B	C	B	D	A	C

21	22	23	24	25	26	27	28	29	30
A	D	D	A	E	D	B	D	A	E

True/False Questions

1	2	3	4	5	6	7	8	9	10
T	T	F	F	T	F	F	T	T	T

Short Answer Questions

1. The four steps are (a) establish standards of performance, (b) measure actual performance, (c) compare performance to standards, and (d) take corrective action.

2. Effective control systems share the following traits: (a) linkage to strategy, (b) understandable measures, (c) acceptance by employees, (d) balance of objective and subjective data, (e) accuracy, (f) flexibility, (g) timeliness, and (h) support of action.

3. Managers have information available to set budget targets for each department to meet the needs of overall company revenues and expenditures in top-down budgeting. The bottom-up approach includes input from lower-level managers that generally helps them feel more committed and motivated. These managers may set a budget closer in line with their needs.

4. Benchmarking is the continuous process of measuring products, services, and practices against the toughest competitors or the industry leaders. The key to benchmarking lies in analysis and in the selection of the comparison company.

Manager's Workbook

Is Your Budget in Control?: Scoring and interpretation provided with exercise.

Anna's Turn to Do the Dishes

1. Delores should have explained more in advance what her expectations were in doing the job (feedforward control). She should have checked up while Anna was still doing the dishes to make sure they were being done correctly (concurrent control). She should have checked up immediately upon Anna's reporting that the job was done to make sure the job met her standards (feedback control).

2. All three types of control would have helped in this situation as illustrated in the answer to the previous question.

Manager's Workshop

Organizational Control Mechanisms: Answers to this application will vary.

Management Control and Organizational Effectiveness:

Suggested answers presented in the table below:

Type of control or outcome	Small Manufacturing Plant	Counseling Center (univ. or other)	Local courier service	College Basketball Team
Quality	Quality circles; reduce cycle time	Group creates shared vision and openly discussed problems	Benchmark other service businesses; reduce cycle time	Continuous improvement
Feedback	Individual production goals and levels posted	Results shared: healing, hospital admits, suicides, etc.	Post number of lost packages, problems, etc.	Scores, individual plays analyzed
Feedforward	Hiring right people	Hiring right people	Hiring right people	Hiring right people
Productivity	Workers discuss ways to increase productivity	Group identifies what higher productivity is and how to attain it	Keeping track on charts of weekly productivity and discuss what was done right	Follow good plays and learn how to have more